Care and Criminal Justice

GOOD PRACTICE in
Assessing Risk
Current Knowledge, Issues and Approaches

Edited by **Hazel Kemshall** and
Bernadette Wilkinson

Jessica Kingsley Publishers
London and Philadelphia

First published in 2011
by Jessica Kingsley Publishers
116 Pentonville Road
London N1 9JB, UK
and
400 Market Street, Suite 400
Philadelphia, PA 19106, USA

www.jkp.com

Copyright © Jessica Kingsley Publishers 2011

Library of Congress Cataloging in Publication Data
Good practice in risk assessment and risk management: 3 / edited by Hazel Kemshall and Bernadette Wilkinson.
    p. cm. -- (Good practice in health, social care and criminal justice)
    Includes bibliographical references and index.
    ISBN 978-1-84905-059-3 (alk. paper)
    1. Social service. 2. Health services administration. 3. Risk assessment. 4. Risk management. I. Kemshall, Hazel, 1958- II. Wilkinson, Bernadette.
    HV40.G66 2011
    361.1--dc22
                          2010026407

British Library Cataloguing in Publication Data
A CIP catalogue record for this book is available from the British Library

ISBN 978 1 84905 059 3

Printed and bound in Great Britain by
MPG Books Group

Dedication

To all those practitioners and managers still running the risk!

CONTENTS

Introduction

HAZEL KEMSHALL AND BERNADETTE WILKINSON

Risk is ubiquitous and we have become a risk preoccupied society. In this climate, professionals working with risk in health, social care, social work and criminal justice are required to adopt high standards of practice and high-quality policies and procedures, and to balance competing concerns about risk, including difficult balances between protection, rights and risk taking (see Baker and Wilkinson, Chapter 1; Titterton, Chapter 2). This needs to include complex decision making in situations of stress and potential blame, and in contexts where perceptions of risk by clients and users can differ from practitioners' views, or be seriously at odds with community expectations of safety (e.g. where communities have defensive and exclusionary attitudes to sex offenders, or punitive attitudes to abusive parents).

Risk can also compete with other agendas, such as those concerned with engaging service users (e.g. in mental health, or in work with children and families) versus political imperatives for low risk and safety (see Maden, Chapter 6; Calder, Chapter 11). This book explores some of these competing perceptions and the role of power and control in risk assessment and management, including the role of centralised power and bureaucracy (see Peckover *et al.*, Chapter 5). Calder for example (Chapter 11), outlines the roles of bureaucracy and organisational function in hindering high-quality professional practice with risk. Other chapters deconstruct the languages and definitions of risk used in particular settings (e.g. child protection, see Peckover *et al.*, Chapter 5), or the insidious negative connotations carried by the word 'risk' in most social care and social work policy (see Titterton, Chapter 2).

Contributors to this book draw out many of the difficulties and limitations of a focus on risk but they also develop from those critiques ideas for improving practice. The controlling function of official discourses of risk is countered by the increased voice achieved by service users in recent years (see Littlechild and Glasby *et al.*, Chapter 9, for example); and an increased focus on resilience rather than risk (see Boeck and Fleming, Chapter 3). This 'voice' is rooted in a greater research and policy recognition of the situated accounts of risk and risk taking of users – for example, through the use of client narratives and story telling – with a focus in this book on young people deemed to be 'at risk' or as 'posing a risk' (Boeck and Fleming, Chapter 3; Baker and Kelly, Chapter 4). These chapters reflect emerging research techniques for gaining more in-depth and sophisticated views of risk. Maden (Chapter 6) explores how a more positive approach to the possibilities of risk assessment can reduce the negative framing of mental health and violence risk, and enable positive approaches to risk management that increase community safety and patient well-being. Barnett and Mann (Chapter 8) consider how even in the very emotive field of practice with sex offenders, collaborative and positive approaches to risk assessment are being developed. Robinson (Chapter 7) pursues this theme of collaboration by considering the use of risk tools with victims to better ensure effective safety plans.

The role of alternative approaches to risk assessment and management is explored, including positive risk taking (Titterton, Chapter 2), and increased professional approaches to the challenges of risk decision making, particularly by taking a more positive framing of defensibility than has been apparent in much social and public policy of late (Baker and Wilkinson, Chapter 1). This is echoed by Peckover et al. (Chapter 5) who explore the potential for improving risk assessment tools by involving practitioners in their design. Broader policy developments are beginning to promote alternative interventions such as the 'Good Lives Model' (GLM) (see Barnett and Mann, Chapter 8), and Robinson shows how a risk approach to victims in the context of domestic violence can positively change service responses and help victims to be heard. Differing practice and policy paradigms are emerging such as public health approaches to risk assessment and management (Wood, Chapter 10) and more positive future oriented understandings like the GLM (Barnett and Mann, Chapter 8), which takes us towards a more active involvement of potential perpetrators in managing their own risk and changing their lives and behaviours.

The Public Health Approach (PHA) takes us beyond a public protection paradigm vested in professionals towards broader community responses to safety, using a combination of public awareness campaigns and community-based approaches to managing risk within which the public plays a more active role. This has the potential to engage communities as 'active participants' in risk management, rather than as passive recipients of safety (Kemshall 2008; The Derwent Initiative 2007). While these more recent approaches no doubt present practitioners and policy makers with challenges, not least to increase their transparency and engagement with communities and users about risk, it may in the long run make risk less contested and its management easier to achieve.

Risk remains a complex policy and practice issue. After some 15 years of practice, policy and research on risk, our understanding of this complex issue has increased. The contributors to this book all demonstrate how new and challenging ideas are enabling considerable practice and policy development. We hope that readers will find the material in this volume helpful in the daily practice of 'running the risk'.

REFERENCES

Kemshall, H. (2008) *Understanding the Community Management of High Risk Offenders.* Maidenhead: Open University/McGraw-Hill.

The Derwent Initiative (TDI) (2007) *Tackling Sex Offending Together.* Newcastle upon Tyne: TDI.

CHAPTER 1

Professional Risk Taking and Defensible Decisions

KERRY BAKER AND BERNADETTE WILKINSON

INTRODUCTION

The increasing focus on risk in social care, health and criminal justice services has an impact on all aspects of decision-making (Kemshall *et al.* 1997). It affects not just the 'big' decisions – such as whether to remove a child from his or her family or whether to release an offender on parole – but also the smaller everyday decisions as to which practice is employed (such as whether or not to do a home visit, or to make an extra phone call for information). Even the task of risk assessment generates its own risk and 'creates new dangers' (Beckett 2008, p.41) because, for example, the more time that is spent assessing one case, the less time there is available for risk assessment in other cases.

Practitioners and managers are faced with the challenge of making demanding decisions about risk with the added pressures of working in a climate of limited resources and intense media and political scrutiny. Power (2004) suggests that this produces risk averse cultures in which organisations and individuals become more concerned with managing reputational risk, thereby sometimes taking attention away from the risks they originally set out to manage. The widespread adoption of the concept of 'defensible decision making' (Kemshall 1998) has arguably been a result of both real concern to manage risks, such as those posed by offending, and a concern with organisational risk (Whitty 2009).

One consequence of this is that, instead of focusing on defensibility, practice can instead sometimes become defensive, contributing to a culture where 'back covering' becomes the priority and appropriate risks are not taken. Titterton (2005) suggests that the fears of individual professionals combined with a risk averse organisational culture may limit the capacity for risk taking, while Taylor's impression from a study of practice in relation to care of the elderly was that '[t]he rationale for decision making seemed to be more about what was defensible than what was right' (Taylor 2006, p.1424). In response to such concerns, some local government services in the UK have begun to rename and rewrite their risk assessment and risk management policies in order to encourage what they see as a more positive approach to risk (Aberdeen City Council 2009).

One of the difficulties in moving thinking on is that there can be a tendency for over-simplified and caricatured responses to these concepts (influenced partly by our own personal level of risk aversion and by the circumstances in which risks are being judged). Views about 'risk taking' tend to divide into two – that is to say it is either reckless and dangerous *or* creative and life affirming. Similarly, defensible decisions are often viewed as either boring, negative, deficit focused and defensive *or* reliable, safe, thorough and rigorous. But the reality is of course far more complex. In an ideal world, most practitioners would probably say that they want to be able to take positive risks *and* act defensibly. But why is this difficult to achieve in practice, and why do the two often seem to be contradictory?

This chapter aims to explore the area 'between the macro level of governmental risk management initiatives and the micro level of professional communication with an individual service user' (Taylor 2006, p.1413), to consider some influences on practice that may often be overlooked, and to use these as a basis for considering some suggestions for how to improve decision-making processes.

BEING 'PROFESSIONAL' AND DEFENSIBLE DECISION MAKING

We all take decisions that may involve risk in our personal lives but '[p]rofessional risk-taking is undertaken for the benefit of others from a duty (moral, legal or employment-based) to assist them' (Carson and Bain 2008, p.31). Beyond this, what is implied by saying that a decision is 'professional' or that it has been made by a professional (Friedson 1994)? There is an extensive literature on professions and professionalism and we can only summarise a few key points here. For example, professionals have been described as having 'a number of key identifiable traits, one of which is autonomous decision-making, underscored by a distinct, theoretical, expert knowledge base' (May and Buck 1998, p.5). Debates continue to rage over the extent to which managerialism has reduced practitioners' autonomy, but it can never be totally eliminated in human service occupations given the irreducible complexity of individuals' behaviour. The second key aspect of professionalism highlighted by May and Buck is an expert knowledge base – that is, the theory, research findings, evidence and practice wisdom relevant to particular occupations. To this should be added a set of core skills around collating, weighing and analysing different types of information and evidence (Beckett, McKeigue and Taylor 2007; Sheppard *et al.* 2001). Third, professional decisions usually involve moral and ethical considerations that affect even seemingly mundane activities such as completing an assessment form, as noted by White, Hall and Peckover in relation to the Common Assessment Framework (CAF) who argue that 'practitioners make strategic and moral decisions about whether and when to complete a CAF and how to do so' (2009, p.1198). Finally, there needs to be an ability to adapt in response to new information and changing circumstances: '[w]hat separates the creative social worker from the mere technician is the capacity to shift from one perspective to the other' (Milner and O'Byrne 2009, p.71).

Current practice, however, occurs in a context in which experts and professionals are not trusted as much as they might have been in previous generations, and practitioners are perhaps unclear about 'what professional judgement is and how it should be exercised' (Hollows 2008, p.52). Against this backdrop, the concept of defensible decision making has been widely adopted as a means of codifying the expected features of decision making more explicitly. Typically these would be defined as decisions based on:

- appropriate levels of knowledge and skill
- appropriate use of information
- risk assessment grounded in evidence
- communication with relevant others
- risk management plan linked to risks and risk level
- risk management plan delivered with integrity
- all reasonable steps taken
- information collected and thoroughly evaluated
- clear recording. (From Kemshall 1997)

The list intertwines aspects of professionalism (e.g. using knowledge and skills) with issues of procedural compliance. One implication therefore is that, if organisations place more emphasis on some elements than others, this can have significant implications for day-to-day practice. The way in which the concept of defensible decision making is applied may influence whether, for example, practitioners see themselves as professionals or administrators, and this will affect their understanding and perception of their role.

PLAYING TO YOUR AUDIENCE

It has been noted earlier that discretion and a degree of autonomy are aspects of professionalism. But of course that's not the whole story. Discretion is not totally unfettered and practitioners will be working within a range of policies, expectations and standards. Early probation national standards, for example, referred to 'practitioners' *professional judgement* to be exercised within a framework of *accountability*' (Home Office 1995, p.2, original emphasis, cited in Eadie and Canton 2002, p.16), and the importance of accountability is frequently emphasised in inspection reports and inquiries into disasters or serious incidents. What is meant by accountability? Sometimes it is just used to refer to activities being 'signed off' by managers, but there is a need to explore in more detail some of the different types of accountability and how they influence decision-making behaviour. People are concerned about how their work will be received by others. How does this influence how they go about professional tasks?

One interesting line of research about decision making starts from the premise that the context within which people make decisions is critical, and that accountability is a universal feature of decision-making environments:

> Accountability is a critical rule and norm enforcement mechanism – the social psychological link between individual decision-makers and the social systems to which they belong. Expectations of accountability are an implicit or explicit constraint on virtually everything people do (If I do this, how will others react?). (Tetlock 1997, p.661)

Tetlock also argues that, in general, people seek approval and respect from those to whom they are accountable. This can be for a number of reasons – from wishing to keep a job, to protect and enhance one's self-image or to acquire power and status.

In this model, there are two key variables that influence how accountability affects people's thinking. The first is whether you know the views of the audience that you are accountable to. A combination of the desire for social approval and the tendency to prefer least effort solutions makes it more likely that you will adopt a position that you think the audience will approve of, and not expend much time considering other options. So, if you know the views of the audience that you are accountable to, it is likely that you will use fewer items of information and adopt a view that you think will be non-controversial. On the other hand, if you don't know the views of your audience in advance, then you are more likely to engage in 'vigilant, complex and self-critical thought' (Tetlock 1997, p.664) in order to prepare for any challenges or questions that they might raise.

Much of the risk assessment activity in social care and criminal justice is concerned with conducting assessments and preparing reports for other decision makers (such as courts or tribunals). In general, practitioners will believe that they know how these audiences are likely to react and may often perceive them as being risk averse. Any discussion with a group of practitioners about court reports, for example, will tend to include comments about the particular preferences of their local court and what they expect to see from assessments. What other audiences might be in the mind of practitioners? An increasingly audited and quality assured approach to practice means that they are likely to have in mind the perspective of their immediate managers, as well as national bodies such as inspectorates. Colleagues in other organisations would be another potential audience to consider, as identified by White *et al.* who suggested that 'completing a CAF for the purposes of referral to another agency placed particular requirements upon the author to present information in a manner designed to engage their interest and resources' (2009, p.1212). All these perceptions may make assessors focus on what they need to do to gain approval, or get the results they want from audiences (Tetlock and Boettger 1989), which may then discourage the taking of positive risks (see Titterton, and Littlechild and Glasby *et al.*, this volume).

As well as whether an audience is known or not, the second key variable in the model is about the timing of accountability. The discussion earlier applies an awareness of accountability *before* making the decision but other factors arise when thinking about situations of accountability *after* a decision has been made. For example, 'once accountable subjects had publicly committed themselves, the major function of thought became the generation of as many justifications for those stands as possible' (Tetlock 1997, p.666). There may be considerable mental effort involved (and an individual's motives may be similar, such as to protect status or social image) but, rather than thinking through a range of information and a choice of explanations, the focus is on justifying a decision already made. This is similar to the process of confirmatory bias observed by other commentators on risk decision making – that is to say, paying attention to information that confirms decisions already made (Strachan and Tallant 1997). It also has parallels in processes observed in offenders whose post-offence justifications may be very different from their original motivations for offending (Wood and Riggs 2009).

The findings from, and publicity given to, reviews of child deaths, injury to vulnerable adults or serious further offences, together with the sometimes over-narrow application of the idea of defensible decision making, have arguably led to Tetlock's post-event justification pattern of thinking influencing practice long before an incident has occurred. Practitioners may aim their work at the account they need to give to the imagined inspector or manager, should the worst happen. This is not all a bad thing of course because it is important to be able to explain decisions in such circumstances. There is a danger, however, that critical thinking is replaced by a focus on justifying one's course of action, rather than examining a range of possible explanations or hypotheses, or planning for a range of possible future scenarios (Risk Management Authority 2007). Defensible decision making could be seen as an attempt to bring more rigour to the pre-decision stage but, if the prevailing culture is risk averse and blame oriented, then this process could be misunderstood. If practitioners perceive their audiences to be focused on narrow elements of defensibility and compliance with basic requirements, it will tend to lead to limited patterns of closed thinking – playing to the anticipated audience – rather than engaging in complex thought about the current problem to be addressed.

This model isn't a complete account of decision making by any means – for example, it doesn't make much reference to emotions, ethics or the influence of theory on behaviour, but it is useful because it takes account of social contingency, reflects reality and appears to fit with commonsense everyday experiences. Even with professional training and the skills to resist some of the more obvious biases or shortcuts in decision making, the pressures and complexities of practice mean that the extent, timing and type of accountability are likely to affect the judgements people make. Appreciating that people will also be influenced by the desire to seek approval can help in understanding our own and other people's decisions.

The known, the unknown and the unexpected

In thinking further about real-world applications, a useful first stage is to identify the different types of accountability mechanisms relevant to a particular area of practice, and to think about how they work. There are, for example, different types of 'challenge mechanisms' including complaints systems (by clients or their families); operational managers; senior managers; other agencies; courts; and the media. In some settings you may be fairly certain that one of these processes will be applied (e.g. if you know that managers will quality assure your work or that there will be an inspection). In other cases, accountability might only come up as a big issue if people complain or appeal against a decision (or the media get involved when something goes wrong) and you are unlikely to know in advance whether or not this will happen. The degree of certainty about whether or not an accountability mechanism will apply is likely to affect how you think. Useful questions to consider, therefore, would include 'What types of accountability do I experience?' 'In what circumstances am I held accountable?' 'If there are several types of accountability mechanisms in play, do they affect my thinking in similar or different ways?' 'If you are adapting your decisions – or the presentation of those decisions – to suit the anticipated reactions of particular audiences, what effect is that having on the way in which you analyse information and make judgements?'

In general, practitioners face audiences whose views will often be known or anticipated. The relative rarity of situations where practitioners encounter the views of audiences whose views are unknown or less familiar may potentially have a negative impact on practice. If dealing with people whose views are not predictable can have positive effects in terms of prompting critical thought, then there is an implication that creative in-depth thinking is less likely to be found in contexts where staff have little contact with unknown audiences. This applies to teams, services and even multi-agency arrangements, as well as to individuals (Peay 2003), because evidence shows a tendency for 'groupthink' to develop when people have learned how colleagues will react and familiarity leads to reluctance to challenge others' decisions or judgements.

Are there ways of introducing the challenge to thinking provided by an 'unknown audience' in order to counter some of these problems? This might be achieved by the nature of case supervision, for example, with managers specifically trying to encourage staff to consider less familiar viewpoints. Or perhaps through gatekeeping systems that are varied, so that it is not always the same people checking each other's work. Or team discussions in which particular people are tasked with the role of 'devil's advocate' (within reason of course). Including lay people in formal processes and structures can also provide a fresh perspective (as, for example, with the role of lay advisors in Multi-Agency Public Protection Arrangements [MAPPA], Ministry of Justice 2009). Unexpected reactions from generally predictable audiences can also provide a useful learning opportunity – rather than just regarding them as one-off events outside the usual pattern, they can instead be a prompt to consider new perspectives or information that may previously have been ignored.

Overcoming stage fright (or 'making the decision')

Presenting decision makers with more unknown and challenging audiences is not, however, the whole answer, and the way that this is put into practice will make a significant difference. It was noted earlier that accountability to unknown audiences prompts people to take account of a more complex range of information but this does not automatically lead to better decisions. Tetlock states that 'pre-exposure accountability to an unknown audience motivated subjects to be more integratively complex, but it did not make them more discriminating consumers of the information at their disposal' (1997, p.672). So, the danger is that assessors take account of more and different types of information but do not necessarily use it to best effect. Research in the fields of child protection and public protection provides examples of this with evidence that, although the range of information gathered by practitioners making critical decisions may have improved over time, there has not necessarily been a corresponding increase in the quality of analysis (Baker 2008; Munro 2008).

Problems in actually reaching a decision can include taking account of irrelevant information, and feeling overwhelmed by the greater awareness of possible outcomes that comes from having more information and a fear of being wrong. This last point is aptly summarised by Beckett *et al.* (writing about child protection but it could apply equally well to other settings): 'To actually come to a conclusion carries the risk of discovering that one's conclusion is wrong, and this creates an incentive to delay' (2007, p.62). Overcoming these difficulties requires, among other things, tools and frameworks that guide people in gathering and analysing information without being over-prescriptive, and practice cultures that facilitate adaptation and revision of judgements (Taylor and White 2006). There is a need to balance the benefits of having challenges from unknown audiences to increase complexity with having tools that support consistency and accuracy, but also to have ways of supporting decision-making and the taking of action that still allows for change over time.

For practitioners, the question would therefore be: Are any of these elements over- or under-emphasised in your work environment, and what would help you to achieve a better balance? For managers: What are you doing to ensure that policies and culture achieve such a balance for your staff?

OF BATTLES, BUILDINGS, SAT-NAVS AND OTHER CURIOUS CONCEPTS

The assessments made and the decisions reached are of course framed in language and communicated to others through the use of language. This has an impact on risk communication (Carson and Bain 2008) and debates over terminology (Baker 2010) affect both decision making and those about whom decisions are made. Language helps to shape perceptions (e.g. whether we talk about 'service users' or 'clients') and therefore affects what we do and how we do it. The use of language in professional discourse can be analysed from a number of angles (e.g. via conversation analysis) but one particularly interesting perspective to consider is the role of metaphor. Although this might not seem immediately to be an obvious route for analysing social policy, examples such as the thought-provoking discussions on the role of metaphors in relation to immigration (Charteris-Black 2006)[1] and criminal justice policy documentation (Armstrong 2009)[2] illustrate how this approach can be a fruitful means for improving our understanding of practice and policy implementation.

We typically tend to think of metaphor as a means to elaborate speech or a way of adding 'colour and emphasis to language' (Armstrong 2009, p.3), although Lakoff and Johnson suggest that 'metaphor is pervasive in everyday life, not just in language but in thought and action. Our ordinary conceptual system, in terms of which we both think and act, is fundamentally metaphorical in nature' (1980, p.3). They suggest that the 'essence of metaphor is understanding and experiencing one kind of thing in terms of another' (1980, p.5) and cite a number of examples to show how metaphor is central to our thinking, often in ways we don't realise. Consider, for example, how our talk about arguments is shaped by the metaphor of 'argument is war' (e.g. we refer to attacking and defending positions). Or the metaphor 'time is money' is evident in the way we talk about spending time.

If metaphors are so central to our patterns of thinking, then it follows that they can also be relevant to understanding professional risk assessment practice. Coe states that '[m]etaphors create meaning, move minds, motivate people' (1996, p.438). If so, then they are most definitely worth exploring. Consider again, for example, the term 'defensible decision making'. The features and components of these (decisions) were described earlier, along with some criticisms that practice can too easily slip into being defensive. In thinking about why

1   Such as the 'container' image, which leads to assumptions about the country being 'full up'.
2   For example, the animal imagery implied by terms such as 'predatory' in relation to sex offenders.

this might occur, one reason might be that the underlying metaphor here is something like 'risk assessment/professional practice is a battle'. The language of defence and defending is normally used in contexts such as war, attacks against people or property, flooding or natural disasters, disease, or legal disputes. Even when used in a sporting context, the impression is still of an adversarial, gladiatorial contest with winners and losers. The activities that make up defensible decisions may in themselves be neutral but, when we think about them in terms of the battle metaphor, we can see how this underlying concept could steer attitudes and practice in ways that practitioners don't consciously realise.

Another way of exploring how risk decision makers think about what they do is through the idea of 'interpretive repertoires' (Edley 2001). These are essentially 'a lexicon or register of terms and metaphors drawn upon to characterise and evaluate actions and events' (Potter and Wetherell 1987, p.138). They become part of the fabric of everyday practice, shaping the way people talk about their work. In a study of an organisation working with homeless women, for example, Juhila (2009) identified various interpretive repertoires used by staff in conceptualising their role: care, assessment, control, therapy, service provision and fellowship. Research into decision making about long-term care of older people has similarly identified a range of 'paradigms' or interpretations of the practitioner's role: identifying and meeting needs, minimising situational hazards, protecting this individual and others, balancing benefits and harms, accounting for resources and priorities, wariness of lurking conflicts (Taylor 2006). The repertoire being used at any one time – which will be influenced by factors including concepts of professionalism, understanding of accountability mechanisms and the use of metaphors – will affect how people deal with risk.

Thinking about the metaphors and repertoires of everyday practice

This chapter is suggesting that, because our approach to risk decision making can become so familiar, we lose sight of the ways in which we are thinking and how this is affecting our judgements and behaviour. Consciously thinking about 'how we are thinking', and identifying the metaphors and repertoires we use, may help us clarify how we are going about risk tasks. This is a rich area for analysis and there is much scope for considering metaphors quite generally in relation to health, social care and crime (and indeed in relation to 'risk', see Young 2001). Titterton in this volume uses the metaphor of a 'lever of change' to think about the purpose of risk taking. For this chapter, we will focus on metaphors associated with the *processes* of risk assessment and decision making. Consider, for example, the use of structured approaches to risk assessment. There are many different types of risk assessments in use across agencies that vary in length, content and design. However, some similarities in practitioners' views about their use are apparent in the literature: positive opinions tend to focus on the ability of such approaches to remind people of key factors to consider and to provide a structure to the process of recording and analysing information, while critics tend to view them as restrictive, narrow methods that prioritise producing statistics over understanding individuals (Mair, Burke and Taylor 2006; Robinson 2003).

In thinking about the metaphors for assessment processes that practitioners may currently be using, we have drawn on findings from this literature and from our practical experience of designing tools and delivering training to practitioners. Some common metaphors for structured assessment processes we have encountered are:

- Calculator: I tick the boxes, add up the numbers and it gives me the correct answer

- Safety net: if things go wrong I will be protected from the 'fall out' because I used the designated tool

- Protective body armour: for back-covering.

Much of the focus is on finding the so-called right answer and on guarding against reputational risk. Are these metaphors ones that you or your team currently use? What difference to practice would it make if other metaphors for assessment frameworks were used? Consider the following possibilities and think about how they might affect practice (note: these are examples to prompt discussion, not necessarily recommended approaches):

- Symptom checker: to assist in problem diagnosis

- Line prompter: if I get lost in my dialogue with the client and don't know what to say, the tool reminds me of the correct 'lines' to use

- Smoke detector: can alert you to signs of danger or risk, early warning, screening, action required

- Tourist guide book: sets out the essential landmarks to look out for (especially useful if time is limited) plus the interesting highways and byways that give you a fuller understanding (if you have time to explore).

One of the conclusions you will no doubt have reached is that metaphors are inevitably partial. A similar discussion can be applied to interpretive repertoires. Risk assessment can be thought of in a variety of ways (e.g. as art, science, a journey or writing a biography) and practitioners' roles could also be conceptualised in significantly different ways. Think back to the examples given earlier (p.22) from the work of Juhila (2009) and Taylor (2006). Which, if any, of these reflect your current practice? If none of them, then which repertoires are you using? And what difference would it make if you used a different repertoire?

Choosing metaphors and repertoires

If metaphors and repertoires are both prevalent and powerful in professional practice, how do we choose which ones to use? In evaluating metaphors, Coe reminds us that it is not a case of their being true or false but rather that 'some are much better than others' (1996, p.443). All metaphors emphasise certain characteristics and hide others, and a critical question therefore is 'whether they direct/deflect attention in ways that help people achieve their purposes' (Coe 1996, p.443).

For example, identify a risk assessment tool or framework that you use. Now consider the difference between thinking of it as a map and thinking of it as a sat-nav. If it's a map, then it will be seen as providing guidance and important cues, but the responsibility for interpreting it, and for choosing which of the possible routes available to use, rests with the traveller. In the case of a sat-nav, there is typically less use of knowledge and fewer choices to make because it's more a case of following the instructions. You may get to the same destination, but you may not understand how you got there, nor have developed an awareness of landmarks on the route or know how to do it again if you didn't have the sat-nav. This is not to say that sat-navs are never useful but rather that over-reliance on them can result in a failure to develop other skills. In thinking about risk assessment tools then, we would want to argue that a map metaphor would be preferable to that of a sat-nav one because it puts more focus on using skills and applying knowledge rather than just complying with instructions or procedures.

What about metaphors for robust and rigorous decision making? What difference would it make if we used a metaphor of 'practice as building' and talked about decisions being 'structurally sound' or 'safely constructed'? Possible advantages of this perspective could be that it:

- assumes that there is a clear and constructive purpose in mind (e.g. to produce a building for people to live or work in)

- emphasises the importance of rigour and accuracy (otherwise the building will not be safe or fit for purpose)

- highlights the need for good foundations

- allows for some individuality and creativity within the structure and procedures required (a row of houses may share similar characteristics but will also have differences in features such as style, appearance and size).

This perspective could have a number of benefits for practice by, for example, encouraging people to be clearer about the goal of the assessment before getting too bogged down in the details. This is similar to the importance of defining the purpose of risk taking as identified in Titterton's chapter (this volume). It also shows the importance of professional theory and knowledge (the 'foundations') and can illustrate the possibility of balancing creativity with rules and structures. As noted earlier, however, all metaphors emphasise certain things and deflect attention from others. Criticisms of the building metaphor for risk assessment might be that it is too static, fails to give enough attention to change over time and doesn't easily convey the idea that risk taking can (sometimes) be positive. An alternative metaphor about journeys, which conveyed ideas about the importance of preparation, knowing the terrain, alertness to potential hazards and having contingency plans in place to deal with unpredictable events, could perhaps contribute to a more dynamic conceptualisation of practice. The key point here is not that any particular metaphor or interpretive repertoire is 'right' but that some will be more useful than others, and also that we are likely to need a range that reflects different activities rather than looking for just one idea to cover all aspects of practice. It reinforces the discussion earlier about the need for challenging audiences who may be able to identify metaphors or repertoires that we take for granted, and who can suggest alternatives that could help to promote professional and analytical patterns of thinking.

Working with metaphors and repertoires

Greater awareness of metaphors and interpretive repertoires and their influences on decision making would contribute to the development of 'risk literacy' (see Titterton, this volume). Once we begin to identify and understand these influences on our own practice, we may become more conscious of different metaphors or repertoires used either by colleagues within the same organisation or staff from other agencies. There may, for example, be different metaphors in use by managers compared with those of practitioners. In relation to risk assessment tools, for example, possible management metaphors might include:

- CCTV: I can see what the staff are doing

- Nanny/mentor: guides the new or less experienced staff
- Product 'brand': reassurance of quality from using a well-known named product.

In multi-agency working there will be different and, sometimes, conflicting metaphors and repertoires in play. This is probably an inevitable feature of practice, but being aware of them at least helps us to understand other people's decision-making processes. A judgement that may not seem to make much sense in the context of a particular interpretive repertoire may appear more rational in another. It also implies that there could be different understandings of defensibility within and across organisations. 'Response tendencies that look like judgmental flaws from one metaphorical perspective frequently look quite prudent from another perspective' (Tetlock 1997, p.660) and even, or perhaps especially, in cases where things have gone wrong it will be important to draw out which repertoires or metaphors were shaping practice, because this may go a long way to explaining the basis for a decision. Managers and inspectors need to be aware of their own preferred repertoires and understand how this affects their judgements about the quality of other people's decision making.

A second area to consider is that individuals – and indeed teams or services – may switch between interpretive repertoires in the course of providing an intervention or service. Juhila (2009), for example, found that staff easily moved between different repertoires, even within quite short spaces of time. This is clearly a useful skill and allows for flexibility in practice, but are there circumstances where this might be confusing for the service recipient or other professionals? Also, if this adaptability is largely subconscious, are there potential problems in repertoires being applied inappropriately? Third, just as assessments need to be reviewed and updated in the light of changing circumstances, so metaphors and repertoires need to be revised over time to take account of developments in research, policy, practice and culture.

BEING AN OPTIMISTIC PROFESSIONALLY DEFENSIBLE RISK TAKER

Holding on to the belief that people and situations can change for the better is not always easy in practice environments that are focused on risk, as noted by Hayles (writing about public protection work in criminal justice services) who argues that '[t]he inception of allegedly more sophisticated systems of risk assessment and risk management in the form of multi-agency public protection panels appears to have done nothing to instil greater optimism' (2006, p.68). And in the wake of high-profile cases such as the death of Baby P (Laming 2009) or the murder of two French students by offenders under statutory supervision (National Offender Management Service 2009)[3] it is easy to become cynical about the concept of 'professional' practice. On the other hand, when thinking about how to improve practice, some of the ideal descriptions may seem difficult to attain. For example:

> One should be sensitive to the views of important constituencies, but avoid appearing so chameleonic that one loses their trust and confidence. One should be self-critical but not to the point of paralysis. And one should stick by one's principles but not to the point of dogmatism or self-righteousness. (Tetlock 1997, p.673)

But how do we nudge closer to this kind of practice in real-world settings?

How individuals think about the job that they are doing, and how their working context affects their decision-making, determines to quite a large degree the way in which they go about professional tasks, including risk assessment and risk management. Policy statements, guidance, assessment tools and training manuals on risk assessment and defensible decisions all have a role to play in developing the practice context and shaping the ways in which professionals understand and interpret the job that they do. This chapter has argued that this process needs to remain dynamic and self-critical, with varied systems of accountability to encourage rigorous thinking, and an exploration of the interpretive repertoires individuals use to understand their task. In doing so, there will also be a need to take account of the social and political context. Thus a 'risk assessment as art' repertoire in unlikely to gain much currency with senior managers or politicians in the current climate but a 'risk assessment as safe construction' theme might be more acceptable. Organisations should aim to develop and promote professional, skilled, non-defensive approaches to risk taking and decision making, rather than merely technical accuracy or procedural compliance. Individual risk assessors and practice supervisors should also aim for this approach to be reflected in all their risk practice, and their conversations about risk practice, with the outcome (it is hoped) that decisions will be more likely to be both positive *and* robust enough to withstand scrutiny.

3   See www.justice.gov.uk/news/docs/noms-investigation-report-sonnex.pdf, accessed on 30 March 2010.

REFERENCES

Aberdeen City Council (2009) *Positive Risk Taking Policy*. Available at www.aberdeencity. gov.uk/web/files/SocialWork/Positive_Risk_Taking_Policy_Aberdeen_City_Jan09.pdf, accessed on 30 March 2010.

Armstrong, S. (2009) *Managing Meaning: Metaphor in Criminal Justice Policy*. Available at http://ssrn.com/abstract=1508340, accessed on 30 March 2010.

Baker, K. (2008) 'Risk, uncertainty and public protection: assessment of young people who offend.' *British Journal of Social Work 38*, 8, 1463–1480.

Baker, K. (2010) 'More harm than good? The language of public protection.' *Howard Journal 49*, 1, 42–53.

Beckett, C. (2008) 'Risk, Uncertainty and Thresholds.' In M. Calder (ed.) *Contemporary Risk Assessment in Safeguarding Children*. Lyme Regis: Russell House.

Beckett, C., McKeigue, B. and Taylor, H. (2007) 'Coming to conclusions: social workers' perceptions of the decision making process in care proceedings.' *Child and Family Social Work 12*, 1, 54–63.

Carson, D. and Bain, A. (2008) *Professional Risk and Working with People*. London: Jessica Kingsley Publishers.

Charteris-Black, J. (2006) 'Britain as a container: immigration metaphors in the 2005 election campaign.' *Discourse and Society 17*, 5, 563–581.

Coe, R. (1996) 'Metaphor.' In T. Enos (ed.) *Encyclopaedia of Rhetoric and Composition: Communication from Ancient Times to the Information Age*. New York: Garland.

Eadie, T. and Canton, R. (2002) 'Practising in a context of ambivalence: the challenge for youth justice workers.' *Youth Justice 2*, 1, 14–26.

Edley, N. (2001) 'Analysing Masculinity: Interpretive Repertoires, Ideological Dilemmas and Subject Positions.' In M. Wetherell, S. Taylor and S. Yates (eds) *Discourse as Data: A Guide for Analysis*. London: Sage Publications.

Friedson, E. (1994) *Professionalism Reborn: Theory, Prophecy and Policy*. Oxford: Polity Press.

Hayles, M. (2006) 'Constructing Safety: A Collaborative Approach to Managing Risk and Building Responsibility.' In K. Gorman, M. Gregory, M. Hayles and N. Parton (eds) *Constructive Work with Offenders*. London: Jessica Kingsley Publishers.

Hollows, A. (2008) 'Professional Judgement and the Risk Assessment Process.' In M. Calder (ed.) *Contemporary Risk Assessment in Safeguarding Children*. Lyme Regis: Russell House.

Home Office (1995) *National Standards for the Supervision of Offenders in the Community*. London: Home Office.

Juhila, K. (2009) 'From care to fellowship and back: interpretive repertoires used by the social welfare workers when describing their relationship with homeless women.' *British Journal of Social Work 39*, 1, 128–143.

Kemshall, H. (1997) *The Management and Assessment of Risk: Training Pack*. London: Home Office.

Kemshall, H. (1998) 'Defensible decisions for risk: or "it's the doers wot get the blame".' *Probation Journal 45*, 2, 67–72.

Kemshall H., Parton, N., Walsh, M. and Waterson, J. (1997) 'Concepts of risk in relation to organizational structure and functioning within the personal social services and probation.' *Social Policy and Administration 31*, 3, 213–232.

Lakoff, G. and Johnson, M. (1980) *Metaphors We Live By*. Chicago, IL: University of Chicago Press.

Laming, Lord (2009) *The Protection of Children in England: A Progress Report*. London: The Stationery Office.

Mair, G., Burke, L. and Taylor, S. (2006) 'The worst tax form you've ever seen? Probation Officers' views of OASys.' *Probation Journal 53*, 1, 7–23.

May, T. and Buck, M. (1998) 'Power, professionalism and organisational transformation.' *Sociological Research Online 3*, 2. Available at www.socresonline.org.uk/3/2/5.html, accessed on 19 July 2010.

Milner, J. and O'Byrne, P. (2009) *Assessment in Social Work* (3rd edition). Basingstoke: Palgrave Macmillan.

Ministry of Justice (2009) *MAPPA Guidance Version 3*. London: Ministry of Justice.

Munro, E. (2008) *Effective Child Protection* (2nd edition). London: Sage Publications.

National Offender Management Service (2009) *Investigation into the Issues Arising from the Serious Further Offence Review: Dano Sonnex*. London: National Offender Management Service.

Peay, J. (2003) *Decisions and Dilemmas: Working with Mental Health Law*. Oxford: Hart Publishing.

Potter, J. and Wetherell, M. (1987) *Discourse and Social Psychology: Beyond Attitudes and Behaviour*. London: Sage Publications.

Power, M. (2004) *The Risk Management of Everything*. London: Demos.

Risk Management Authority (2007) *Standards and Guidelines: Risk Management of Offenders Subject to an Order for Lifelong Restriction*. Paisley: Risk Management Authority.

Robinson, G. (2003) 'Implementing OASys: lessons from research into LSI-R and ACE.' *Probation Journal 50*, 1, 30–40.

Sheppard, M., Newstead, S., Di Caccavo, A. and Ryan, K. (2001) 'Comparative hypothesis assessment and quasi triangulation as process knowledge assessment strategies in social work practice.' *British Journal of Social Work 31*, 6, 863–885.

Strachan, R. and Tallant, C. (1997) 'Improving Judgement and Appreciating Biases within the Risk Assessment Process.' In H. Kemshall and J. Pritchard (eds) *Good Practice in Risk Assessment and Risk Management 2*. London: Jessica Kingsley Publishers.

Taylor, B. (2006) 'Risk management paradigms in health and social services for professional decision making on the long-term care of older people.' *British Journal of Social Work 36*, 8, 1411–1429.

Taylor, C. and White, S. (2006) 'Knowledge and reasoning in social work: educating for humane judgment.' *British Journal of Social Work 36*, 6, 937–954.

Tetlock, P. (1997) 'An Alternative Metaphor in the Study of Judgment and Choice: People as Politicians.' In W. Goldstein and R. Hogarth (eds) *Research on Judgment and Decision Making: Currents, Connections and Controversies*. Cambridge: Cambridge University Press.

Tetlock, P. and Boettger, R. (1989) 'Social and cognitive strategies for coping with accountability: conformity, complexity, and bolstering.' *Journal of Personality and Social Psychology 57*, 4, 632–640.

Titterton, M. (2005) *Risk and Risk Taking in Health and Social Welfare*. London: Jessica Kingsley Publishers.

White, S., Hall, C. and Peckover, S. (2009) 'The descriptive tyranny of the Common Assessment Framework: technologies of categorization and professional practice in child welfare.' *British Journal of Social Work 39*, 7, 1197–1217.

Whitty, N. (2009) 'MAPPA for Kids: Discourses of Security, Risk and Children's Rights.' In K. Baker and A. Sutherland (eds) *Multi-Agency Public Protection Arrangements and Youth Justice*. Bristol: The Policy Press.

Wood, E. and Riggs, S. (2009) 'Adult attachment, cognitive distortions, and views of self, others, and the future among child molesters.' *Sexual Abuse: A Journal of Research and Treatment 21*, 3, 375–390.

Young, J. (2001) 'Risk(ing) metaphors.' *Clinical Perspectives on Accounting 12*, 5, 607–625.

CHAPTER 2

POSITIVE RISK TAKING WITH PEOPLE AT RISK OF HARM

MIKE TITTERTON

INTRODUCTION

Across numerous welfare regimes within the UK and internationally, an exciting development has been unfolding, one which has the potential to transform the lives of children and adults who may be described as being at 'risk of harm'. In countries as far apart as Scotland and Australia, and within international networks, there has been an upsurge of interest in what has been labelled 'positive risk taking' (Titterton 1999, 2005a), and what this approach has to offer in terms of lasting change in the way people are helped through professional practice and also how social services are conceived and delivered (Barry 2007; Clarke 2006, 2009; Green 2007; Hughes 2009; Mitchell and Glendinning 2007; Powell 2005; Sawyer 2008; Stanford 2008; Taylor 2006). This is an approach that promises much, not just for service users and practitioners, but also for risk researchers. This is reflected in the growth of interest, not just in risk per se, a topic that has grown markedly over the last decade, but in the positive attributes of risk.

In this chapter, the author explores the notion of positive risk taking in relation to people who are deemed to be in a state of vulnerability or at risk of harm. After a brief consideration of some conceptual and definitional issues, the potential of this approach, along with some of its challenges, are examined. The problem facing practitioners, attempting to 'get the balance right' when making risk decisions, will receive special attention. An example from Scotland, which provides a useful illustration of the practical application of this approach, is outlined. In conclusion, the author affirms the central importance of positive risk taking for improving health and welfare outcomes for vulnerable children and adults, as well as the need for support and training of professionals, users and informal carers.

RISK AND ITS FIVE FACES

'Risk' has many aspects. There is only space to highlight five here briefly. These are worth noting because they have an impact upon understandings and perceptions of users of social services and their formal and informal carers, as well as upon the general public. The first aspect is that risk is politically contested; it is subject to vigorous political discourse and debate, which extends to issues of trust, authority and expertise (Franklin 1998). The governance and regulation of risk and risk groups could be cited as an example of this, and after a slow start this is a topic that is witnessing a flourishing literature (Dean 1999; Green 2007; Joyce 2001; Kemshall 2002; Taylor-Gooby 2006; Van Loon 2008). Criticisms of 'over-regulation' and 'over-protection' of vulnerable people have been made, especially in terms of the negative perceptions of risk that some recent legislative and policy measures have embodied (Titterton 2005a).

The second is that risk is socially constructed; what this means, among other things, is that there are social factors that shape and influence perceptions of risk. Such factors include gender, age, ethnicity, social class, education, income and so on. The social construction of risk has largely built upon the foundations laid by risk theorists, especially those in the sociological field, and has received much attention in the burgeoning literature (Adam, Beck and Van Loon 2000; Alaszewski 2009; Stalker 2003; Taylor-Gooby 2006). Some of this risk theory is admittedly dense and triumphantly impenetrable, as well as blissfully untroubled by empirical evidence. Furthermore, some writers have debated the merit of 'risk' as a research topic in its own right (e.g. Green 2009; Zinn 2009). Nonetheless, risk has been a particularly fruitful source of social research (Alaszewski 2009; Alaszewski and Horlick-Jones 2003; Taylor-Gooby and Zinn 2006b). A helpful addition to research studies, for example, has been made by those investigating risk communication (Bennett and Calman 1999; Franklin 1998; Giles, Castleden and Baker 2010) including the social amplification of risks, and how the latter become exaggerated and distorted through the lens of the media (Pigeon, Kasperson and Slovic 2003).

Third, risk has cultural aspects, as the work of Mary Douglas showed (Douglas 1992; see also Giles *et al.* 2010; Gjernes 2008; Macaden and Clarke 2006). It is variable across countries and regions; thus issues facing children and young people with long-term conditions in eastern European and central Asian countries differ from those in western countries, which means that western models applied there for the purposes of prevention and intervention miss their target (Titterton and Smart 2010).

Fourth, risk has an experiential dimension: it is an essential part of the subjective experience of being human. This has a number of important implications, of which only three can be mentioned here. It implies that we need to be sensitive to individual and group experiences of risk, and to the diversities of professional experience, as well as strategies for managing uncertainty in everyday life (Alaszewski and Coxon 2008; Ballinger and Payne 2002; Zinn 2008). We need to acknowledge competing narratives and framing interpretations, as well as tracing these across the life course (Clarke 2009; Schoon and Bynner 2003; Vickerstaffe 2006). It also indicates that we need to draw much more readily from the field of psychology and should seek to integrate social scientific disciplines when studying risk and welfare (Taylor-Gooby and Zinn 2006a; Titterton 1992).

The fifth aspect concerns the dual nature of risk, or the embodying of both positive and negative features, which is being increasingly appreciated in the literature (Clarke 2009; Mitchell and Glendinning 2007). However, there remains a preoccupation with risk in its negative aspects in risk research and in professional practice; this is in part a reflection of the dominance of a pathological paradigm in welfare research (Titterton 1992). In this chapter, the author seeks to redress the balance and to set out the principal elements of positive risk taking.

POSITIVE RISK TAKING

One of the implications of the predominance of the pathological paradigm, and the preoccupation with the negativity of risk, has meant that certain features remain relatively neglected within welfare research. This includes a tendency to overlook the importance of competence, coping, capacity and capital; this is often accompanied by an assumption of homogeneity of responses to risk and adversity among risk groups across the life course (Titterton 1992; see also Schoon and Bynner 2003; Taylor-Gooby 2006). Risk is an important feature for the development of children and adolescents (Titterton, Hill and Smart 2002); while resilience has rightly been receiving greater attention (Atkinson, Martin and Rankin 2009; McMurray et al. 2008; see also Baker and Kelly, this volume), the need for children and adults to face risk in order to develop diverse forms of resilience also requires highlighting. More attention should be paid towards understanding and fostering resilience in adults (Dowrick et al. 2008; Hildon et al. 2008). The relationship between risk, resilience and vulnerability needs to be better explicated and developed into more effective models for working with, for example, children with long-term conditions across health, social care and educational settings (Titterton and Smart 2010).

These considerations, which underpin the positive risk-taking approach, apply to other risk groups across the caring spectrum, including groups as diverse as those with organic brain disorders (such as dementia), those affected by blood-borne virus infection (such as HIV) and even those labelled with 'high-risk' classifications (such as mentally disordered offenders) (Titterton, Maas-Lowit and Robertson 2007). There are important lessons to be learned across risk groups and risk settings, something that emerged from the first two books in this Good Practice Series (Kemshall and Pritchard 1996, 1997). One of the reasons that Health and Life for Everyone (HALE),[1] an international charity that works with children and adults at risk of harm, was established was to promote innovative and creative practice through positive risk taking across these groups and settings, to aid transfer of knowledge about effective practice and to promote more coordinated and holistic ways of working.

Positive risk taking sits at the heart of emerging agendas around self-management, personalisation and self-directed support (Hunter and Ritchie 2007; Scottish Executive 2006; Scottish Government 2009), recovery and patient experts (Davidson 2005), and users and informal carers as their own risk assessors (Langan 2008) and risk managers (Clarke and Heyman 1998; Ryan 2002). Such agendas are open to the objection that they reflect the transfer of responsibilities from the welfare state to the individual (Kemshall 2002; Ritchie and Woodward 2009). However, in positive risk taking, the emphasis is on empowerment through building capacity of service users and their carers, sharing redistributed resources, and learning jointly with public sector professionals in diverse and differentiated strategies to co-produce and manage personal welfare (Hunter and Ritchie 2007; Titterton 1992).

Risk work with children and adults can be constrained, however, by stifling restrictions on practice, which may exist for several reasons: these include limited understandings of risk; absence of risk policies and guidance; lack of managerial support; and a shortage of appropriate training. A critique of 'safety-first' approaches was made earlier by the author (Titterton 2005a; see also Clarke 2006). The failure to conceptualise risk holistically leads to defensive practice and to the 'blame culture' (Carson and Bain 2008; Titterton 2005a). When this comes to be overlaid by the protection and regulation agendas, which are currently still dominating practice in the UK, it can lead to

1   See www.haletrust.com, accessed on 17 July 2010.

additional difficulties for the pursuit of positive risk taking. An important issue concerns shared language and understandings (Titterton 2005a), which are affected by the limitations of risk communication, a problem that Carson and Bain (2008, p.181) rightly see as critical. There are at least two issues here. One is the clash of perceptions over risk, not only between service users and professionals but also among practitioners themselves, who often come from different and diverse disciplinary backgrounds (Horlick-Jones 2005). The media researchers mentioned earlier (such as Bennett and Calman 1999; Pigeon *et al.* 2003) have provided much food for thought around the problems that can arise from the 'amplification' of risk. The role of the media, in its diverse forms, in relation to risk is clearly a highly sensitive one (Hughes, Kitzinger and Murdock 2006) and it is readily identified by practitioners as a key factor in warping perceptions of risk work.

Authors such as Carson and Bain (2008) stress that there is a need to clarify the terms we are using in order to aid our risk decisions. There are, for example, few helpful definitions of 'risk taking' in the academic and professional literatures, as opposed to 'risk' (for a discussion, see Heyman *et al.* 2009). For the particular purposes of risk work in health care and social work, the author defined 'risk taking' as: 'a course of purposeful action based on informed decisions concerning the possibility of positive and negative outcomes of types and levels of risk appropriate in certain situations' (Titterton 2005a, p.25).

The significance of this definition in relation to health and social care is this. It proposes that the conceptualisation of the taking of risks should include the elements of purpose and the setting of objectives. It should involve informed decision making, where service users exchange and understand information with regard to risks. Further, it should embrace the appraisal of options, particularly in relation to potential harms and benefits from a course of action or from a set of circumstances. Finally, it should set boundaries for decision making about risk taking.

This definition, it should be noted, rules out the taking of risks that could be judged to be 'rash' and impetuous, at least for planned risk work with children and adults who may be defined as 'vulnerable' in the sense of needing some form of help or support. There is of course a moot point about just how informed an individual should be: this is one of the key aspects for practitioners and service users to consider, as well as taking into account issues relating to competency and capacity (understood in the sense of legal competence to make a decision regarding treatment, something addressed in law in the UK, US and Canada, as in Scotland's Adults with Incapacity Act 2000); this is addressed in Chapter 2 of Titterton (2005a; see also Buchanan 2004; Carson and Bain 2008).

RISK LITERACY AND STRIKING BALANCES IN RISK DECISIONS

The notion of 'risk literacy' can be advanced here in order to help promote a critical understanding of risk and risk taking. By 'risk literacy' is meant the capacity for critical understanding of, and reflective judgements about, risk and risk taking, based on evidence and experiential learning. Aspects of this notion have been further developed in Heyman *et al.* (2009). This notion can usefully be elaborated on in relation to risk work with children and adults in need of help and support. Our efforts need to focus on capacity building among users, informal carers and practitioners through skill building, including evaluating and managing risks in partnership.

The constitutive elements of risk literacy for decision making can be unpacked (see also Heyman *et al.* 2009), which are also useful when training professionals and working with service users on the topic of risk. This includes the development of critical understandings of the theoretical and practice factors that influence risk decisions by professionals (see also Baker and Wilkinson, this volume; Carson and Bain 2008). What is needed is not more top-down regulation driven by the latest inquiry into adverse events but bottom-up empowerment involving the development of skills, knowledge and confidence in risk decision makers (Titterton 2005a, 2005b). This applies across all risk settings but with particular force in respect of child protection, which has become perhaps uniquely 'sequestered' (Ferguson 2005), as well as increasingly anxiety-driven (Waterhouse and McGhee 2009) and open to bias in assessments because of underlying attitudes concerning removal from home (Davidson-Arad and Benbenishty 2010).

A major challenge for professionals in health care, social work and education is that of attempting to 'get the balance right' (such as between danger and safety) when making difficult risk decisions. This is so whether in respect of adult protection and child protection cases, or in more 'everyday risk work' with older people with dementia, younger adults with learning disabilities and/or mental health problems, alcohol and drug users, young offenders and so on. In order to develop and expand the appropriate repertoire of professional skills, risk literacy for practitioners must be fostered and nourished. This includes, inter alia, learning skills for digging behind presenting risks to get at the underlying welfare dilemma at stake. The latter has been defined as 'A welfare dilemma involves choices that welfare professionals, vulnerable people, their informal carers and their communities face between options that entail possible benefits and possible harms. These choices may be equally acceptable but their outcomes essentially remain unknown' (Titterton 2005a, p.50).

This involves identifying and working through essential dilemmas such as:

- autonomy versus intervention

- individual freedom versus public safety

- rights versus responsibilities

- user views of risk versus professional views of risk.

Welfare dilemmas are important to note because they help us think about the underlying issues that often lie *behind* the presenting problems of the service user. It is these that provide opportunities for practitioners and users to develop skills and knowledge in a learning process.

The emphasis is on an approach that focuses on the whole person within the context of his or her everyday life. Risk taking is a negotiated process, situated and framed by this context or 'lifeworld' with differing degrees of risk (Belschner *et al.* 1991; Hallrup *et al.* 2009), which includes the recognition, and negotiation, of the rights and responsibilities of the individual and those of the community in which he or she lives. It is acknowledged that this is not an easy process and that as professionals we may have to deal with conflict and with grey areas. Positive risk taking, while acting as an enabler in the lives of children and adults, can also be a challenge for staff. For example, we can be called upon to review the assumptions we hold and the decisions we make.

In HALE's work (e.g. when health care and social work staff are being trained in assessing and managing risks) there is a focus on what is called PAIR (purposeful, acceptable, informed and reasonable) risk taking (see Figure 2.1).

First, as the earlier discussion made clear, risk taking in relation to children and adults at risk of harm should be purposeful: it should have a clear purpose or goal. Next, the risk should be acceptable within the limits agreed by the service user and the welfare professional involved. Third, the risk should be informed: the advantages and disadvantages of the risk should be made clear in the understanding shared by the service user and the welfare professional with others to be kept informed as appropriate. Fourth, the risk should be reasonable to take according to the circumstances, abilities and understanding of the service user, and be realistic, feasible and subject to review. This pithy acronym (PAIR) helps practitioners and service users to focus on positive risk taking that has aims and limits, which are shared and understood by those involved in making the risk decision. It can aid professionals in conceptualising the key dimensions when attempting to think through the balances to be considered in their welfare dilemmas.

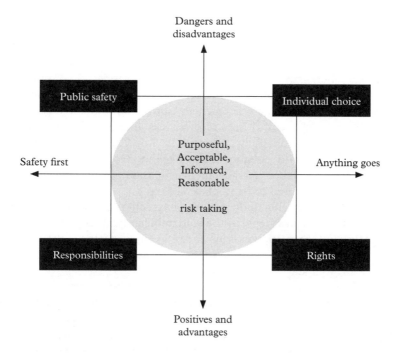

Figure 2.1: PAIR risk taking

THE TEN STEPS FOR RISK TAKING

The author has developed a 'good practice' model based on research and developmental work with practitioners and users, namely the Person-centred Risk Assessment and Risk Management System (PRAMS) (Titterton 1999, 2005a, 2005b, 2005c). This can be summarised in these ten steps to help guide risk decision makers, which are further elaborated on in Titterton (2005a, 2005b) (see Figure 2.2).

In Step 1, the main principles governing risk taking should be set out in a risk policy. Step 2 involves an assessment, closely involving the service user and encompassing not just possible harms but also those benefits likely to accrue as a result of taking the risk. These risks are discussed at length in Step 3, where advantages and disadvantages can be gone through, and boundaries and limitations specified. In Step 4, and where it can be shown that the vulnerable individual has the competency to make a clear decision about risks, the client should be empowered to take the decision for him/herself about taking the risk. Where the individual is reckoned to be lacking the competency to take the decision in this particular instance, steps to check why this is the case need to be taken. Whether an advocate or some other person should be involved in the risk decision is a question that requires addressing at this point.

In Step 5, a risk plan is drawn up, setting out responsibilities for implementation and steps for minimising possible harms and boosting possible benefits, as well as timescales and milestones. Step 6 involves ensuring, as far as possible, that all parties to the risk decision are consulted and a consensus is reached. Compared to the assessment of risks, the management of risks receives less attention than it deserves and this has to be forcefully addressed in Step 7. Key actions for both reducing harms and enhancing the likelihood of positive outcomes have to be undertaken. Arrangements for monitoring, reviewing and recording are required to be in place at Step 8.

Step 9 entails the undertaking of agreed risks, as assessed and discussed in previous steps, by the vulnerable individual and monitored accordingly. At Step 10, reviewing and reflecting form the core activities, this is an opportunity for practitioner and service user to learn from what went well and what did not go well.

This element of reflection is important for both professional and service user and it is this learning opportunity that facilitates the development of crucial judgemental skills concerning the striking of appropriate balances in risk work with vulnerable individuals.

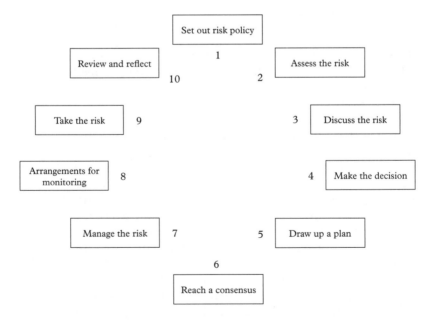

Figure 2.2: The ten steps

RISK AS A LEVER OF CHANGE

An intriguing challenge for staff, especially at senior practitioner level, is to consider the importance of using risk as a way of bringing about a positive change in the life of an individual and his or her circumstances or, in other words, using risk as a lever of change. This mainly involves deliberately using risk to bring about a stepped or incremental change in the abilities or capacities of the child or adult concerned. This involves, for example, giving the child or adult and their carers the opportunity to take a chance, in a planned and coordinated manner, that will lead to improved outcomes for the child or adult, their carers and the community. We can therefore introduce 'step changes' that represent something new and different from what went before, and which can be subject to monitoring and review at each progressive step if necessary. The cumulative effect should be one that helps the individual to 'move on' from their present circumstances (see Figure 2.3).

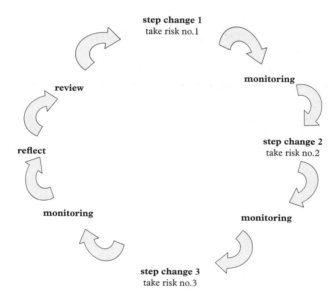

Figure 2.3: Risk as a lever of change

An example might be, in the case of residential care or youth justice settings, allowing a young person under supervision to undertake certain activities (e.g. to undertake a hill walk or some outdoor activity). In fieldwork, another example might be where a child is permitted supervised visits by a formerly abusive parent or carer, if this is in the interests of the child. Such examples need to be part of a structured risk plan with clear aims and with effective monitoring. The results of undertaking this activity might give the young person a sense of achievement, thereby raising their self-esteem, as well as a sense of responsibility. In the case of an adult with learning disabilities and a sexual offending history, changes through managed risk taking are possible, such as a staged increase in unsupervised activity. This can be especially powerful when life and goal planning techniques, such as the Good Lives Model (GLM) (Ward and Maruna 2007), in rehabilitation activities are deployed in combination, and where there is a building up of, or a reconnecting with, social networks.

This approach does take time and it does take patience, on behalf of both the practitioner and the client, but it has longer lasting effects and it is more cost-effective than wrapping up vulnerable individuals in expensive care packages and costly 24/7 supervisory arrangements, where opportunities to learn, develop and move on are tightly restricted.

REFLECTIVE PRACTICE AND PROFESSIONAL DEVELOPMENT

An important aspect of positive risk taking is that of the development of reflective practice by both welfare professionals and service users. Its importance, mentioned in the discussion on the ten steps earlier, is increasingly affirmed in the literature (Russell 2005; Wilson, Walsh, and Kirby 2007), even if its elements remain to be more fully explored and spelled out. The irony is that the importance of reflection is often underlined but life in modern social work and health care offices is anything but reflective because of staff shortages, growing workloads and increasing administrative burdens. Reflective practice is also very useful for groups and teams, not just individuals, making practitioner forums a potentially helpful fulcrum for this. Better use should also be made of supervisory opportunities (see Baker and Wilkinson, this volume). Some of the implications for education and training of professionals have been spelled out by the author (Titterton 1999), and include involving users and carers in education for social workers and health care staff (Taylor and Le Riche 2006). Multi-agency training, which should include independent sector staff, is very important but it tends to suffer at a time of budget restrictions, as does training generally. The author earlier raised a query about the evidence relating to how practitioners conceive of risk in a range of settings (Titterton 1999). Multi-agency perspectives could provide a valuable cross-referencing of the models and paradigms that staff deploy when thinking about risk situations (Baker and Wilkinson, this volume; Taylor 2006).

In the next section, an example from Scotland is presented for consideration, in order to help illustrate the potential in positive risk taking.

AN EXAMPLE FROM SCOTLAND

Within the context of the UK, Scotland has much more 'policy space' to innovate and experiment in than is often realised, something reinforced by the actions of the Parliament re-established in 1999; there is also a large measure of consensus over social policy goals among the political parties (Titterton 2001). Scotland has sought to forge ahead with legislative measures such as the Adults with Incapacity (Scotland) Act 2000, Mental Health (Care and Treatment) (Scotland) Act 2003, and Adult Support and Protection (Scotland) Act 2007. Despite severe fiscal pressures imposed by UK central governments over three decades, some local authorities in Scotland have endeavoured to maintain high levels of service provision and to develop approaches to risk work in partnership with health care, education, police and the independent sector. One such is Fife Council, which forms the third largest local authority in Scotland and is one that has followed an innovative approach to risk; an initiative featuring social work services, in partnership with HALE, provides a valuable illustration of an approach based on the positive risk agenda.

The ten main elements of the Fife approach were chiefly developed between 2006 and 2008 and can be described as follows:

1. Spelling out guiding principles for risk taking.

2. Devising procedures to guide the assessment and management of risks.

3. Providing guidance for staff.

4. Creating forms for risk assessment and management recording.

5. Training of managers and front-line staff.

6. Measuring the success of the initiative and learning from results.

7. Holding reviews and discussions.

8. Developing a training pack.

9. Encouraging colleagues in other agencies to adopt this approach.

10. Producing information for the public.

Currently the process in Fife is being extended to children and family services, and a series of training events for professionals with a focus on risk in child protection and child care has already taken place, including staff from a mix of services, such as youth justice. An interesting aspect has been that of the setting up of multidisciplinary Significant Risk Advisory Groups (SRAGs) for three topic areas: mental health, learning disabilities and young people; the task of the SRAGs is to provide a multidisciplinary arena for the discussion of cases that feature notable levels of adverse risk. A public launch of the professional guidance (Fife Council 2008) and training pack took place in December 2008, attended by a range of agencies and councillors, including the chair of the Social Work Committee and director of Social Work. This helped to raise publicity, and included an article in the local newspaper: journalists were invited, because it was considered important to involve representatives of the media, which plays such a key role in the portrayal and perceptions of risk in society.

There is much to be gleaned from considering the Fife initiative. The main learning points include the following:

- the importance of having an approach to risk that is informed by a framework – namely, PRAMS – which is supported by theoretical work and empirical research (Titterton 1999, 2005a)

- the centrality of having senior managers signed up to the positive risk-taking approach

- the value of training for staff, which is clearly linked to the framework described earlier

- putting a process in place, which has specialised guidance provided for staff

- the importance of multi-agency working

- having champions for risk, who are committed to the values and the process for implementing a risk approach.

Multi-agency working would appear to be functioning well in Fife, particularly on the ground, although there are differences in how agencies and disciplines perceive and treat risks. The partnership with HALE has given Fife Council the opportunity to embrace an innovative approach to risk taking. The next challenge in Fife is to ensure full multi-agency and multidisciplinary ownership of risk.

The importance of having a long-term view should be noted. So far the process has taken three years and the risk champions within the agency have had to be prepared to stay the distance, pushing and shoving for change.

CONCLUSION

Positive risk taking is a credible, robust and evidence-based approach for improving health and welfare outcomes for service users and for the range of vulnerable groups in society that form the target of social policy. It constitutes best practice for welfare professionals in terms of promoting dignity, autonomy and respect when working with children and adults at risk of harm. It encourages a focus on capacity building in terms of the skills, knowledge and understanding of service users, informal carers and professionals alike. Importantly, it facilitates a focus on resilience and encourages a move away from the pathological paradigm that has dominated social policy and welfare research for so long. It generates resources for risk literacy needed to guide decision making and to strike appropriate balances, through the development of frameworks like PRAMS, tools such as PAIR and techniques such as 'Risk as a lever for change'. As the example from Fife shows, it provides for innovative, practical and values-led partnerships for risk involving social work services, education, health care, the independent sector and the police. As such, positive risk taking represents the best and most effective rebuttal of the drift towards the 'risk averse society', particularly in its most zealous and frankly disturbing forms (BBC 2010; Pearce 2007; Saner 2009). In view of the recent growth of interest in aspects of risk in health and social care within some government-related agencies (Better Regulation Commission 2006; Commission for Social Care Inspection 2006; Department of Health 2007a, 2007b; Manthorpe 2007; Mental Welfare Commission for Scotland 2006; Scottish Executive 2006), this constitutes a very good time to be investigating and promoting this valuable approach.

ACKNOWLEDGEMENTS

The author wishes to thank the following people: the staff of Fife Social Work Services, especially Sheena Robertson; his colleague Helen Smart of HALE; Charlotte Clarke of Northumbria University; and Mike Maas-Lowit of Robert Gordon's University. He would like to dedicate this chapter to the memory of Liz Bain, service user representative and resident of Appin House, Kirkcaldy.

REFERENCES

Adam, B., Beck, U. and Van Loon, J. (2000) *The Risk Society and Beyond: Critical Issues for Social Theory*. London: Sage Publications.

Alaszewski, A. (2009) 'The future of risk in social science theory and research.' *Health, Risk and Society 11*, 6, 487–492.

Alaszewski, A. and Coxon, K. (2008) 'The everyday experience of living with risk and uncertainty.' *Health, Risk and Society 10*, 5, 413–420.

Alaszewski, A. and Horlick-Jones, T. (2003) *Risk and Health: Research Review and Priority Setting*. Medical Research Council and London: Economic and Social Research Council.

Atkinson, P.A., Martin, C.R. and Rankin, J. (2009) 'Resilience revisited.' *Journal of Psychiatric and Mental Health Nursing 16*, 137–145.

Baker, K. and Kelly, G. (2010) 'Risk Assessment and Young People.' In H. Kemshall and B. Wilkinson (eds) *Good Practice in Assessing Risk*. London: Jessica Kingsley Publishers.

Baker, K. and Wilkinson, B. (2010) 'Professional Risk Taking and Defensible Decisions.' In H. Kemshall and B. Wilkinson (eds) *Good Practice in Assessing Risk*. London: Jessica Kingsley Publishers.

Ballinger, C. and Payne, S. (2002) 'The construction of the risk of falling among and by older people.' *Ageing and Society 22*, 305–324.

Barry, M. (2007) *Effective Approaches to Risk Assessment in Social Work: An International Literature Review*. Edinburgh: Scottish Executive.

BBC (2010) 'Are you a danger to children?' *Panorama*, 8 February. London: BBC Productions.

Belschner, W., Engel, A., Henicz, H. and Muller-Doohm, S. (1991) 'Life world and risk behaviour of young adults.' *International Conference on AIDS, 7*, 421.

Bennett, P. and Calman, K. (eds) (1999) *Risk Communication and Public Health*. Oxford: Oxford University Press.

Better Regulation Commission (2006) *Risk, Responsibility and Regulation – Whose Risk is it Anyway?* London: Department for Business, Enterprise and Regulatory Reform.

Buchanan, A. (2004) 'Mental capacity, legal competence and consent to treatment.' *Journal of the Royal Society of Medicine 97*, 415–420.

Carson, D. and Bain, A. (2008) *Professional Risk and Working with People: Decision-making in Health, Social Care and Criminal Justice*. London: Jessica Kingsley Publishers.

Clarke, C.L. (2006) 'Risk and ageing populations: practice development research through an international research network.' *International Journal of Older People Nursing 1*, 3, 169–176.

Clarke, C.L. (2009) 'Risk and long-term conditions: the contradictions of self in society.' *Health, Risk and Society 4*, 11, 297–302.

Clarke, C.L. and Heyman, B. (1998) 'Risk Management for People with Dementia.' In B. Heyman (ed.) *Risk, Health and Health Care: A Qualitative Approach*. London: Hodder Arnold.

Commission for Social Care Inspection (2006) *Making Choices and Taking Risks: A Discussion Paper*. London: Commission for Social Care Inspection.

Davidson, L. (2005) 'Recovery, self-management and the expert patient – changing the culture of mental health from a UK perspective.' *Journal of Mental Health 14*, 1, 25–35.

Davidson-Arad, B. and Benbenishty, R. (2010) 'Contribution of child protection workers' attitudes to their risk assessment and intervention recommendations: a study in Israel.' *Health and Social Care in the Community 18*, 1, 1–9.

Dean, M. (1999) *Governmentality: Power and Rule in Modern Society*. London: Sage Publications.

Department of Health (DH) (2007a) *Independence, Choice and Risk: A Guide to Best Practice*. London: DH.

Department of Health (DH) (2007b) *Best Practice in Managing Risk: Principles and Guidance for Best Practice in the Assessment and Management of Risk to Self and Others in Mental Health Services*. London: DH.

Douglas, M. (1992) *Risk and Blame: Essays in Cultural Theory*. London and New York: Routledge.

Dowrick, C., Kokanovic, R., Hegarty, K., Griffiths, F. and Gunn, J. (2008) 'Resilience and depression: perspectives from primary care.' *Health 12*, 4, 439–452.

Ferguson, H. (2005) 'Trust, Risk and Expert Systems: Child Protection, Modernity and the (Changing) Management of Life and Death.' In S. Watson and A. Moran (eds) *Trust, Risk and Uncertainty*. London: Palgrave Macmillan.

Fife Council (2008) *Guidance on Risk in Professional Practice for Adults and Older People Service*. Glenrothes: Fife Council Social Work Service.

Franklin, J. (ed.) (1998) *The Politics of Risk Society*. Cambridge: Polity Press.

Giles, A.R., Castleden, H. and Baker, A.C. (2010) '"We listen to our elders. You live longer that way": examining aquatic risk communication and water safety practices in Canada's North.' *Health and Place 16*, 1, 1–9.

Gjernes, T. (2008) 'Perceptions of risk and uncertainty among Sami women involved in reindeer herding in Northern Norway.' *Health, Risk and Society 10*, 5, 505–516.

Green, D. (2007) 'Risk and social work practice.' *Australian Social Work 4*, 60, 395–409.

Green, J. (2009) 'Is it time for the sociology of health to abandon "risk"?' *Health, Risk and Society 11*, 6, 493–508.

Hallrup, L.B., Albertsson, D., Tops, A.B., Dahlberg, K. and Grahn, B. (2009) 'Elderly women's experience of living with fall risk in a fragile body: a reflective lifeworld approach.' *Health and Social Care in the Community 17*, 4, 379–387.

Heyman, B., Alaszewski, A., Shaw, M. and Titterton, M. (2009) *Health Care Through the Lens of Risk: A Critical Guide to the Risk Epidemic*. Oxford: Oxford University Press.

Hildon, Z., Smith, G., Netuveli, G. and Blane, D. (2008) 'Understanding adversity and resilience at older ages.' *Sociology of Health and Illness 30*, 5, 726–740.

Horlick-Jones, T. (2005) 'On "risk work": professional discourse, accountability and everyday action.' *Health, Risk and Society 7*, 3, 293–307.

Hughes, R. (ed.) (2009) *Rights, Risk, and Restraint-free Care of Older People: Person-centred Approaches in Health and Social Care*. London: Jessica Kingsley Publishers.

Hughes, E., Kitzinger, J. and Murdock, G. (2006) 'The Media and Risk.' In P. Taylor-Gooby and J.O. Zinn (eds) *Risk in Social Science*. Oxford: Oxford University Press.

Hunter, S. and Ritchie, P. (eds) (2007) *Co-production and Personalisation in Social Care*. London: Jessica Kingsley Publishers.

Joyce, P. (2001) 'Governmentality and risk: setting priorities in the NHS.' *Sociology of Health and Illness 23*, 5, 594–614.

Kemshall, H. (2002) *Risk, Social Policy and Welfare*. Buckingham: Open University Press.

Kemshall, H. and Pritchard, J. (eds) (1996) *Good Practice in Risk Assessment and Management 1*. London: Jessica Kingsley Publishers.

Kemshall, H. and Pritchard, J. (eds) (1997) *Good Practice in Risk Assessment and Management 2*. London: Jessica Kingsley Publishers.

Langan, J. (2008) 'Involving mental health service users considered to pose a risk to other people in risk assessment.' *Journal of Mental Health 17*, 5, 471–481.

Macaden, L. and Clarke, C.L. (2006) 'Risk perception among older South Asian people in the UK with type 2 diabetes.' *International Journal of Older People Nursing 1*, 3, 177–181.

Manthorpe, J. (2007) 'Managing risk in social care in the United Kingdom.' *Health, Risk and Society 9*, 3, 237–239.

McMurray, I., Connolly, H., Preston-Shoot, M. and Wigley, V. (2008) 'Constructing resilience: social workers' understandings and practice.' *Health and Social Care in the Community 16*, 3, 299–309.

Mental Welfare Commission for Scotland (2006) *Rights, Risks and Limits to Freedom: Principles and Good Practice Guidance for Practitioners Considering Restraint in Residential Care Settings*. Edinburgh: Mental Welfare Commission for Scotland.

Mitchell, W. and Glendinning, C. (2007) *A Review of the Research Evidence Surrounding Risk Perceptions, Risk Management Strategies and their Consequences in Adult Social Care for Different Groups of Service Users.* York: University of York, Social Policy Research Unit.

Pearce, A. (2007) *Playing It Safe: The Crazy World of Britain's Health and Safety Regulations.* London: Friday Books.

Pigeon, N.F., Kasperson, R.K. and Slovic, P. (2003) *The Social Amplification of Risk.* Cambridge: Cambridge University Press.

Powell, S. (2005) *Risk in Challenging Behaviour: A Good Practice Guide for Professionals.* Kidderminster: British Institute of Learning Disabilities.

Ritchie, A. and Woodward, R. (2009) 'Changing lives: critical reflections on the social work change programme for Scotland.' *Critical Social Policy 3*, 29, 510–532.

Russell, T. (2005) 'Can reflective practice be taught?' *Reflective Practice 6*, 2, 199–204.

Ryan, T. (2002) 'Exploring the risk management strategies of informal carers of mental health service users.' *Journal of Mental Health 11*, 1, 17–25.

Saner, E. (2009) 'Playing it too safe?' *The Guardian*, 30 December.

Sawyer, A-M. (2008) 'Risk and new exclusions in community mental health practice.' *Australian Social Work 4*, 61, 327–341.

Schoon, I. and Bynner, J. (2003) 'Risk and resilience in the life course: implications for interventions and social policies.' *Journal of Youth Studies 6*, 1, 21–31.

Scottish Executive (2006) *Changing Lives. Report of the 21st Century Social Work Review.* Edinburgh: Scottish Executive.

Scottish Government (2009) *Personalisation: A Shared Understanding. Commissioning for Personalisation.* Edinburgh: Scottish Government.

Stalker, K. (2003) 'Managing risk and uncertainty in social work: a literature review.' *Journal of Social Work 3*, 2, 211–233.

Stanford, S. (2008) 'Taking a stand or playing it safe?: resisting the moral conservatism of risk in social work practice.' *European Journal of Social Work 11*, 3, 209–220.

Taylor, B.J. (2006) 'Risk management paradigms in health and social services for professional decision making on the long-term care of older people.' *British Journal of Social Work 36*, 1411–1429.

Taylor, I. and Le Riche, P. (2006) 'What do we know about partnership with service users and carers in social work education and how robust is the evidence?' *Health and Social Care in the Community 14*, 5, 418–425.

Taylor-Gooby, P. (2006) 'Social and Public Policy: Reflexive Individualization and Regulatory Governance.' In P. Taylor-Gooby and J.O. Zinn (eds) *Risk in Social Science.* Oxford: Oxford University Press.

Taylor-Gooby, P. and Zinn, J.O. (2006a) 'Current directions in risk research: new developments in psychology and sociology.' *Risk Analysis 26*, 2, 397–411.

Taylor-Gooby, P. and Zinn, J.O. (eds) (2006b) *Risk in Social Science.* Oxford: Oxford University Press.

Titterton, M. (1992) 'Managing threats to welfare: the search for a new paradigm of welfare.' *Journal of Social Policy 21*, 1, 1–23.

Titterton, M. (1999) 'Training Professionals in Risk Assessment and Risk Management: What Does the Research Tell Us?' In P. Parsloe (ed.) *Risk Assessment in Social Work and Social Care.* London: Jessica Kingsley Publishers.

Titterton, M. (2001) *Social Care Policy in Scotland.* York: Joseph Rowntree Foundation.

Titterton, M. (2005a) *Risk and Risk Taking in Health and Social Welfare.* London: Jessica Kingsley Publishers.

Titterton, M. (2005b) 'The fine art of risk taking.' *Professional Social Work*, February, 12–13.

Titterton, M. (2005c) 'One step at a time: the steps to better risk taking.' *Community Care*, 26 May–1 June, 42–43.

Titterton, M. and Smart, H. (2010) 'Risk, resilience and vulnerability in children and adolescents in relation to long term conditions: the example of eastern Europe and central Asia.' *Journal of Nursing and Health Care of Chronic Illness 2*, 153–163.

Titterton, M., Hill, M. and Smart, H (2002) 'Mental health promotion and the early years: the evidence base. Risk, protection and resilience.' *Journal of Mental Health Promotion 1*, 1, 20–35.

Titterton, M., Maas-Lowit, M. and Robertson, S. (2007) 'Risk work with mentally disordered offenders.' *Newsletter for Mental Health Officers in Scotland*, Issue 16, winter.

Van Loon, J. (2008) 'Governmentality and the Subpolitics of Teenage Sexual Risk Behaviour.' In A. Petersen and I. Williamson (eds) *Health, Risk and Vulnerability*. Abingdon: Routledge.

Vickerstaffe, S. (2006) 'Life Course, Youth and Old Age.' In P. Taylor-Gooby and J.O. Zinn (eds) *Risk in Social Science*. Oxford: Oxford University Press.

Ward, T. and Maruna, S. (2007) *Rehabilitation: Beyond the Risk Paradigm*. Abingdon: Routledge.

Waterhouse, L. and McGhee, J. (2009) 'Anxiety and child protection – implications for practitioner–parent relations.' *Child and Family Social Work 14*, 481–490.

Wilson, G., Walsh, T. and Kirby, M. (2007) 'Reflective practice and workplace learning: the experience of MSW students.' *Reflective Practice 8*, 1, 1–15.

Zinn, J.O. (2008) 'Heading into the unknown: everyday strategies for managing risk and uncertainty.' *Health, Risk and Society 10*, 5, 439–450.

Zinn, J.O. (2009) 'The sociology of risk and uncertainty: a response to Judith Green's "Is it time for the sociology of health to abandon 'risk'?"' *Health, Risk and Society 11*, 6, 509–526.

CHAPTER 3

THE ROLE OF SOCIAL CAPITAL AND RESOURCES IN RESILIENCE TO RISK

THILO BOECK AND JENNIE FLEMING

INTRODUCTION

There has been increasing attention to the role of social capital in fostering resilience to risk for young people. This chapter will provide an overview of the role of social capital – particularly networks – and its significance to young people's lives, and consider its contribution to their resilience and their ability not to avoid risks but to become 'a risk navigator'. Our concern is both with young people as sources of risk and with their abilities to take appropriate actions (which they themselves may perceive as risky) to negotiate pathways through the challenges of everyday life. We use the notion of resilience to consider how many young people are able to navigate and develop access to a variety of resources with which to cope, manage, make informed choices and act upon them.

The chapter particularly focuses on how practitioners can work with young people to enhance their social capital and develop networks that can foster resilience and enable them to 'get on' in life.

BACKGROUND AND CONTEXT

Heavy targeting of young people by corporate businesses, and the resultant consumerism on their part, makes possible new ways for young people to constitute themselves within a 'fluidity of opportunities and moments of consumption' (Vaughan 2005, p.181). However, it is argued that this fluidity has also created a sense of 'risk' (Beck 2000; Giddens 1998; Kemshall 2002a, 2002b) with people 'regarding the social world as unpredictable and filled with risks which can only be negotiated on an individual level' (Furlong and Cartmel 2007, p.3). In everyday life we are flooded with information about risk and situations that seem to pose risks. These risks make contemporary life particularly challenging for young people, because many of them are beyond their ability to influence and control (Furlong and Cartmel 2007).

The terms 'risk' and 'youth' have become meshed, with an almost constant demonising of youth (Kemshall, Boeck and Fleming 2009). In the crime arena, young people are seen as problematic; and persistent young offenders have been singled out for much policy and practice attention (Kelly 2001; Youth Justice Board 2001). The association of crime with youth has persisted, despite evidence that youth crime is falling (Armstrong 2004), resulting in what Goldson (1997) has called a 'moral panic' about children and young people either being seen as 'a risk' to others, through offending or other anti-social activity, or being 'at risk' and vulnerable themselves. While the routes of these risks are often beyond what young people can control, there is a current trend for youth policy and interventions to be framed only within these risk perspectives with a desire to 'manage and control' these risks.

However, many young people seen as 'at risk' of offending are in other ways 'risk averse', in the sense that they can be unwilling or unable to take the risk of leaving their present situation, their immediate networks of family and friends and the locale where they live. Being able to take actions to loosen such ties can be crucial for 'pathways out of crime' (Boeck, Fleming and Kemshall 2006b). The work of MacDonald and Marsh found that while 'connections to local networks could help in coping with the problems of "social exclusion" and generate "inclusion", they could simultaneously limit the possibilities of escaping the conditions of "social exclusion"' (2001, p.384). Considering locality and place, they found that social networks proved indispensable to 'negotiate the wreckage of the collapsed "economic scaffolding" that previously enabled transitions to a stable, working-class, adult life.' (MacDonald et al. 2005, p.885).

However, while paid work is still central to inclusion in society, it no longer constitutes the major source of identity for young people. Instead, music, fashion and leisure may be more important and this results in a picture of transitions shifting from linearity to constant movement, like 'yo-yos' (EGRIS 2001; Walther, Stauber and Pohl 2005). Vaughan (2003, 2005) argues that many young people appear to be doing something akin to 'milling and churning', which is what the Organisation for Economic Co-operation and Development (OECD) have described as the process of 'moving between a diverse set of activities, only one of which is work, before settling into permanent work: unemployment; labour market programmes; out of the labour force; back into education for short spells; part-time jobs; brief full-time jobs' (2000, p.76, in Vaughan 2003). Some young people may quite deliberately try to postpone the development of work identities in favour of other identities. This can be seen as resilience and a coping strategy in response to a plethora of choices and the decision making required of young people. While keeping busy following different and alternative pathways and shopping for jobs are barriers for settling down, they might also be a preoccupation with avoiding 'settling down'.

Young people 'at risk' who overcome difficult life situations challenge traditional views that focus on problems through a lens of deficit and disorder. Difficult life problems pose dangers, but can also lead to new strengths and coping ability (Brendtro and Larson 2004). What is often overlooked is the ability to 'bounce back', thus producing relatively good outcomes despite adversity. Preventative, risk-infused models of work with young people tend to adopt 'deficit' and 'blaming the victim' approaches (Kemshall *et al.* 2009) and overlook the resiliency of young people.

SOCIAL CAPITAL, PLACE AND ACCESS TO RESOURCES

'It's not what you know, it's *who* you know' – this common saying sums up much of the conventional wisdom regarding social capital (Woolcock 2001). Most definitions revolve around the notion of social networks, the reciprocities that arise from them and the value of these for achieving personal mutual goals (Baron, Field and Schuller 2000). Originating with people forming connections and networks based on the principles of trust, mutual reciprocity and norms of action, social capital is created from the complexity of social relations and their impact on the lives of the people engaged in them (Boeck and Fleming 2002). People engage with others through a variety of associations, forming many different types of networks, sometimes each of which has different sets of norms, trust and reciprocity (Field 2003). Thus there can be significant differences between the types of networks people have, not only in quantity but also in quality. The quality of social networks and sense of belonging to place can influence how aspirations and intentions in education, training and the labour market are shaped. Where people look out from affects what they are able to see, and how they interpret their own lives; therefore, social capital is not only important in terms of emotional support, but also crucial in giving people more opportunities, choice and power (Boeck *et al.* 2006b). Conversely, the absence of social capital can have an equally important negative impact on people's lives (Woolcock 2001).

In the following section, we will consider the importance of social capital in young people's lives with a focus on networks, outlook on life and trust. In a 4-year Economic and Social Research Council

(ESRC)-funded study of pathways into and out of crime for young people, the link between the enhancement of social capital and resiliency was extensively explored (a full explanation of the methodology and key results can be found in Boeck *et al.* 2006a, 2006b; Boeck, Johnson and Makadia, 2008 and Kemshall *et al.* 2009).[1]

BONDING AND BRIDGING SOCIAL CAPITAL

Place and locality can influence how or whether young people are able to access the relationships that are important to their sense of belonging (Morrow 2004). Place and locality in young people's lives can be the immediate neighbourhood, the school or other places where they tend to socialise, such as places of worship, groups or even the city centre or the local park. For many young people, their identity and what they understand as their future lies within the context of their localised social networks (Raffo and Reeves 2000). While networks that are based upon the immediate locale of the street, local park and home can be safe and give a sense of security, they can also create an environment in which young people feel trapped. This bonding social capital tends to be more static and young people tend to interact with familiar, and therefore often similar, young people (Boeck *et al.* 2006b; Morrow 2002).

Social capital uses the concepts of 'bonding' and 'bridging' social capital (Gittell and Vidal 1998, p.10). Bonding social capital refers to inward-looking social networks focusing on relationships and networks of trust and reciprocity that reinforce ties within the group. These strong ties to family and friends are important; however, we also need to look at the weaker links that form part of young people's lives – referred to as bridging social capital. Bridging social capital is concerned with outward-looking connections among different (heterogeneous) groups (Holland, Reynolds and Weller 2007, p.101). It has been argued that bonding social capital is good for 'getting by', but bridging networks are crucial for 'getting ahead' (Field 2003; Putnam 2000). The distinction between bonding and bridging social capital is important in enabling the negotiation of youth transitions (Holland *et al.* 2007).

A concrete example of developing bridging social capital was a youth work initiative in the St Ann's area of Nottingham (Fleming and Boeck 2002). One of the major focuses of the project was the building of networks that the young people were part of. This was

1   This article draws on data from the ESRC project: 'Young people, social capital and the negotiation of risk' in the ESRC network 'Pathways Into and Out of Crime: Risk, Resilience and Diversity', grant number: L330253001.

broken down into two elements: the links between the young people in their communities (bonding networks) and developing networks with people further afield (bridging networks). Through partnership work with other projects, the young people developed closer links with other young people in St Ann's, using other youth projects. Although they and some of the workers already knew each other, relationships were strengthened through a community carnival and community sports event. Bridging social capital was developed through the young people having the opportunity to make contact and develop links with people in other cities, visiting Leicester and Blackpool. The workers actively encouraged the young people to make these links. They arranged for them to play football with teams from other areas and to go swimming with other young people in Blackpool, and they devised a questionnaire about the Leicester Carnival, which involved the young people having to ask people from Leicester questions. Some of the young people stayed in touch with the people they met on these trips and overall they felt that, through this, they had gained access to new resources and had broadened their horizons.

The project also showed that challenging some of the young people's preconceived ideas of authority, and introducing them to other agencies, increased their feelings of trust and safety. This enhanced their ability to access agencies' support by having a better understanding of roles and responsibilities.

Workers also pointed out that youth participation in the projects was a way of increasing both networks and trust within those networks. The activities were organised in partnership with the young people, who were involved in the choosing, planning, promotion and running of the events. The young people had a say about issues that were important to them, and also in what happened.

Exploring transitions in young people's lives (Holland et al. 2007) highlights how many draw upon their social networks as resources to negotiate different stages of their life. Young people who draw on localised static social capital might have fewer resources when it comes to finding work through agencies, or friends and family. Raffo and Reeves' (2000) research suggests that, within more deprived areas, young people's avenues for finding jobs are often based on previous experiences and contacts, and that they relied on highly localised networks. Thus, while strong bonding social capital can provide young people with a strong sense of belonging and security, it may provide few opportunities for interactions with significant others. These others include peers who might be able to help the young people concerned to generate new, informal and practical knowledge, to start the process of dealing with the constraints in their lives and thereby to gain access to material, cultural or social resources (Fram 2004; Morrow 2004). Boeck *et al.* (2008) observed that 'young offenders' were not very likely to access family and friends support when it came to the resolution of problems in their lives, and so less likely to benefit from the social capital resources that could be available to them.

Having the resources to interact with different groups of other young people and adults, and drawing from more dynamic social capital, enhances young people's resiliency. In our research, some young people have shown a more complex diversity within these different networks, especially within groups from different places such as their school, their local area, interest groups, or identity groups (Boeck 2009). The heterogeneity of network relationships is relevant to young people's lives:

> because they provide a diversity of resources, experiences and qualities: the youth cultural network primarily provides information and exchange of practical support; circles of friends (be they wider circles or in the more intimate form of a love relationship) are important for belonging, trust and encouragement; the parental generation often provides access to financial resources. (Walther *et al.* 2005, p.226)

The importance of a diverse set of networks is also referred to in transitions to work, in research in Spain and Germany (Field 2003). Half the young people in a Spanish survey had entered work thanks to family and friends, and a further study of young people who had grown up in the German Democratic Republic, found:

> that the individual's education played a more important role than the father's resources in finding work; nevertheless, nearly half of their sample had found work through informal channels, and in these cases it was often important to possess strong ties with highly prestigious contacts. (Field 2003, p.51)

Participation within diverse networks can facilitate the development of an understanding of and an ability, simultaneously, to negotiate a complex set of relationships derived from differential peer-group and institutional norms. This might stem from the experiences of some young people of having to negotiate different types and levels of relationships, and the necessity of having to develop a complex response to authority (Raffo and Reeves 2000). The frequently adverse experiences of growing up can also enable some young people to develop new and diverse relationships. However, this depends strongly on the quality of the relationship with peers and 'significant others'. A Rowntree study (Webster *et al.* 2004, 2006) found that desistance from offending and heroin use was aided by the support of family members and partners, and the leaving behind of earlier social networks that encouraged crime and drug use. They also referred to informal contacts as being more effective in the search for jobs than training or education.

However, it should not be forgotten that class position is still highly relevant when it comes to having access to these diverse resources and exercising choice (Furlong and Cartmel 2007). Webster *et al.* (2006) argue that in order to understand growing up in poor areas neither 'deficient' parenting nor lack of opportunity alone sufficiently explains experiences of poor transitions. Instead they emphasise 'intermittent crises, contingent and chance events and choice, albeit in an emerging structural context that provides few resources to resolve crises or overcome contingency, and that constrains choice' (Webster *et al.* 2006, p.2). Walther *et al.* (2005) show that for young people from poorer backgrounds the access to different leisure activities, opportunities to travel and alternative groups is denied them because of their class position. The networks of some young people from more affluent backgrounds were widespread, enabling them to access heterogeneous networks in terms of social space and territory. There are examples that reveal that through tapping into the social and cultural capital of their parents, young people establish a countrywide network realised through the contacts of their parents. For other young people, networks expand through their membership of interest groups (such as music and sport): '...for transitions to work, it is crucial that the socio-spatial structure of networks extends beyond the immediate context of everyday life and contains exit options from social origin' (Walther *et al.* 2005, p.225).

Practice implications

This discussion has relevance for practitioners and how they can consider this aspect of social capital with young people; discussions between practitioners and young people about whom they know and their networks could lead to new ideas for interventions and activities. Practitioners have told us that considering aspects of young people's social capital has encouraged them to focus on aspects of their lives that they may not have given much consideration to previously (Fleming and Boeck 2002).

There are many activities practitioners can do with young people to help them think about and develop their networks. These include the following:

- Seek to help young people to enhance their networks of support and interaction. Discuss with young people: Who is supporting them? Who is important to them? What do they gain from these relationships?

- Explore ways for young people to meet and interact with new people and groups, different from their immediate locale of street, school and family.

- Work with young people where they are and within the networks they already have. Isolating young people from their existing networks might damage their bonded social capital, which is important for coping and resilience.

- Consider group work approaches, which can often be as important as individual interventions.

- Mentoring can also be a way for some young people to increase their bridging contacts.

OUTLOOK ON LIFE

For some young people, place-based social networks and attachment to place are very important factors in their decisions about life choices. Localised outlooks may mean that they do not consider opportunities beyond their neighbourhood or home town, or opportunities that are different from those conventionally followed by local people (Green and White 2008). Kemshall *et al.* (2006), in their research with young people 'at risk', observed an overarching sense of young people's lack of knowing what their future might hold. There was a certain unrealistic flavour to many of the accounts of young people's construction of future aspirations. Sometimes this seemed to be related to a feeling of apathy or boredom, and in others to a sense of hopelessness and frustration.

In our research, young people often blamed missed opportunities or missed chances on personal failures, which intensified their sense of being stuck. In some cases, this resulted in their conforming to present situations, which were experienced as negative but without any exit strategy to draw upon, as strongly expressed in the following account of a young offender:

Because work is shit... You face the real world now don't you?

(*Interviewer*) Would you now, if you had the chance again to go back, would you say OK I would be more...

Yeah, I would actually, if I had the chance, but I am not going to have the chance.

(*Interviewer*) In this sense, if you look back at what has happened and now you are in the situation, do you think that now you have something where you say OK I want to aim for something?

I don't know yet, probably I will get fed up with this job and go to college or training.

(*Interviewer*) Do you have something where you say I would like to be this...?

No.

Some young people would talk about their dreams and what they would like to be in the future. Young women from an outer-city council estate spoke in a decision group of some harsh realities to their lives – although they often spoke of them in a jovial way; the oldest in the group was just 19 years old. Personal negative experiences contributed to their feeling that aiming for something would bring with it a lot of disappointment. Again in these accounts, as in other accounts, it is noticeable how young people feel that it is up to them to 'try hard' and achieve:

(*Interviewer*) So what is your aim, do you think about something in the future?

- I don't want to dream.

- I don't have dreams because if you don't get it you will be disappointed.

- If you want it you can get it but if you don't try hard enough you won't get it.

- I just want a nice house, a nice family and live happily ever after.

- I just want a healthy life.

- I just wish my boyfriend would stop cheating on me and be a man.

- There is no point dreaming because when you wake up in the morning it is just a disappointment.

In our research, it also was noticeable that, while 87 per cent of young people from a grammar school had concrete aims for the next 5 years, only 20 per cent of young people accessed through Youth Inclusion Programmes (YIPs) and Youth Offending Teams (YOTs) had concrete aims; and, while 10 per cent of young people accessed through a grammar school had less concrete aims, over half (55 per cent) of the young people accessed through YIPs and YOTs had less concrete aims over the next 5 years.

Practice implications

Before moving on to consider developing a more focused outlook on life, we consider some of the practice implications of working with young people who may not see many opportunities for themselves:

- Do not blame young people for their low aspirations.

- Give young people the opportunity to talk about their lives. Listen to what young people say about their lives.

- Consider the diversity of young people's life experiences in how you work with them.

- Consider how you can work with young people to build their self-esteem.

- Ensure you value the young people you work with, and remember that all young people have skills and abilities they can use to tackle the problems they face.

NEW AND MORE FOCUSED OUTLOOK ON LIFE

Linked to the development of a dynamic social capital is the possibility of individuals having aspirations, and developing and engaging in practices that are outside their safety zone. The need for diverse and wider ranging networks, a sense of belonging to a wider locale, and a focused and active outlook on life is well recognised. This is not just about the 'size and density' of the network, it is also about the resources that the network brings (Halpern 2005). Vaughan (2005), in her study, found that nearly all the young people considered a state of goal-less-ness to be 'a bad thing' and confidently stated their belief that it was important for people their age to have goals. However, few had any definite plans towards any goals. Reflecting on the fluidity of young people's own views of navigating transitions, Vaughan's (2005) research showed that some young people associated definite plans for the future with a notion of adulthood as dull, or as the closing down of options. In our study, those young people with a more positive outlook on life tended to express a strong sense of wanting to achieve things in their life, which sometimes was related to a certain sense of ambition and hope for social mobility:

> Yes, my ambition is to become an engineer. I have ambition of places to go and see and I know that in order to do that I have to find the job that will pay to get there. One ambition feeds other ambitions. Your ambitions grow... (Young man, age 17)

Access to resources and a sense of having choices were often related by young people in our research to a more positive and focused outlook on life. Some young people expressed a more positive attitude to their futures than others. One might think that this positive outlook could be related to their social position, school achievements, or gender; however, the following account of a 'young offender' challenges some of these assumptions:

> I don't think that I've got to a point where everything is closed off and the end of the line, there are end of line signs written all over the place. I think there are things that are closed now that weren't before, but it's not terminal, it doesn't stop quite as much, the sidings on some of the lines don't work, whereas they would have done before, now they don't so you've got less options but still a big range, there's still a lot of them. It's not like there's only one option and that's it. (Young man, age 17)

Crucial to this outlook on life is the individual's perception of their own future, coupled with a sense of having something to aim for. Elder (1985), in a seminal work on life transitions, argues that all change entails a potential loss of control. Key to how this risk is perceived and managed depends on past experiences, perceptions of self-efficacy and the imagined future possibilities (see also Evans 2002). Raffo and Reeves argue that some types of social capital are more helpful in achieving aspirations than others, because they facilitate learning and the development of 'competence, self-confidence, self-esteem and identity' (2000, p.151).

Practice implications

Once again this discussion can have implications for how we ourselves work with young people. As workers, we can have an effect on how young people see themselves and how they are perceived by others. Actions we could take include the following:

- Talking with young people about how they see their future. Do they think they can influence their future?

- Talking with young people about how they see themselves. If they feel a lack of opportunities, you could work with them to build up their resilience, setting positive goals with a sense of achievement. Can they see themselves differently from how they are now?

- Working with young people in building their self-confidence. Work with them to discover their skills and thus enhance their aspirations by encouraging them to take the risk of change.

- Exploring with young people how they can apply these developing aspects and relate them to new networks and new trusting relationships, as well as to their existing networks.

THE LEAP OF TRUST

The German sociologist, Niklas Luhmann (1980), stresses that trust is a way of dealing with the difficulties created in an increasingly complex society, and thus '...the uncertainty of interpersonal interactions and the emotional investment of such put the individual at risk...trust places the self at risk' (Weber and Carter 1998, p.8). Solomon and Flores (2003, p.9) assert that:

> ...trust not only lets us increase complexity in our lives (and thus simplify them at the same time); it also changes our lives in dramatic ways, allowing us to explore in new directions, to experiment and express ourselves in our relationships in ways that would otherwise be unthinkable.

Therefore, trust entails a willingness to take risks in a social context based on a sense of confidence that others will respond as expected and will act in mutually supportive ways, or at least that others do not intend harm (Fukuyama 2001; Misztral 1996). Within the different conceptualisations of trust, in terms of resiliency (or the lack of it) it can be useful to consider the concept of 'suspension', which is referred to as the 'leap of trust' (Moellering 2001). The consideration of 'suspension' explores how the 'willingness to take risks' or making the 'leap of trust' happens.

Young people tend to socialise with other young people, with their family and other people around them in different ways. Of considerable importance is how close young people feel to others and therefore the significance of those within their lives. Relationships and networks are underpinned by a strong trust related to feelings of safety, belonging and identity. Young people in our study spoke of the different 'types' of trust they have with friends and other people. Often they referred to an almost unconditional trust in the parents '...because they are your parents...' This trust can be seen as an 'unconditional trust': parents are always there for you:

> ...they won't let you down, friends can... (Young man, age 16)

It seems that for some young people trust, safety and reciprocity evolve within a limited inward-looking circle and, as a result, tightly bonded networks are often small and static in nature.[2] Within these tightly bonded networks, there is a prevalence of a type of trust that is about looking out for each other and, to a certain extent, protecting each other, or of gaining protection from an outsider; we call this a strong 'group-based trust'. In the focus groups and interviews with young offenders, this more inward-looking trust was apparent. They may be closely bonded and tied together through the 'need' to protect each other, and reciprocity is characterised by an immediate or even no sense of return. This is reflected in the following account which took place in a focus group conducted at a YOT office:

We stay together.

(*Interviewer*) But what type of things?

A lot of us got arrested for criminal damage, 4 or 5 of us, we all go down the police station and we would all just blame it on each other 'cos then they can't arrest none of us, so that is the best way we can get out of trouble. I would just blame M, M would blame my cousin, my cousin would blame M's brother and M's brother would blame one of our other friends.

(*Interviewer*) You would have to trust each other?

Yes, we have all done it before; even the police officer said to me that every single one of us said it was each other.

(*Interviewer*) So is that part of the trust you have?

Yes.

(*Interviewer*) Because no-one would…

No-one would grass anybody up. (Young man, age 14)

It would be easy to stigmatise young 'offenders' or young people 'at risk' as having a stronger, group-based trust because of their attitudes or behaviour. However, our study revealed that 'young offenders' are not dissimilar in their feelings of trust, reciprocity and being trusted, to other young people. Solely behavioural explanations need to be challenged, and structural or contextual interpretations must also be given due weight. The distinction between a more protective trust and a trust based on socialising and feeling comfortable with others should become important when exploring the dynamics between the different

---

2   Reciprocity is when a person acts for the benefit of others at a level of personal cost to themselves, but in the general expectation that a similar kindness will be returned at some undefined time in the future. Reciprocity is not surprisingly closely linked with trust and safety.

environments and social settings where different pathways are forged, negotiated and navigated (Boeck *et al.* 2006b).

A recent study identified that an important factor in enhancing resilience is for young people to be able to make their own decisions and to be trusted by others to make those decisions. Feeling and experiencing that they have high levels of influence and are being trusted by adult workers is extremely important to young people. The support and trust they get from workers was identified as a crucial element (Boeck *et al.* 2008). In order to enhance resilience, relationships between young people and workers should be meaningful. They should not be based only on providing information or advice. Advice from adults who are seen by young people as part of an external system, with few, if any, authentic links to their lives, carries little or no importance for many and actually might be perceived as disrupting their social capital:

> What they really might be on about is having *relationships* that enable them to try things, make mistakes, and change their minds – and then be able to put it all together in creative ways. So making the transition work for young people means supporting them *through* the confusing times and the changes of heart; but it doesn't necessarily mean eradicating those things. (Vaughan 2003, no pagination)

Practice implications

As in previous sections, this discussion can have implications for how we ourselves work with young people. In terms of creating resilience through the enhancement of social capital, practitioners need to weigh up if they can realistically engage in trusting, meaningful and authentic relationships with young people by acting as significant others. The following practice implications are some pointers that we consider to be useful especially when exploring with young people how to make the 'leap of trust':

- Explore with young people whom they trust and what trust means to them. Do they only trust a small number of people? How might they be able to take the risk to trust new people? Work towards establishing strong trusting relationships within safe environments.

- Make sure that you are trustworthy. Be honest with young people about what you can offer and achieve; be clear about your role and limitations.

- Establish clear situations where you can demonstrate your trust in young people; young people value the trust of adults.

Reflection for practitioners

It is important, for the enhancement of social capital, that practitioners see themselves as working 'with' young people and not 'for' them. Thus they become part of young people's social capital and active agents in enhancing their social capital. We are aware that this is not an easy task. To help in this, workers might consider their own social capital as discussed in this chapter – their networks, trust and outlook on life.

Questions you might like to consider in relation to your own social capital could include:

- Do you like socialising with diverse people? What are the resources you get out of these interactions?

- Within diversity is there a 'common ground'?

- Whom do you trust and whom don't you trust? Are you prepared to make a 'leap of trust'?

- Who trusts you?

- Can you influence what is happening in your local neighbourhood, your community, your work, through working collectively with others?

- Overall, you might ask yourself if you have the social resources to set sail and take risks to explore new horizons. Are you prepared to leave behind your own comfort zone?

CONCLUSION

In this chapter, we have used the notion of resilience to indicate how many young people are able to respond to the challenges they face and 'bounce back' in a way that maintains or even enhances their well-being, thus producing relatively good outcomes despite adversity. We looked at resilience not as 'avoiding' risks but as the ability to 'navigate' and having the resources to cope, manage, make informed choices and act upon them. A focus on social capital illuminates the absence of advantaged social ties, and that absence becomes more than simple personal preference or happenstance. Processes of inclusion and exclusion are seen to sustain class boundaries by constraining access to opportunities and resources for mobility.

For practitioners, a focus on social capital as a resource and as the social context within which people negotiate everyday life would involve paying attention to community and locale, peers, networks and the social resources to which young people have access. Young people 'at risk' who often have predominantly bonded, static networks, with a restricted outlook on life and an aversion to taking the 'leap of trust', can be characterised as being in a state of 'risk stagnation'. For these young people, leaving their present lifestyle, which might conventionally be labelled as 'high risk' is itself a risk, and one they may be ill equipped to take (Kemshall *et al.* 2009). Work with 'at risk' young people should look at how to strengthen resilience by enabling them to enhance 'dynamic' and 'bridging' social capital. This aids young people's ability to navigate complex social situations and to be able not only to avoid risks but also to take and negotiate important social risks, such as forming new networks, making the 'leap of trust' and broadening their outlook on life.

Having explored the importance of networks, place, outlook on life and trust within young people's access to social capital, we argue that risks should neither be individually framed, nor seen as subject to individual negotiation. The lack of real and meaningful relationships is often experienced by 'young people at risk' in their encounters with professional institutions with their emphasis on 're-orientation' and 're-education' (Kemshall 2002a). Official vocational guidance agencies and employment services are often viewed as being too bureaucratic, or even not relevant, and young people feel these services are not interested in their personal needs and individual aspirations. This chapter has argued for the need to shift attention from predominantly individual and psychological frameworks, often used in risk assessments, to the greater inclusion of a contextual lens, which focuses on the more significant socio-political and economic factors that enhance or diminish young people's ability to develop resiliency. Young people should not be seen solely as the active, autonomous and responsible entrepreneurs of their DIY projects of the self (Kelly 2001). We advocate a move away from the individualist explanation of youth transitions, acknowledging that actions and choices made by young people are not completely open and free. Choices are often constrained by practical knowledge and understanding of what is possible – clearly mediated by locality, gender and class (MacDonald and Marsh 2001; Raffo and Reeves 2000).

Much research on the life course and criminality has shown that desistance from crime is associated with a positive conception of self, and a belief in one's self-efficacy (Maruna 2001; Uggen, Manza, and Behrens 2004). Thus, we are critical of 'deficit' and 'blaming the victim' approaches to young people. Our approach is based on a commitment to children's and young people's rights, with young people having the right to be heard, to define the issues facing them, to set the agenda for action and, importantly, to build on their existing strengths to take action on their own behalf. As such, empowerment, participation and capacity release are core elements for the enhancement of 'risk navigation' and hence resiliency.

REFERENCES

Armstrong, D. (2004) 'A risky business? Research, policy and governmentality and youth offending.' *Youth Justice 4*, 2, 100–116.

Baron, S., Field, J. and Schuller, T. (2000) *Social Capital – Critical Perspectives*. Oxford: Oxford University Press.

Beck, U. (2000) *World Risk Society*. Cambridge: Polity Press.

Boeck, T. (2009) 'Social Capital and Young People.' In J. Wood and J. Hine (eds) *Work with Young People*. London: Sage Publications.

Boeck, T. and Fleming, J. (2002) *Social Capital and the Nottingham Social Action Research Project (SARP)*. Nottingham: Nottingham Primary Care Trust.

Boeck, T., Fleming, J., Hine, J. and Kemshall, H. (2006a) 'Pathways into and out of crime for young people.' *ChildRight*, July August, 18–21.

Boeck, T., Fleming, J. and Kemshall, H. (2006b) 'The context of risk decisions: does social capital make a difference?' *Forum: Qualitative Social Research 7*, 1, Art. 17.

Boeck, T., Johnson, C. and Makadia, N. (2008) *Enhancing Dynamic and Bridging Social Ties through Participative Youth Volunteering*, NCVO/VSSN 'Researching the Voluntary Sector' Conference, 9–10 September, Warwick.

Brendtro, L. and Larson, S. (2004) 'The resilience code.' *Reclaiming Children and Youth 12*, 4, 194–200.

EGRIS (2001) 'Misleading trajectories: transition dilemmas of young adults in Europe.' *Journal of Youth Studies 4*, 1, 101–118.

Elder, G.H. (1985) *Life Course Dynamics: Trajectories and Transitions, 1968–1980*. Ithaca, NY: Cornell University.

Evans, K. (2002) 'Taking control of their lives? Agency in young adult transitions in England and the new Germany.' *Journal of Youth Studies 5*, 3, 245–269.

Field, J. (2003) *Social Capital*. London: Routledge.

Fleming, J. and Boeck, T. (2002) *St Ann's Youth Workers' Forum*. Nottingham: Nottingham Social Action Research Project (SARP), Nottingham Primary Care Trust.

Fram, M.S. (2004) 'Research for progressive change: Bourdieu and social work.' *Social Service Review 78*, 4, 553–576.

Fukuyama, F. (2001) 'Social capital, civil society and development.' *Third World Quarterly 22*, 1, 7–20.

Furlong, A. and Cartmel, F. (2007) *Young People and Social Change: New Perspectives*. Maidenhead: Open University Press.

Giddens, A. (1998) 'Risk Society: The Context of British Politics.' In J. Franklin (ed.) *The Politics of Risk Society*. Oxford: Polity Press.

Gittell, R. and Vidal, A. (1998) *Community Organizing – Building Social Capital as a Development Strategy*. London: Sage Publications.

Goldson, B. (1997) 'Children, crime, policy and practice: neither welfare nor justice.' *Children and Society 11*, 2, 77–88.

Green, A.E. and White, R. (2008) 'Shaped by place: young people's decisions about education, training and work.' *Benefits 16*, 3, 213–224.

Halpern, D. (2005) *Social Capital*. Cambridge: Polity Press.

Holland, J., Reynolds, T. and Weller, S. (2007) 'Transitions, networks and communities: the significance of social capital in the lives of children and young people.' *Journal of Youth Studies 10*, 1, 97–116.

Kelly, P. (2001) 'Youth at risk: processes of individualisation and responsibilisation in the risk society.' *Discourse: Studies in the Cultural Politics of Education 22*, 1, 23–33.

Kemshall, H. (2002a) 'Effective practice in probation: an example of "Advanced Liberalism Responsibilisation".' *Howard Journal 41*, 1, 41–58.

Kemshall, H. (2002b) *Risk, Social Policy and Welfare*. Buckingham: Open University Press.

Kemshall, H., Boeck, T. and Fleming, J. (2009) 'Risk, youth and moving on.' *British Journal of Community Justice 7*, 2.

Kemshall, H., Marsland, L., Boeck, T. and Dunkerton, L. (2006) 'Young people, pathways and crime: beyond risk factors.' *The Australian and New Zealand Journal of Criminology 39*, 3, 354–370.

Luhmann, N. (1980) *Trust and Power*. New York: Wiley.

MacDonald, R. and Marsh, J. (2001) 'Disconnected youth?' *Journal of Youth Studies 4*, 4, 373–391.

MacDonald, R., Shildrick, T., Webster, C. and Simpson, D. (2005) 'Growing up in poor neighbourhoods: the significance of class and place in the extended transitions of "socially excluded" young adults.' *Sociology 39*, 5, 873.

Maruna, S. (2001) *Making Good: How Ex-Convicts Reform and Rebuild Their Lives*. Washington, DC: American Psychological Association.

Misztral, B. (1996) *Trust in Modern Societies: The Search for the Bases of Social Order*. Cambridge: Polity Press.

Moellering, G. (2001) 'The nature of trust: from Georg Simmel to a theory of expectation, interpretation and suspension.' *Sociology 35*, 2, 403–420.

Morrow, V. (2002) 'Children's Experiences of "Community" Implications of Social Capital Discourses.' In C. Swann (ed.) *Social Capital and Health – Insights from Qualitative Research*. London: HDA.

Morrow, V. (2004) 'Children's "social capital": implications for health and well-being.' *Health Education 104*, 4, 211–225.

Putnam, R. (2000) *Bowling Alone – The Collapse and Revival of American Community*. New York: Simon & Schuster.

Raffo, C. and Reeves, M. (2000) 'Youth transitions and social exclusion: developments in social capital theory.' *Journal of Youth Studies 3*, 2, 147–166.

Solomon, R.C. and Flores, F. (2003) *Building Trust: In Business, Politics, Relationships, and Life*. New York: Oxford University Press.

Uggen, C., Manza, J. and Behrens, A. (2004) 'Less than the Average Citizen: Stigma, Role Transition, and the Civic Reintegration of Convicted Felons.' In S. Maruna and R. Immarigeon (eds) *After Crime and Punishment: Pathways to Offender Reintegration*. Cullompton: Willan.

Vaughan, K. (2003) *Changing Lanes: Young People Making Sense of Pathways*, NZCER Annual Conference, 'Educating for the 21st Century', August: New Zealand Council for Educational Research.

Vaughan, K. (2005) 'The pathways framework meets consumer culture: young people, careers, and commitment.' *Journal of Youth Studies 8*, 2, 173–186.

Walther, A., Stauber, B. and Pohl, A. (2005) 'Informal networks in youth transitions in West Germany: biographical resource or reproduction of social inequality?' *Journal of Youth Studies 8*, 2, 221–240.

Weber, L.R. and Carter, A. (1998) 'On constructing trust: temporality, self-disclosure, and perspective-taking.' *International Journal of Sociology and Social Policy 18*, 1, 7–26.

Webster, C., Simpson, D., MacDonald, R., Abbas, A., Cieslik, M., Shildrick, T. and Simpson, M. (2004) *Poor Transitions Social Exclusion and Young Adults*. Bristol: The Policy Press.

Webster, C., MacDonald, R., Shildrick, T. and Simpson, M. (2006) *Social Exclusion, Young Adults and Extended Youth Transitions*. London and Birmingham: Barrow Cadbury Trust.

Woolcock, M. (2001) 'The place of social capital in understanding social and economic outcomes.' *Canadian Journal of Policy Research 2*, 1, 11–17.

Youth Justice Board (2001) *Risk and Protective Factors Associated with Youth Crime and Effective Interventions*. London: Youth Justice Board for England and Wales.

CHAPTER 4

RISK ASSESSMENT AND YOUNG PEOPLE

KERRY BAKER AND GILL KELLY

INTRODUCTION

Risk-taking and risk-making behaviour are associated with adolescence and the process of negotiating key transitions from childhood to adulthood (Thom, Sales and Pearce 2007). At the same time, however, the perceived risks to the public from young people, and the risks that young people themselves face, are (and always have been) a concern for society (Fionda 2005). 'Risk' has also become an increasingly central feature of many areas of social policy (Kemshall 2009).

Risk assessment practice is influenced by a number of contemporary developments. The United Nations Convention on the Rights of the Child presents a challenge to policy and practice by emphasising the need to pay attention to children's 'best interests', including their right to have a say in decision making. There is also an increasing interest in research on listening to young people's voices (Hart 1997; Henderson 2006; Lewis 2004; Thomas 2007), which is creating greater awareness of some of the differences between adults' and young people's perspectives. Second, the negative language of risk can create a 'them' and 'us' situation in relation to young people. McNeill, for example, has argued that much of the debate around crime 'tends to dichotomise the interests of offenders and the interests of victims and communities in a zero-sum game' (2009, p.22) Third, assessment increasingly occurs in a multi-agency context, which can create a clash of perspectives (Souhami 2007). Finally, all this occurs within a professional arena characterised by the imposition of more prescriptive approaches to practice.

For both practitioners and policy makers, there are a number of dilemmas in assessing and managing risk in this context, dilemmas which arguably can militate against effective work with young people. These include:

- balancing the unhelpful dichotomy between young people as 'troubled' or 'troublesome'

- allowing young people to make genuine contributions to assessment while acknowledging their ongoing need for guidance, protection and support

- producing outcomes that are beneficial for both young people and their communities

- providing frameworks and tools to promote consistent, shared approaches to practice while retaining a focus on individuals and avoiding the drift towards standardised descriptions of young people.

In exploring ways of working in this context, the chapter will argue for the need to incorporate a diversity of perspectives into the assessment process, and consider the potential for notions of 'biography' and narrative to provide a means of integrating different views into a coherent account or, in other words, 'a story that is helpful to all concerned' (Milner and O'Byrne 2002, quoted in Parker and Bradley 2007, p.6). The chapter will then look at how these ideas can be applied within structured practice frameworks so that assessments can properly incorporate a young person's perspective and lay the foundation for constructive approaches to risk management.

A (VERY) BRIEF OVERVIEW OF RISK ASSESSMENT

Risk assessment is a multifaceted activity that can be undertaken for a variety of purposes. A full discussion of practice would need to consider the rationale for assessments ('why' they are being undertaken), their content ('what' is being assessed) and the methods used (the 'how'). The focus of this chapter will mostly be on the third of these – the 'how' – in relation to young people who pose risks to themselves and/or others through their behaviour or lifestyle.[1]

One of the most significant developments in recent years has been the increasing use of structured assessment tools: key examples include the Common Assessment Framework or CAF (Department for Children, Schools and Families 2009), the Asset framework used in youth justice (Youth Justice Board 2006) and the Assessment Framework for Children in Need (Department of Health 2000). There are also many other specialist tools used to assess a range of

---

1   Young people can also engage in positive, constructive risk taking (see Titterton, this volume) but a decision was made to focus here on problematic behaviours given the space limitations of one chapter.

risks, strengths and needs in relation to physical health, mental health, substance use, literacy, communication needs, behaviour or specific types of offending by young people (e.g. violence or sexual abuse of others). Debates about such tools have focused on issues such as their impact on professionalism and practitioner autonomy, but one of the main areas of interest for this chapter will be the 'picture' of a young person that emerges from the assessment process.

Tools are not the only determinants of assessment quality. Other factors such as practitioner skills, agency culture, the amount of time available, IT systems and access to specialist staff will also be important. In addition, practice will be affected by the recurring tension between the aim of developing trusting relationships with young people and the importance of acting quickly. As Yates explains:

> [o]n the one hand, there is the need to make accurate assessments of young people's situations as early as possible in order that appropriate, and sometimes urgently needed, responses and interventions can be put in place, and many services have working protocols to adhere to in this regard. On the other hand, though, this need must be balanced against the very real possibility of such assessment being negatively perceived as too intense or personal and damaging the vital fledgling young person–adult worker relationship. (2009, p.183)

Inappropriate use of assessment tools could exacerbate this problem if they are applied insensitively or in a way that hinders the development of the worker–young person relationship. Given that such frameworks and tools are likely to be part of the practice landscape for the foreseeable future, it is worth considering how they can be used in ways that take more account of complex and varied perceptions of risk.

PERSPECTIVES ON RISK AND 'RISKY' BEHAVIOURS
Practitioners, managers, policy makers and young people will hold a wide variety of views about 'risky' behaviours, which can lead to tensions. These could be due to factors such as moral beliefs – for example, conflicting attitudes about sexual activity by young people (Hoggart 2007). Another example would be differences in knowledge – for example, with regard to the use of new technology where young people may have greater know-how than adults but sometimes less understanding of the risks involved (Livingstone and Brake 2010).

Professional perspectives
One view of children and young people is that they should be seen as active agents, able to take decisions, morally responsible for their

behaviour and, in some cases, as presenting very serious risks to others. Other perspectives include seeing young people displaying risky behaviour as being 'in need' (Fitch 2009), as disempowered (Action for Children 2009), as the victims of disadvantage (Barrow Cadbury Trust 2009) or as those whose behaviour can be attributed to medical causes (Joughin and Morley 2007). These views need not always be mutually exclusive and many would argue that young people can both be at risk from harm themselves and at the same time present a risk to others.

Differences in organisational purposes can shape how risk is defined or prioritised (Barry 2007) and Souhami notes that '…because agencies inhabit "different assumptive worlds" staff from these agencies are likely to have different conceptions of the problems at hand and thus the appropriate approach to them' (2007, p.190). This can lead to practitioners adopting a variety of approaches to risk assessment, some of which may vary from organisational guidance or policy. Practitioners retain some discretion over how they work within formalised structures (Baker 2009) and may amend or subvert procedures. As Kemshall states in relation to assessment practice, practitioners '…may for example focus on resilience rather than risk, care rather than control, and empowerment rather than marginalisation' (2009, p.161). Different perspectives will lead to different approaches to risk assessment and it is not possible to assume that practice will be homogenous just because a particular tool or framework is in use.

Young people's perspectives

Barter argues that '[w]e should not assume that young people's experiences and evaluations of seriousness reflect professional ones…' (2009, p.226) and research relating to young people's views about risk is beginning to reveal something of the complexity of their perceptions and the meanings they attach to their behaviour and experiences (Boeck, Fleming and Kemshall 2006; Sharland 2006; Williamson 1978). It is worth considering just a few examples. Evidence suggests that adult perceptions of young people's substance use need to take greater account of the differences between groups of young people with regard to drinking cultures, patterns of behaviour and the meaning they attach to substance use (Duffy et al. 2008; Melrose 2004). A study of 'recreational rioting' in Belfast revealed that young people have complex and sometimes conflicting views about involvement in such violence, seeing it as both fun and yet also dangerous. The meaning of these events for young people also needs to be understood through '…the ways in which children's sectarian identity is expressed and experienced through rioting' (Leonard 2010, p.47). A third example relates to how a sense of futility about the future – in particular the expectation of an early death – can be a factor in explaining young people's involvement in gang activity (Brezina, Tekin and Topalli 2009).

In addition to understanding young people's perceptions of risk, it is also important to recognise that resilience is a socially constructed concept, that young people's views of positive outcomes may differ from those of adults and that they have abilities to negotiate their environments in order to obtain outcomes that they regard as good (Ungar 2004). An example of this would be the young people described as 'resisters' (Murray 2010, p.115), those who were able to avoid involvement in offending while maintaining credibility with their chosen peer groups. Awareness of this kind of evidence is important but it is also necessary to bear in mind that research findings about young people's views will not apply to every young person – rather, an assessment needs to be specific and individualised in each case.[2]

Arriving at a shared understanding

These different perspectives can give rise to some 'common problems and areas of conflict between adults and youth' (Mitchell, Tanner and Haynes 2009, p.15) and practitioners need to be aware of the consequent challenges involved in negotiating the 'youth/risk' dynamic (Wood and Hine 2009). These include:

- taking a collaborative approach within a prescriptive context

- seeing young people's responses to risk as rational within their lived experiences

- allowing young people to describe and give meaning to their own lives rather than simply asking them for information to be analysed from an adult perspective.

Risk assessment and risk management decisions are likely to be more relevant to a young person if his or her perspective can be integrated with that of the assessor into a mutual understanding, thus providing a basis for future interventions (see also Titterton, this volume). But this is often difficult to achieve in practice. There is, for example, 'evidence from social welfare research that children's views are still routinely absent in decision-making that concerns them directly' (Holland, 2004, p.327). In thinking about how to meet this challenge, the chapter

---

2   A similar issue arises in relation to actuarial data that cannot be automatically applied to individual cases. Data about groups – either quantitative or qualitative – need to be interpreted in the context of specific case circumstances.

now moves on to consider some approaches for incorporating young people's perspectives and enhancing the quality of assessments.

CHARACTER, CONTEXT AND TIME

One recurring concern about recent trends in risk assessment practice has been that, because structured frameworks and tools typically have separate sections for different issues or risk factors, assessments become compartmentalised and fail to present a rounded picture (Aas 2004; Hayles 2006; White, Hall and Peckover 2009). In response to this, there have been calls for a return to more 'holistic' approaches to assessment (Barry 2007). One of the aims of this chapter is to explore how the use of stories and biographies could help in enabling practitioners to make assessments of young people that capture the complex, rich detail of their lives and their behaviour.

The enduring power and attraction of stories

In his discussion of the reasons for the often less than optimal use of formalised risk assessment tools, Schwalbe suggests that one explanation for this is that 'people are influenced to a greater extent by a good story than by statistical information' (2004, p.569). Dawes goes further, suggesting that our 'cognitive capacity shuts down in the absence of a story' (1999, p.29). It could be argued that this has been illustrated recently in regard to the use of the Common Assessment Framework (CAF) in children's services in England where researchers have found that, even though the tool was designed in a way that discourages narrative, practitioners added to or amended the form in order to incorporate stories which they saw as essential to understanding a young person (White et al. 2009).[3]

This raises an interesting question about the design of structured assessments. Many tools have sections to record details about particular problems but just having space for free text may not be enough – CAF includes this and yet users were still dissatisfied. The reason seems to be that the free text boxes provided were for explanation, description and analysis of specific factors in a young person's life,[4] but practitioners felt that the overall sense of a young person's story was missing: 'we are told a set of needs, but have no idea of the child's personal life story, family, experiences and so forth' (White et al. 2009, p.1209).

3   For example, some sites added a background information section to each domain of the form to provide space for recording context and timelines.
4   These text boxes may have different names in specific tools (e.g. in Asset they are known as 'evidence boxes'), but their common purpose is to allow practitioners space to choose which information to record.

So what can be done to promote a sense of a more complete picture or story of a young person's situation and behaviour? Recent thinking about assessment has often been structured in terms of 'domains', as seen for example in the 12 scored sections of Asset addressing specific dynamic factors related to offending (Youth Justice Board 2006) or the three domains of CAF (child development/parenting/environment; Department for Children, Schools and Families 2009). A useful alternative angle, however, would be to think about assessment in terms of the key elements of a biography or drama: time, situation and character.

TIMELINES

This refers to both a sequence of events occurring in time and to the interactions between different events. Understanding the context surrounding a young person's behaviour requires some knowledge of what has happened previously – that is, it requires a sense of *time*. It is also useful to make a distinction between 'linear time' and 'event time' (Elwyn and Gwyn 1999) as both are important for understanding events in context. The linear detail shows 'what' happened and 'when', whereas event time focuses more on the meaning and significance of those events for a young person.

SITUATIONS AND CIRCUMSTANCES

If timelines capture specific events, this category is more about the ongoing features of life that constitute the backdrop to particular incidents or behaviours. This includes circumstances specific to the individual young person, such as being excluded from school, being caught up in complex family relationships or having a particular health problem. It also covers wider situational factors affecting the local community – for example, the environment, neighbourhood, social structures, inequalities and experiences of discrimination, social tensions, patterns of crime in the locality, policing priorities, educational and leisure resources, and employment opportunities.

CHARACTER STUDY

Understanding character requires knowledge of factors such as attitudes, preferences, dislikes, hopes and fears, skills, strengths and weaknesses, temperament, beliefs, abilities and motivations. When assessing a young person, clearly there needs to be an understanding of developmental change during adolescence and the subsequent implication that these traits and characteristics may not yet be consistently apparent in his or her life, but nevertheless are relevant issues to consider.

Thinking about biography

A good biography would include each of these components and one of the implications of this for assessment with young people is to see that a deeper understanding can emerge from the interplay between the three elements. For example, understanding a young person's character helps to make sense of why particular events may have escalated out of control, and knowing the situational backdrop helps to see why certain events may recur in one young person's timeline but not another's. Figure 4.1 illustrates how the interplay between the key components of character, situation and time can contribute to an event involving risky behaviour. Over time, the individual encounters different situations and responds to them with small decisions and choices, influenced by their existing personal characteristics or developing attitudes and capabilities. These can culminate in more significant and concerning risky behaviour.

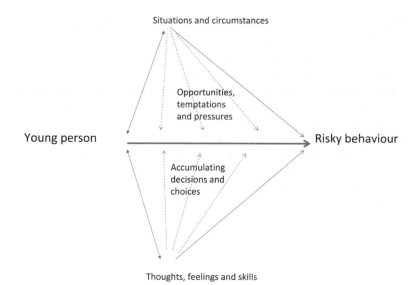

Figure 4.1: Understanding risky behaviour
Source: Adapted from Rutter, Giller and Hagell (1998) and Farrow, Kelly and Wilkinson (2007).

One advantage of thinking in terms of biography is that it is an approach that allows for the combination of both analysis and synthesis. Analysis can be defined as breaking things down into component parts whereas synthesis refers to integrating specific parts to produce a complex whole. Both are required for good assessment. One weakness of some structured assessment tools is that they help in breaking the process down to focus on particular risks or needs, but they may not provide the space to integrate these different items of information back together. With biography, however, time, situation and character can be seen as elements that need to be considered and assessed as specific components, but that then also have to be combined in order to produce a meaningful account of the subject's life and behaviour. A further benefit of this approach is that it can help people to think about the relationship between one individual's situation and the lifestyles and experiences of other young people. A good biography, for example, would compare the subject's characteristics and behaviours with those of other people, thus taking account of both the 'particularities of unique cases' and the 'probabilistic patterns' found in the groups to which young people belong (Schwalbe 2004, p.568).

USING STORIES WITHIN STRUCTURED APPROACHES TO PRACTICE

'Using stories' has a double meaning here. It refers both to taking account of the perspectives of professionals and young people (that is, how they make sense of events) *and* to the use of narrative in explaining and presenting assessments (that is, making sense to others). When thinking about applying these ideas in practice, it is important to be aware that, although a focus on story and biography has advantages, there are also weaknesses such as the potential for bias, error and misinterpretation (Schwalbe 2004, p.569). Such approaches are also open to the charge that assessments can lack direction and may become rather rambling, unfocused accounts. Second, as noted earlier, risk assessment with young people occurs within systems, procedures and frameworks that may not immediately seem to allow for this approach. In the light of these factors, how might such approaches work in practice?

Assessment preparation and obtaining information

Taking account of stories does not imply a vague and unplanned approach to practice. Rather, it requires being clear about the purpose of the assessment and thinking ahead about how to obtain the young person's story, whether certain aspects of the story are especially relevant for this particular type of assessment, and what questions will be needed to tease out the narrative. A focus on stories does not, however, equate to being naïve, and Hayles provides a useful reminder of the continued need for 'painstaking questioning, probing, testing and verification – irrespective of the model of intervention' (2006, p.77).

A good biography depends on asking good questions, but this can be done in a variety of ways. The process of collecting information could begin perhaps with drawing out the timeline of events and then move on to a discussion to build up the character study. Or alternatively, it could start with looking at particular characteristics of a young person and then explore the context and situational factors. The order can be flexible, as can the methods, which could include visual and interactive approaches to producing timelines or other ways of teasing out the young person's story (cartooning, collage, life-story work) that are appropriate to the young person's abilities and level of maturity, and the amount of time available for the assessment. Figure 4.1 illustrated a single incident whereas Figure 4.2 illustrates a timeline capturing a number of different events. It shows an approach to plotting a story that can help capture information about what happened *and* the meaning of those events in the context of a young person's situation and his or her response to those circumstances. The narrative begins with the young person (1), then plots the sequence of risk-taking incidents (2) alongside life events (3) and the young person's developing attitudes and skills (4). Finally, having plotted each of these components, it is possible to identify connections between the different elements and underlying patterns and themes (5). The diagram suggests questions that could be used to add detail to the narrative.

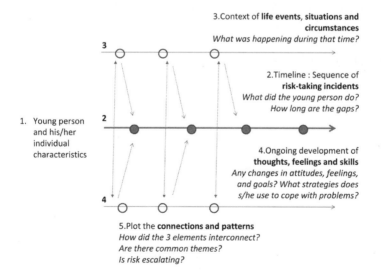

Figure 4.2: Plotting a story over time

All this requires skills in making participation meaningful and helping young people to feel that their voices are genuinely being heard. This presents challenges for practitioners but, encouragingly, there is now a gradually expanding literature on methods and approaches for promoting engagement with, and participation by, different groups of young people (e.g. Callahan, Kelly and Wilkinson 2009; Coleman, Catan and Dennison 2004; Fleming and Hudson 2009; Mason and Prior 2008; Weld 2008).

Analysing stories

The analysis of stories could be considered from a number of perspectives but we will limit the focus here to just two angles. First, there is a difference between *how* a story is told and *what* is told (Gubrium and Holstein 1998, p.165). Assessors need to focus not just on the content but on the way in which stories are told because explanations 'reveal something of the explainer's mind to the enquirer' (Antaki 1988, p.8). The way in which a story is told will be influenced by the context – for example, a young person's account of his or her behaviour may be different after exclusion from school has occurred from the descriptions given before the decision was made. It will also be influenced by the 'functional utility of accounting to the individual' (Cody and McLaughlin 1988, p.114). This refers to how excuses and justifications are used by individuals to preserve their self-esteem or social reputation. The same information can be told in different ways and how behaviour is explained or justified may give significant insights into a young person's self-image and attitudes.

Second, information for an assessment should come from a range of sources and stories from different parties will sometimes conflict. Listening to the voices of young people and families does not mean being uncritical. The role of the assessor is not simply to repeat the stories of others but to produce a new narrative that takes account of conflicting perspectives. This is similar to the way in which biographers will express opinions about the validity or otherwise of views held by their subjects. This can be done in a way that acknowledges the reasons why certain views may be held (and perhaps very sincerely believed) but which is nevertheless realistic about flaws and weaknesses in someone's perceptions and reasoning.

Making judgements and risk decisions

Kemshall refers to the weak link between risk factors and risk trajectories (2009, p.158) and this is one of the many factors making assessment so difficult. Stories can help here because they show patterns over time (that is, the trajectory) and can assist practitioners in thinking ahead to possible future behaviour by a young person.

TAKING ACCOUNT OF CONTEXT AND SITUATION

Situational factors are highly relevant to decisions made by young people about risky behaviours. Hoggart, for example, describes the impact of drugs and alcohol on young people's ability to 'maintain control of their sexual encounters' (2007, p.193). In relation to offending, Craissati and Sindall (2009) highlight the importance of situational context in serious group-based violence by young men. For young people living in residential care, their circumstances (and the feelings of powerlessness provoked by these experiences) can be significant in understanding the 'explosions of strong feeling about apparently trivial events' that often occur in such settings (Ward 2004, p.238).

Some assessment tools designed to help practitioners make judgements about future risk/s have tried to capture these situational factors through questions such as 'In which circumstances is this behaviour likely to occur?' 'When is it likely to happen?' 'What will the triggers be?' However, these often seem to be difficult for assessors to identify in advance. The biography approach could help here because knowledge of both the timelines and the young person's character could assist practitioners in assessing how or why a young person is likely to respond to particular events or triggers in ways that could lead to adverse outcomes, either for themselves or others.

ALTERNATIVE ENDINGS AND CHARACTER DEVELOPMENT

The biography approach also lends itself to creative 'what if?' ways of thinking about the future. This could include encouraging a young person to think about questions such as 'What are the different possible endings to the story?' 'Which ones are most likely to occur and why?' 'What would need to happen to get to the ending that you most prefer?' A similar discussion could apply around the idea of character development – for example, talking with a young person about how their character in the biography can change and mature over time. This helps to promote participation but also contributes to rigorous risk assessment in that, if a young person cannot see any potential for development or any alternative story endings, then their risk level may be greater than for a young person who can see the potential to re-write their story. Such approaches will require time and resources and may not always be possible at the early stages of an assessment process, but they could be a useful component of ongoing work to assess and manage risk over time.

Form and frameworks

The reason for focusing on these more 'technical' aspects of practice is not just because they are such a key part of current practice but also because 'experience is not simply known or conveyed to others, but *takes on its meaning* within descriptive frames or contexts' (Gubrium, Buckholdt and Lynott 1989, p.197, emphasis added). And once meaning has been given within a form or assessment tool, this may persist over quite long periods of time: '[t]he importance of the written records, reports and files are crucial to the way cases are constructed. After a while a file takes on a life of its own, and it can be very difficult to question what it appears to represent' (Teoh *et al.* 2003, p.157). How judgements about young people are recorded and communicated through written reports and electronic case records matters therefore.

One potential consequence of the use of structured assessment forms can be that practitioners lapse into the use of standardised terminology, which results in descriptions of complex problems being too narrow. In their study of medical care plans, for example, Gubrium *et al.* found that many patients were described as having remarkably similar problems, treatment and goals (1989, p.207). White *et al.* noted a similar trend in relation to the use of CAF, commenting on the 'danger that the much lauded "common language" may evolve into little more than a sentence bank' (2009, p.1212).

There is often a considerable difference, too, between 'practitioners' knowledge and what they write in the report' (Thomas and Holland 2009, p.15). Evidence for a similar pattern has been found in youth justice (Baker 2008) with practitioners often recording only a limited account of their understanding and analysis of a case. This is likely to be partly explained by 'the disruption of narrative and chronology' (White *et al.* 2009, p.1208) in the design of assessment tools and, as discussed earlier, the lack of opportunity within the tools to draw together different items of information. How then can practitioners overcome some of these problems to make use of narrative – and its capacity for translating '*knowing* into *telling*' (White 1980, p.5) – within structured practice frameworks? Some key general principles would be as follows:

- Ensure that different perspectives are incorporated and acknowledged.

- Include a discussion of time, situation and character.

- Don't be taken over by the stylistic demands and terminology of assessment frameworks.

Some more specific examples are given later. These are not meant to be taken as definitive guidance but rather to prompt reflection about practice: To what extent would it be appropriate for you to adopt these approaches and how would you go about it? Are there alternatives that reflect similar principles but which are more suitable for your practice setting?

REPORTS

Many practitioners are required to produce formal reports of some kind such as child protection reports, school exclusion reports, social enquiry reports (for children's hearings in Scotland) or pre-sentence reports for youth courts. Writing in the context of child protection, Holland notes that '…it is possible to make quite dramatic changes to the credibility of children's views through the choice of wording in assessment reports' (2004, p.328). The same issues would apply in relation to other formal reports about young people, and care is therefore needed in seeking to explain their views to others.

The format of these reports is often highly structured but because 'report writers trade in interpretations as well as "facts"' (McNeill 2002, p.431) there is still scope to be flexible, and Gorman argues that practitioners should 'mould their storytelling expertise' (2006, p.106) to fit the defined structures. Practical examples could include framing issues in a young person's life as obstacles to progress rather than causes of a problem, or giving attention to periods in the timeline of a young person's life when s/he demonstrated resilience in the face of difficulties, seeking to explain how this was achieved. Writing with reference to court reports for offenders, Gorman argues that, even though the report format may be tightly prescribed, these documents can still provide a:

> medium through which the report writer and the offender can *collaboratively* construct and reconstruct a coherent, personal story which endeavours to make sense of past mistakes/misdeeds; integrate present strengths, difficulties and contradictions; and envision a crime-free future. (2006, p.114)

This perspective could be equally relevant to report writers across a range of health, education and social care settings.

PLANS

Young people's participation in assessment processes will be critical when it comes to constructing plans designed to reduce, contain or manage risk. These are more likely to be effective if young people feel they have been genuinely consulted and have a sense of ownership about targets and actions identified. The concept of biography is also relevant in that plans should seek to help a young person achieve a suitable and realistic 'story ending'. Or, if that seems like too distant a goal, the plan can at least aim to assist a young person in moving on to the next 'chapter' of their story.

REFERRALS

Making referrals to other agencies requires practitioners to present information to colleagues who may not know the young person very well and/or may work from a very different perspective. This can present a number of moral and professional challenges because there are myriad ways of communicating the 'same' information. Some key points to consider would include *whom* you are communicating with: your audience, their professional perspectives and how these might affect their interpretation of your information. You would also need to be clear *why* you are providing them with information and how you would expect them to use it. This in turn is likely to affect how you decide *what* they actually need to know.

These could be summarised into the following question: What are the essential aspects of the story that the receiver needs to know in order to make sense of specific events, problems or requests for resources? In most cases, they are unlikely to want to know everything but the most useful information will be that which enables them to understand and interpret other details of the young person's life. Once the essential backdrop has been established, it will then be easier to decide how much else, and which particular aspects of the story, need to be included in the referral.

CONCLUSION

Given the complexity of the risk assessment task, a range of skills and methods are likely to be required and this chapter has argued that it is time to look again at the potential benefits of story and biography. Narrative is central to our understanding of the world and to the way we communicate (Porter Abbott 2008), to the extent that ignoring it means that we are likely to miss out on some of the rich and risk-relevant detail of the lives of young people. It is not a panacea for instantly remedying concerns about the quality of risk assessments, but it can and should be a more valued part of practice.

The discussion of this chapter suggests that tool designers need to think again about how to combine the analysis of different aspects of a young person's life – character, context and time – in order to promote assessments that are both more nuanced and more robust. This should apply not only to the design of the core of an assessment profile but also to that of intervention and risk management plans, so that these documents do not simply list a static set of objectives but are able to capture a sense of the young person's trajectory and hence provide a basis for dynamic, risk-responsive interventions.

Kemshall suggests that 'personal biography may yet triumph over risk prediction' (2009, p.161). Perhaps – we will have to wait and see. But this chapter has shown that an awareness of the value of different perspectives and of narrative can play a valuable role in the complex task of risk assessment with young people. Such approaches do not ignore the risk that a young person's behaviour may create, but they avoid making this the only focus of attention and can thus contribute to the development of a 'more participative, holistic and proactive' culture of risk assessment practice (Barry 2007, p.42). If implemented thoughtfully, the suggestions presented here may help to promote a practice culture in which assessments take greater account of the detail of young people's lives, have a clearer sense of the development of risk trajectories over time and, consequently, provide a stronger basis for interventions to reduce risk.

REFERENCES

Aas, K. (2004) 'From narrative to database: technological change and penal culture.' *Punishment and Society* 6, 4, 379–393.

Action for Children (2009) *Step Inside our Shoes:Young People's Views on Gun and Knife Crime.* London: Action for Children.

Antaki, C. (1988) 'Explanations, Communications and Social Cognition.' In C. Antaki (ed.) *Analysing Everyday Explanation.* London: Sage Publications.

Baker, K. (2008) 'Risk, uncertainty and public protection: assessment of young people who offend.' *British Journal of Social Work* 38, 8, 1463–1480.

Baker, K. (2009) 'MAPPA as "Risk in Action": Discretion and Decision Making.' In K. Baker and A. Sutherland (eds) *Multi-Agency Public Protection Arrangements and Youth Justice.* Bristol: The Policy Press.

Barrow Cadbury Trust (2009) *Coping with Kidulthood: The Hidden Truth Behind Britain's Abandoned Adolescents.* London: Barrow Cadbury Trust.

Barry, M. (2007) *Effective Approaches to Risk Assessment in Social Work: An International Literature Review.* Edinburgh: Scottish Executive.

Barter, C. (2009) 'In the name of love: partner abuse and violence in teenage relationships.' *British Journal of Social Work* 39, 2, 211–233.

Boeck, T., Fleming, J. and Kemshall, H. (2006) 'The context of risk decisions: does social capital make a difference?' *Forum: Qualitative Social Research* 7, 1, 17. Available at www.qualitative-research.net/fqs-texte/1-06/06-1-17-e.htm, accessed on 6 January 2010.

Brezina, T., Tekin, E. and Topalli, V. (2009) '"Might not be a tomorrow": a multimethods approach to anticipated early death and youth crime.' *Criminology* 47, 4, 1091–1129.

Callahan, D., Kelly, G. and Wilkinson, B. (2009) *The Jigsaw Approach: A Programme for Young People in the Community.* Birmingham: Youth Justice Services and KWP.

Cody, M. and McLaughlin, M. (1988) 'Accounts on Trial: Oral Arguments in Traffic Court.' In C. Antaki (ed.) *Analysing Everyday Explanation.* London: Sage Publications.

Coleman, J., Catan, L. and Dennison, C. (2004) 'You're the Last Person I'd Talk To.' In J. Roche, S. Tucker, R. Thomson and R. Flynn (eds) *Youth in Society.* London: Sage Publications.

Craissati, J. and Sindall. O. (2009) 'Serious further offences: an exploration of risk and typologies.' *Probation Journal* 56, 1, 9–27.

Dawes, R. (1999) 'A message from psychologists to economists: mere predictability doesn't matter like it should (without a good story appended to it.' *Journal of Economic Behavior and Organization 39*, 1, 29–40.

Department for Children, Schools and Families (DCSF) (2009) *Common Assessment Framework: Managers' and Practitioners' Guides*. London: DCSF.

Department of Health (DH) (2000) *Framework for the Assessment of Children in Need and their Families*. London: DH.

Duffy, M., Schafer, N., Coomber, R., O'Connell, L. and Turnbull, P. (2008) *Cannabis Supply and Young People: 'It's a Social Thing'*. York: Joseph Rowntree Foundation.

Elwyn, G. and Gwyn, R. (1999) 'Stories we hear and stories we tell: analysing talk in clinical practice.' *British Medical Journal 318*, 186–188.

Farrow, K., Kelly, G. and Wilkinson, B. (2007) *Offenders in Focus*. Bristol: The Policy Press.

Fionda, J. (2005) *Devils and Angels*. Oxford: Hart.

Fitch, K. (2009) *Teenagers at Risk – The Safeguarding Needs of Young People in Gangs and Violent Peer Groups*. London: NSPCC.

Fleming, J. and Hudson, N. (2009) 'Young People and Research Participation.' In J. Wood and J. Hine (eds) *Work with Young People*. London: Sage Publications.

Gorman, K. (2006) 'Constructing a Convincing Narrative.' In K. Gorman, M. Gregory, M. Hayles and N. Parton (eds) *Constructive Work with Offenders*. London: Jessica Kingsley Publishers.

Gubrium, J., Buckholdt, D. and Lynott, R. (1989) 'The descriptive tyranny of forms.' *Perspectives on Social Problems 1*, 195–214.

Gubrium, J. and Holstein, J. (1998) 'Narrative practice and the coherence of personal stories.' *Sociological Quarterly 39*, 1, 163–183.

Hart, R. (1997) *Children's Participation*. London: Earthscan and UNICEF.

Hayles, M. (2006) 'Constructing Safety: A Collaborative Approach to Managing Risk and Building Responsibility.' In K. Gorman, M. Gregory, M. Hayles and N. Parton (eds) *Constructive Work with Offenders*. London: Jessica Kingsley Publishers.

Henderson, S. (2006) *Inventing Adulthoods: A Biographical Approach to Transitions*. London: Sage Publications.

Hoggart, L. (2007) 'Young Women, Sexual Behaviour and Sexual Decision Making.' In B. Thom, R. Sales and J. Pearce (eds) *Growing Up with Risk*. Bristol: The Policy Press.

Holland, S. (2004) 'Representing children in child protection assessments.' *Childhood 8*, 3, 322–339.

Joughin, C. and Morley, D. (2007) *Conduct Disorder in Older Children and Young People: Research Messages for Practice Problems*. Dartington: Research in Practice.

Kemshall, H. (2009) 'Risk, Social Policy and Young People.' In J. Wood and J. Hine (eds) *Work with Young People*. London: Sage Publications.

Leonard, M. (2010) 'What's recreational about "recreational rioting"? Children on the streets in Belfast.' *Children and Society 24*, 1, 38–49.

Lewis, V. (2004) *The Reality of Research with Children and Young People*. London: Sage Publications.

Livingstone, S. and Brake, D. (2010) 'On the rapid rise of social networking sites: new findings and policy implications.' *Children and Society 24*, 1, 75–83.

Mason, P. and Prior, D. (2008) *Engaging Young People: Source Document*. London: Youth Justice Board.

McNeill, F. (2002) 'Assisting Sentencing, Promoting Justice?' In C. Tata and N. Hutton (eds) *Sentencing and Society: International Perspectives*. Aldershot: Ashgate.

McNeill, F. (2009) 'What works and what's just.' *European Journal of Probation 1*, 1, 21–40.

Melrose, M. (2004) 'Fractured transitions: disadvantaged young people, drug taking and risk.' *Probation Journal 51*, 4, 327–341.

Milner, J. and O'Byrne, P. (2002) *Assessment in Social Work* (2nd edition). Basingstoke: Palgrave Macmillan.

Mitchell, T., Tanner, T. and Haynes, K. (2009) *Children as Agents of Change for Disaster Risk Reduction*. London: Children in a Changing Climate.

Murray, C. (2010) 'Conceptualizing young people's strategies of resistance to offending as "active resilience".' *British Journal of Social Work 40*, 1, 115–132.

Parker, J. and Bradley, G. (2007) *Social Work Practice: Assessment, Planning, Intervention and Review* (2nd edition). Exeter: Learning Matters.

Porter Abbott, H. (2008) *The Cambridge Introduction to Narrative*. Cambridge: Cambridge University Press.

Rutter, M., Giller, H. and Hagell, A. (1998) *Antisocial Behaviour by Young People*. Cambridge: Cambridge University Press.

Schwalbe, C. (2004) 'Re-visioning risk assessment for human service decision making.' *Children and Youth Services Review 26*, 6, 561–576.

Sharland, E. (2006) 'Young people, risk taking and risk making: some thoughts for social work.' *British Journal of Social Work 36*, 2, 247–265.

Souhami, A. (2007) *Transforming Youth Justice: Occupational Identity and Cultural Change*. Cullompton: Willan.

Teoh, A., Laffer, J., Parton, N. and Turnell, A. (2003) 'Trafficking in Meaning: Constructive Social Work in Child Protection Practice.' In C. Hall, K. Juhila, N. Parton and T. Pösö (eds) *Constructing Clienthood in Social Work and Human Services*. London: Jessica Kingsley Publishers.

Thom, B., Sales, R. and Pearce, J. (2007) *Growing Up with Risk*. Bristol: The Policy Press.

Thomas, J. and Holland, S. (2009) 'Representing children's identities in core assessments.' *British Journal of Social Work*. Available at http://bjsw.oxfordjournals.org, accessed on 21 July 2010.

Thomas, N. (2007) 'Towards a theory of children's participation.' *International Journal of Children's Rights 15*, 2, 199–218.

Ungar, M. (2004) 'A constructionist discourse on resilience.' *Youth and Society 35*, 3, 341–365.

Ward, A. (2004) 'Working with Young People in Residential Settings.' In J. Roche, S. Tucker, R. Thomson and R. Flynn (eds) *Youth in Society*. London: Sage Publications.

Weld, N. (2008) 'The Three Houses Tool: Building Safety and Positive Change.' In M. Calder (ed.) *Contemporary Risk Assessment in Safeguarding Children*. Lyme Regis: Russell House Publishing.

White, H. (1980) 'The value of narrativity in the representation of reality.' *Critical Analysis 7*, 1, 5–27.

White, S., Hall, C. and Peckover, S. (2009) 'The descriptive tyranny of the common assessment framework: technologies of categorization and professional practice in child welfare.' *British Journal of Social Work 39*, 7, 1197–1217.

Williamson, H. (1978) 'Choosing to be a delinquent.' *New Society*, 9 November.

Wood, J. and Hine, J. (2009) *Work with Young People*. London: Sage Publications.

Yates, S. (2009) 'Good Practice in Guidance: Lessons from Connexions.' In J. Wood and J. Hine (eds) *Work with Young People*. London: Sage Publications.

Youth Justice Board (2006) *Asset Guidance*. London: Youth Justice Board.

CHAPTER 5

The Fallacy of Formalisation: Practice Makes Process in the Assessment of Risks to Children

SUE PECKOVER, KAREN BROADHURST, SUE WHITE, DAVID WASTELL, CHRIS HALL AND ANDREW PITHOUSE

INTRODUCTION

In the UK in recent years, a number of high-profile inquiries into non-accidental child deaths have led to the blaming of children's social care services for deficiencies in their policies, procedures and practices (Laming 2003; Munro 2004; Reder and Duncan 1999, 2004; Reder, Duncan and Gray 1993). Attention has focused particularly on front-line professionals like social workers who have been blamed for errors of judgement or practice (Munro 1999, 2004). As a result, children's services departments have been subject to a range of measures designed to standardise and monitor performance, including the introduction of e-systems for assessing risk and managing cases. These have been designed to reduce human error while also increasing scrutiny and accountability. This re-configuration of children's social care services underpinned by information and communication technologies (ICTs) reflects broader themes in New Labour's modernisation agenda for the reform of public services (see Hudson 2002). As Littlechild (2008) has argued:

> Central government appears to have taken a view that in order to reduce the risk of child abuse deaths, the production of mandatory guidance and checklists for professionals will ensure that agencies and professionals carry out risk assessments and plan their work in standardized ways, and therefore reduce the risk to children, and risk to the government of negative and critical publicity. (Littlechild 2008, p.663)

These developments have, however, created considerable challenges for those working in front-line social work practice who are required to utilise these initiatives, while at the same time working with clients in complex and vulnerable situations, in order to protect children. This difficult task requires a wide range of knowledge and skills, including the ability to engage with people. Importantly, the context of social work with children and families remains relationship-based and requires practitioners to utilise a range of strategies in assessment work. Practitioners need to use their knowledge and senses about the situations facing them, and in doing this 'the smell of practice' (Ferguson 2004) – the embodied knowledge gained through direct contact with clients – is an important element in shaping decisions and actions. In this process, practitioners are also required to resolve competing moral, emotional and practical concerns. Thus, assessing risks and managing cases is a complex professional task that requires a range of skills and judgements.

This chapter focuses upon the management of risk in everyday social work practice, drawing attention to some of the tensions that arise when practitioners are faced with complex cases and required to use structured approaches to risk management. We will explore the ways that social workers use standardised risk reduction technologies, along with a range of more *informal* processes arising from the relationship base of social work with children and families, in their everyday risk assessment work (see Broadhurst *et al.* 2010a). The chapter draws upon findings from an Economic and Social Research Council (ESRC)-funded multi-method research study of social work practices in children's statutory services, undertaken in five local authorities in England and Wales, between 2006 and 2008 (see White, Pithouse and Wastell 2009b for further details of the research methodology and design). This study took place at a time of increasing formalisation of practice through systems of risk management, particularly those that involve the use of ICTs such as the Integrated Children's System (ICS). The findings seriously challenge the notion that such standardisation of systems straightforwardly improves practice and, this chapter suggests that one way forward is to involve users in the design of ICT base tools.

'RISK' AND SOCIAL WORK

Social workers and managers concerned with the welfare and protection of children are all too familiar with the concept of 'risk' (Kemshall *et al.* 1997; Munro 2008; Parton, Thorpe and Wattam 1997; Stalker 2003; Webb 2007). Over recent years, its categorisation has become a central organising principle within social services (Kemshall *et al.* 1997), leading to a range of practices concerned with differentiating between 'high' and 'low' risk cases. As Parton *et al.* (1997) have pointed out, this is underpinned by an assumption that risk can be both predicted and managed, which also underpins the socio-legal discourses, with their emphasis upon investigation and forensic evidence, which have shaped so much of contemporary child welfare practice.

While the emphasis upon 'risk' within contemporary social work reflects wider themes – particularly the idea that in late modernity we live in a 'risk society' (Beck 1992; Giddens 1990, 1991) – its application to social care is not without critique (Parton 1998). Risk assessment approaches used within child welfare, which are focused upon minimising errors, serve to constrain social work practice because they privilege notions of predictability rather than the uncertainty and ambiguity that characterise much everyday practice with children and families (Parton 2008). Engaging in decision making that is socially constituted, contextual and based upon professional judgement appears to be particularly important given the socially constructed nature of child abuse (Littlechild 2008).

Commentators have argued that the current preoccupation with risk reflects a loss of confidence in professionals and institutions and has led to increasing attempts to regulate practice (see Littlechild 2008, p.665). Indeed the UK, like many other western countries including the US, Canada, Australia and New Zealand, has adopted formal approaches to managing risk (Goddard, Saunders and Stanley 1999; Kemp *et al.* 1998; Little and Rixon 1998; Shlonsky and Wagner 2005; Wald and Woolverton 1990). These include a number of tools and instruments that provide a standardised approach to case management and serve to guide decision making around risk (Cleaver, Wattam and Cawson 1998). More recently in England and Wales, these have been further developed through the application of ICTs, particularly the ICS. Such risk assessment instruments are seen by policy makers to reduce decision-making options and minimise discretion (Houston and Griffiths 2000). These 'technocratic models' rely upon a number of bureaucratic practices including procedures and case management systems, but they also herald 'the rise of the social work "technician" armed with his or her risk assessment devices' (Houston and Griffiths 2000, p.5).

RISK ASSESSMENT TOOLS AND CHILD WELFARE

There are different types of tools used in social work that incorporate a standardised approach to risk management. These include various actuarial tools, which generate risk scores at the front door of practice

(Webb 2007), and comprehensive structured assessments, which to support clinical or professional judgement. While these approaches have different orientations, they both aim to improve the accuracy of assessment, thereby limiting the possibility of error and improving the targeting of scarce resources.

The actuarial tools, which rely upon statistical calculations of, for example, future violent behaviour (Hart, Michie and Cooke 2007) have been used widely in criminal justice settings (for critical accounts, see Aas 2005; Kemshall 2000a, 2001; Kemshall and Maguire 2001; Maguire *et al.* 2001). More recently, tools based upon known risk factors for homicide and incorporating structured professional judgement (Richards 2004) have been used by the police to risk assess perpetrators in domestic violence incidents (Co-ordinated Action Against Domestic Abuse 2008; HM Government 2008; Robinson, this volume).

Actuarial approaches are used alongside structured professional judgement in most cases because they relate to child welfare and are intended to support the detail of risk management and intervention plans. These structured assessment tools have been developed in a wide variety of formats and characterise the types of tools we examined in our research. Overall they aim to direct practitioners' judgements, through providing an aide memoire, and ensuring that 'evidence-based' risk factors are considered. Examples of structured assessment formats introduced in England and Wales include *Protecting Children. A Guide for Social Workers Undertaking a Comprehensive Assessment* (Department of Health 1988) known also as the *Orange Book*, and the *Framework for the Assessment of Children in Need and their Families* (Department of Health 2000). These types of tools are generally based upon expert or clinical evidence (Shlonsky and Wagner 2005), although this has been challenged (Goddard *et al.* 1999).

The Framework for the *Assessment of Children in Need and their Families* (Department of Health 2000) provides practitioners with standard assessment domains, questions and templates. While this has developed as a structured assessment tool, it was initially envisaged as an attempt to encourage social workers to think more holistically about children, families and the wider community. Other examples of structured assessment tools include the 'Strengths and Difficulties Questionnaire' and the 'Home Conditions Assessment' tool although it should be noted that these are generally utilised on a voluntary basis.[1] The tools we discuss in our research are embedded within the e-system and demand use on a compulsory basis.

---

1   See www.dh.gov.uk/en/Publicationsandstatistics/Publications/Publication-sPolicyAndGuidance/DH_4008144, accessed on 18 July 2010.

A growing body of work has questioned the reliability and validity (usefulness) of the risk assessments used within the child protection arena (Littlechild 2008; Munro 2005). As Cooper, Hetherington and Katz (2003, p.13) point out:

> the real risk assessment must be done by child professionals who base their judgments on daily interactions with children and families. The danger is that over-reliance on automated risk assessment systems will actually reduce the capacity of child protection practitioners to identify and manage the risks to children.

As we have argued elsewhere, the effective use of these types of structured risk assessment tools requires 'excellent critical thinking skills, together with a reflexive awareness of the impact of informal processes' (Broadhurst et al. 2010a, p.16).

Nonetheless, standardised assessment formats such as the Assessment Framework have become even more firmly embedded in part as a consequence of the increasing electronic configuration of practice. In particular, e-enabled systems such as the ICS provides a uniform structure for completion of initial and core assessments through standard formats, procedure and processes of workflow alongside strict timescales for completion. These new IT systems, which incorporate centrally derived, but locally implemented, assessment protocols, schedules and formats, are designed to standardise social work practice and by implication reduce error in human performance. In doing this, however, they also have the potential to reduce professional autonomy in ensuring compliance particularly because these systems neglect the many rationalities that organise practitioners' judgements and decisions (Broadhurst et al. 2010a, 2010b; Horlick-Jones 2005a, 2005b; Parton 2008; Wastell et al. 2010). In our related publications we have said, 'social workers increasingly interact with a range of technologies, but the work remains relationship-based' (Broadhurst et al. 2010a, p.2)

THE CONTEXT FOR RISK ASSESSMENT
The relational aspects of social work with children and families have been referred to as the 'humane project of social work' (Broadhurst et al. 2010a) and involve a range of informal, moral rationalities concerning care, trust, kindness and respect. These aspects of everyday practice create a range of situated, practical–moral dilemmas that are difficult to systematise (Horlick-Jones 2005a; Mattison 2000).The relational activity implicit within social work requires practitioners to engage in a more complex approach to risk management than encompassed by these types of tools (c.f. Broadhurst et al. 2010a; Ruch 2005).

As Littlechild (2008, p.671) argues, 'social workers construct their own realities and attributions within their work, which lead to actions which are not always foreseen by policy-makers and higher-level managers'. Some have applied the term 'street-level bureaucrats' (Lipsky 1980) to describe how social workers use their own professional discretion in order to circumvent procedural-based decision making, to achieve goals and outcomes that reflect the best use of resources, within local situated contexts, and to create a more manageable working life (Evans and Harris 2004; Wastell *et al.* 2010).

RISK ASSESSMENT IN PRACTICE
It was evident in our research that practitioners were continually juggling a range of risk management strategies and resources, including those that are informal and/or tacit. Our fieldwork gained information from direct observations of practice and interview work with practitioners. We first describe the risk technologies being used, particularly at the 'front door' of social services, and then highlight some examples of decision making and risk assessment drawing attention to the interplay between 'the case' and the risk assessment apparatus that shapes so much of practice.

Risk technologies
During the period of our study, the ICS was being introduced in all our research sites. This often replaced or upgraded existing IT systems and, although different configurations were evident, these systems all shared key national policy requirements for standardising assessment processes. These systems embedded templates framed by strict timescales, which provided social workers with 'e-pathways' for categorising and managing cases. This placed particular demands upon practitioners such as requiring recordings to be up to date, and tasks completed before cases could progress through the e-pathway. In the following example, a social worker comments upon the system requirement to display a completed initial assessment (IA) before more urgent child protection inquiries could be undertaken.

> I had to do this s.47 investigation this week and I had to go through an IA first, whereas on the old computer system I could just create a strategy document for discussion and just get straight into the s.47, I had to do this weird IA, that's not really an IA.[2] ... And I have to...

2   Section 47 of the Children Act 1989 places a duty on local authorities to make enquiries into the circumstances of children considered to be at risk of 'significant harm' and, where these enquiries indicate the need, to undertake a full investigation into the child's circumstances.

It's almost, not mocking it, but it's just ticking a box, oh yes, I've done the initial assessment, when really it's not what *I* would call an initial assessment at all...even though that's the name that's been assigned to it! (Social worker)

A similar issue in relation to the completion of completing core assessments is commented upon by the following social worker:

...when I took my case load over at [name of team] because I'd taken over another workers'...it was said 'oh, that needs a core assessment, that needs a core assessment, that needs a core assessment'. Right, OK. All these core assessments have still to be done, so I thought, well, why? Because these families are getting a small, really small package of support. Like, I don't know, 5 direct payment hours or something. So I'm just doing these core assessments for the sake of it. (Social worker)

In both these examples, social workers are pointing to the priority placed upon the system requirements to complete an assessment rather than considering its quality or purpose. Unsurprisingly, many social workers considered the e-systems were time-consuming and took them away from direct work with children and families, particularly in cases where they were required to enter repetitive information as part of the assessment processes for families with large numbers of children. There were also worrying examples of systems failure leading to loss of case notes or recordings.

Our research particularly focused upon practice in intake or referral teams who are required to make decisions about how cases will be processed, a key site for assessing risk. In all five sites, we observed these teams typically receiving very high numbers of referrals within a context of limited resources and heavy workload. This presented acute challenges. Workers were required to safeguard children and support families, while also minimising the possibilities of error and blame that could arise from the demands of the performance framework. In particular, the IT-dependent case management systems constrain workers' professional discretion in responding to referrals requiring them to categorise cases at an early stage and follow prescribed e-pathways.[3]

3　The *Framework for the Assessment of Children in Need and their Families* (Department of Health 2000) defines the initial statutory response to a 'contact' or 'referral' as a distinct stage in the assessment process, and lays down specific temporal frames for this work to be completed; within 1 day of a referral being received, agencies are required to make a decision about what response is required, and within 7 days an initial assessment must be complete.

In some sites support workers staffed the front-line desk, taking responsibility for receiving and undertaking the initial processing of referrals. While we observed variations in local arrangements for this, not least the extent to which this activity was supervised and managed by an experienced social worker, the deployment of support staff was a key feature and reflected other models for taking referrals such as such as centralised call centres (see, for example, Coleman and Harris 2008). Underpinning these staffing developments is a belief in the standardisation practices inherent within the IT-driven systems, which require information entry and processing to generate contacts and referrals that could be used by social work staff in the assessment teams. This initial contact is a crucial point in the overall risk assessment of cases presenting to a social services department. Despite this, we found the risk assessment tools were being utilised by untrained staff with the overall task constructed as one of information processing within a standardised format rather than requiring the exercise of professional judgement, analysis or interpretation. This is described in the following extract from an interview with a social worker:

> ...what happens is when [they] have a fax through...the multi-agency referral form, however that is written is how they have to put it on the system.[4] So if it doesn't make sense for them, they have to put it on the system the way that it's, the way that it's written. So when it comes down to us a lot of the time then we will end up having to phone whoever has made that referral to clarify bits of information so get a better understanding or picture of exactly what is, of exactly what's happening then. (Social work team manager)

The introduction of support or customer service workers rather than trained social workers at the 'front door of social services' illustrates the underlying trend identified by Houston and Griffiths (2000, p.5), which constructs practitioners as 'technicians' rather than professionals who exercise expertise and judgement. It also has unintended consequences. The information that is entered at the point of referral, and which is a crucial element of risk assessment, is decontextualised; the workers are unable to draw upon practice knowledge or interviewing skills in order to interact with the referrer and generate the most useful and interrogated information about each case.

---

4   At the time of this study, agencies were using a multi-agency referral form. This has now been replaced by the Common Assessment Framework (CAF).

Assessing risk and decision making

The processing of referrals requires decision making. In all our sites, this was undertaken by a senior social worker (with variations in their location and role within the intake process) and involved the assessment of risk. In most instances, the decision-making process was professional judgement supported by local eligibility criteria. In one of our sites, a risk-scoring tool was used, which provided a numerical risk score of between 1 and 9 based upon the likelihood, and consequences, of a risk occurring. This is described by the team manager in the following data extract:

> We have got a risk assessment tool...basically sets out background involvement, current concerns, the likelihood and the consequences of, and it's a scoring system.... If I say this needs an initial assessment then I would complete a risk assessment form. The risk assessment score goes from 1 to 9. Nine being immediate risk, section 47, a duty visit, a strategy meeting if needed. To one, which actually I probably wouldn't have accepted for initial assessment if it's going to score 1. They generally come in at 3, 4, 6, and 9. Three would be a child that has got perhaps ADHD, ASD, significant kind of needs, family are obviously having difficulty managing, we would want to be offering them a service of some description, but it wouldn't be urgent. (Social work team manager)

In practice, these risk scores were calculated very quickly and were often based upon limited information. They are therefore likely to involve substantial amounts of lay reasoning and tacit knowledge, as well as moral judgement about normality and deviance. This appears to be leading to an 'early categorisation' of a case (e.g. 'this is a non-familial assault' or 'this is a behaviour support issue') and these are associated with plans about what we do in these sorts of cases. More importantly, while cognisant of the eligibility criteria, the referral team manager explained that she undertook the risk assessment score 'in her head', and then filled in the form to evidence her decision. This again suggests an ex post facto rationalisation for a decision taken on intuitive grounds.

This risk scoring forms part of the e-record that is passed to the assessment team, described in our fieldwork as being 'workflowed'. The risk scoring is also printed out and signed by the team manager, producing an artefact that is symbolically suggestive of scientific risk assessment, but in truth may be an expedient re-packaging of a subjective professional judgement, performed in order to comply with the required formal procedure. In this study site, the risk assessment scores shaped decisions about allocation of cases, and the immediacy of visits to children and families; they were also used to illustrate to senior managers the extent and seriousness of unallocated cases, highlighting an ongoing resource constraint. The risk scores were constantly being revised, particularly if information changed or there were staff shortages meaning that cases could not be allocated to a named social worker. Thus, the scores have rhetorical and moral significance showing, first, that a rational and judicious process has been followed and, second, that the team is managing under difficult circumstances.

Our research found clear evidence that the e-systems designed to standardise risk assessment processes created additional tensions for social workers and managers. These frequently arose because of a mismatch between the need to engage meaningfully with clients (being cognisant of the everyday realities of clients' lives), in order to undertake assessments and protect children, and the demands of the information system that imposes particular pathways for case management. This situation led to a number of 'workarounds' in some of our sites where categories like 'passed to team' evolved to enable more information to be sought before commiting a decision to the system. Similarly, we noted in some of our sites that, in order to meet the 7-day deadline, the initial assessment was 'signed off' as complete after the child had been seen, rather than at the point when the paperwork was completed. However, such workarounds themselves create the conditions for future blame from an inspectorial regime charged with checking that standardised processes have been followed.

The following example illustrates how workers focused upon meeting the immediate needs of a homeless young person and, having provided him with section 17 money (funds provided under the Children Act 1989 to prevent children becoming 'looked after' by the local authority) to help him through an immediate crisis, they lost contact with him, meaning they were unable to complete an initial assessment within the given timescale:

> So we hadn't completed the initial assessment. But you try explaining that to a service manager. And that does happen with young people. Eventually we tracked him down through various sources and other people, other young people funnily enough, and we completed it and we did the work and it was fine, and through that period he had been fine, but to try and explain why it had taken us I think it was something like 21 days to do the initial assessment, it wasn't about not wanting to do it within 7 days, it was about the fact that we couldn't pin this young person down. What he presented to us, the immediate need was that he needed somewhere to stay, that's your primary objective that day, not getting the initial assessment done. So as it turned out, I think it was sort of 20 or 21 days, those sort of things really frustrate me,

because we are dealing with human beings and you can't factor them in. you can't ever. (Social worker)

The extent to which practice is made to fit the system requirements, regardless of what constitutes sensible notions of 'good practice', raises serious concerns about the potential of these structured assessment systems to themselves further heighten risk. This is also evident in how the 'structured' formats themselves contribute to a disaggregation of the assessment information, making them difficult to complete, read and understand. This has been highlighted in previous work (White, Hall and Peckover 2009a) and is further illustrated in the following quote:

> ...like, these cases that I'm looking at now, I'm wanting to get a picture of the history...but I'm dotting from one place to another on the system...whereas on...[name of previous system], everything would have been together. (Social worker)

Difficulties with the ICTs, the demands to meet rigid timescales and the ways the performance indicators shape social work take little account of the needs of clients or reflect approaches to practice that are grounded in professional judgement. In our study social workers understood the need to pay due regard to procedure and protocol, but 'work' did not stop there. They described an iterative process of moving back and forth between the demands of procedure and the demands of 'the case', 'the case' being all those 'real-world' details that arise in the context of the practice of *social* work but which are left out of standardised question and answer formats (Broadhurst *et al.* 2010a).

In our earlier work, we argued that the modernised initial assessment system within children's statutory services has a flawed design and that its dysfunctions provide 'latent conditions' for error (Broadhurst *et al.* 2010b). Errors identified in our study include the many short cuts that workers operate to maintain workflow, for example:

- Quick categorisations based on limited information, which may lead to some cases that may require intervention being filtered out.

- The consideration of new referrals in relation to existing cases and workload. This may drive thresholds to unacceptably high levels in busy teams.

- The ubiquitous 'front and backing' of the IA form, by which practitioners omit completing the central sections of the assessment, indicates the lack of fit between tool and trade.

- The requirement to prioritise data input demands, which leads to a reduction of valuable face-to-face time with children and their parents or carers.

- Entrenched patterns of tacit reasoning as workers become habituated to methods of finding quick disposals. (Broadhurst *et al.* 2010b)

While acknowledging the importance of professional discretion in effective front-line practice in the public services (Lipsky 1980), Broadhurst *et al.* (2010b) suggest in front-line social work practice that the excessive rigidity of the systems lead to workarounds that may become defensive rather than innovative.

RISK AS A NEGOTIATED PHENOMENON

As discussed earlier, children's social care is saturated by both the language and techniques of risk. However, our research found that there is more to the day-to-day management of risk than procedure and protocol. Practitioners' work of risk management, while arguably shaped and constrained by this standardising apparatus, also requires practitioners to engage with the particular exigencies of each case and the individuals involved. An important finding from our study was the ways in which social workers, while mindful of the importance of complying with requirements to complete and log risk assessment schedules, also displayed awareness of the 'limits of procedure' and the need to engage in other types of work in order to assess cases and make decisions. This latter necessarily involved negotiating engagement with clients and attending to the contextual details of each case. As described in related studies (Broadhurst *et al.* 2010a, 2010b), 'risk trade-offs' are calculated and made, having as much to do with dialogue and the quality of relationships than this or that procedure.

We can condense the detail of informal logics of risk management into the following typology (see Broadhurst *et al.* 2010a, p. 1052):

1. The logics of risk management strategies are *emergent/contingent* – they arise in relation to particular cases as reflexive, individualised and tailored responses.

2. Risk assessment practices are embedded in *social* relations – team culture, client–worker relationships create unique contingencies, but also habitual responses.

3. A *multiplicity of rationalities* are invoked that are not just to do with instrumental concerns, but invoke human virtues of compassion, empathy and a sense of responsibility for others.

This interplay between the demands of the structured risk assessment technologies and the exercise of professional judgement reflect themes reported elsewhere. For example, in a study of practitioners' use of structured risk assessment tools in criminal justice settings, Kemshall and Maguire (2001) suggest that:

> what is happening in terms of risk assessment is not simply a direct replacement of expert judgement by actuarial judgement, but new combinations and interactions between the two. It is important not to underestimate the influence, at ground level, of both agency cultures and practical concerns and contingencies. (Kemshall and Maguire 2001, p.249)

Structured risk assessment tools provide a means to guide social workers in their practice, ensuring they take into account different types of risk factors. What their introduction obscures, however, is the exercise of professional judgement used by practitioners when working with clients and making decisions about individual cases (Kemshall 2000b; Kemshall and Maguire 2001, p.249; Littlechild 2008). Littlechild (2008) also points out there are risks associated with the current risk strategies employed in child protection social work that include the unrealistic expectation that such tools can eliminate risk. This resonates with a wider operating environment in which social workers are influenced in their everyday practice by fear – 'fear of getting it wrong' as well as fear relating to clients and their employing organisations.

Social work practice remains an essentially *social*, interpretive and interactive enterprise, in which both the logics and strategies of risk management are fundamentally contingent. The difficulties posed by the current e-enabled risk assessment approaches used in child welfare have been recognised by Laming (2009) who, in a recent review of the English child protection system, made the following comment:

> Practitioners and managers are committed to the principle of an electronic system and have no desire to return to paper-based case management. However, the current state of the technology – particularly the local IT systems that support the use of the Integrated Children's System (ICS) – is hampering progress. Professional practice and judgement, as said by many who contributed evidence to this report, are being compromised by an over-complicated, lengthy and tick-box assessment and recording system. The direct interaction and engagement with children and their families, which is at the core of social work, is said to be at risk as the needs of a work management tool overtake those of evidence-based assessment, sound analysis and professional judgement about risk of harm. (Laming 2009, s3.17, pp.32–33)

USER-CENTRED DESIGN

The importance of adopting a *user-centred approach* to the design of IT-based systems has been understood for many years (Norman 1998), and is attested by a substantial body of research evidence, reaching back over several decades (see Ives and Olson 1984, itself a review of earlier work). In the language and calculus of risk, lack of user involvement is certainly a 'risk factor' imperilling any IT initiative, and we have advocated the user-centred approach in our earlier papers (see Broadhurst *et al.* 2010b) in the specific context of child welfare. To build IT systems that effectively support practice, an informed understanding of the requirements of users is essential, which enjoins their direct engagement in design activities.

The report of Lord Laming, quoted earlier, has created opportunities for agencies to revise the design of ICS implementations, aimed in particular at the simplification of forms; local authorities and suppliers have been authorised 'in discussion with professionals to remove "forms" and "exemplars", giving them more flexibility to use their professional judgement' (Department for Children, Schools and Families 2009). The new spirit of collaboration between system suppliers and end users can be seen to pay off handsomely, as shown by the following comment from a social work professional involved in a working group set up by one of the leading ICS suppliers. She observed that the participative approach had led to the development of 'very much simpler and easy-to-read forms based on a family approach so that a family or multi-agency meeting only have one output which covers all the children in the family with individual narrative on each'. Early feedback from staff using the re-designed forms in real situations is very encouraging, as affirmed by the following two comments:

> I preferred this format to the current format on ICS. Whilst it took a little while to readjust my thinking to be able to use this type of form again; I do feel that it is a more user-friendly form and is a lot clearer from a service user point of view. (Social worker commenting on the redesigned IA)

> This is a joy to read! I've spent far too long reading ICS assessments where I'm no clearer at the end of the document as I was at the beginning what the issues were, whereas this was so easy to read and understand. I really think we are on the right track. (Senior manager commenting on a completed assessment)

CONCLUSION

The work of supporting families and safeguarding children is inherently complex and context dependent, and practitioners' situated work of managing risk comprises contingent acts of judgement, discretion and care, which cannot be reduced to standard formulae and algorithms. While such technological apparatus may help legitimise an external image of social work as rational and efficient, as we ideally expect of our public institutions, their potential for defensive practice, perverse incentives and stifling of 'outside the box' thinking should not be under-estimated.

As this chapter has demonstrated, while social workers are required to use risk reduction technologies, more *informal* processes arising from the relationship-based context of social work with children and families are important in shaping decisions and actions. The study has drawn attention to the artful work of practitioners to moderate or dispense with the regulatory systems in order, paradoxically, to offer a less risky service. However, professional discretion is under threat, given the e-configuration of procedure and protocol that render far more visible 'non-compliant' activity. While the project set out to examine error, we found that error per se was little discussed by social workers or managers; however, *risk*, *blame* and the possibility of organisational *sanctions* were routinely invoked, with these considerations exerting a frequently very negative impact on decision making.

Top-down approaches to risk management, which are now more difficult to 'workaround' in the context of ICS, inhibit effective and skilled professional risk management practices. These arise from careful analysis, balancing and tradeoffs that are an inevitable feature of risk management but are negotiated in each and every case – and subject to reflexive review. The curtailment of the reflexive, dialogical spaces necessary to undertake this work thus increases the likelihood of error. Elsewhere we have argued that the bureaucratic–instrumental bias manifest in the modernisation of children's services, in prioritising metrics and administrative power, leaves the informal and relational aspects of practice under-emphasised and under-theorised (Broadhurst *et al.* 2010a).

The structured risk assessments examined in this research display design errors that have the potential to heighten risk for children and families and for social workers who are operating in the complex and highly charged world of child protection. Their evaluation and future development must focus upon their use in practice and, in doing so, the voices of workers and service users, as well as policy makers and regulators, are essential to ensure that future developments avoid some of the problems of the current systems (for further discussion, see Broadhurst *et al.* 2010b; Munro 2005). User-centred design is not just an imperative for the design of IT systems. It is a sine qua non for the design of any system if, to use the jargon, it is to be 'fit-for-purpose', as our final quotation from Cooper *et al.* (2003) trenchantly argues:

> New methodologies that take the system's complexity as their premise could be developed easily enough. They would involve those charged with inspection and standards working alongside the system, operating as a part of it, initiating and engaging in feedback processes, taking account of the many unpredicted and unpredictable influences that arise to influence the system, as well as those influences deriving from planned and rational intervention. The costs of methodologies like these need be no greater, and are probably lesser, than the burden of current quality assurance and governance costs. And they are likely to prove more effective, because they are adapted to the reality of the systems they are aiming to influence. (Cooper *et al.* 2003, pp.63–64)

REFERENCES

Aas, K. (2005) *Sentencing in the Age of Information: From Faust to Macintosh.* London: Glasshouse Press.

Beck, U. (1992) *Risk Society: Towards a New Modernity.* London: Sage Publications.

Broadhurst, K., Hall, C., Wastell, D., White S. and Pithouse A. (2010a) 'Risk, instrumentalism and the humane project in social work: identifying the *informal* logics of risk management in children's statutory services'. *British Journal of Social Work 40,* 4, 1046–1064.

Broadhurst, K., Wastell, D., White., S., Hall., C. *et al.* (2010b) 'Performing initial assessment: identifying the latent conditions for error in local authority children's services.' *British Journal of Social Work 40,* 352–370.

Cleaver, H., Wattam, C. and Cawson, P. (1998) *Assessing Risk in Child Protection.* London: NSPCC.

Coleman, N. and Harris, J. (2008) 'Calling social work'. *British Journal of Social Work 38,* 3, 580–599.

Cooper, A., Hetherington, R. and Katz, I. (2003) *The Risk Factor: Making the Child Protection System Work for Children.* London: Demos.

Co-ordinated Action Against Domestic Abuse (2008) Toolkits for MARAC. Available at www.caada.org.uk/practitioner_resources/IDVAresources.htm, accessed on 17 August 2010.

Department for Children, Schools and Families (2009) *The Protection of Children in England: Action Plan. The Government's Response to Lord Laming.* Available at http://publications.dcsf.gov.uk/eOrderingDownload/DCSF-Laming.pdf, accessed on 15 May 2009.

Department of Health (1988) *Protecting Children. A Guide for Social Workers Undertaking a Comprehensive Assessment.* London: The Stationery Office.

Department of Health (2000) *Framework for the Assessment of Children in Need and their Families.* London: The Stationery Office.

Evans, T. and Harris, J. (2004) 'Street level bureaucracy, social work and the (exaggerated) death of discretion.' *British Journal of Social Work 34,* 6, 871–895.

Ferguson, H. (2004) *Protecting Children in Time: Child Protection and the Consequences of Modernity.* London: Sage Publications.

Giddens, A. (1990) *The Consequences of Modernity.* Stanford, CA: Stanford University Press.

Giddens, A. (1991) *Modernity and Self-identity: Self and Society in the Late Modern Age.* Cambridge: Polity Press.

Goddard, C.R., Saunders., B.J. and Stanley, J.R. (1999) 'Structured risk assessment procedures: instruments of abuse?' *Child Abuse Review 8*, 4, 251–263.

Hart, S., Michie, C. and Cooke, D. (2007) 'Precision of actuarial risk assessment instruments: evaluating the "margins of error" of group v. individual predictions of violence.' *British Journal of Psychiatry 190*, 49, 60–65.

HM Government (2008) *Saving Lives. Reducing Harm. Protecting the Public. An Action Plan for Tackling Violence 2008–2011.* London: Home Office.

Horlick-Jones, T. (2005a) 'Informal logics of risk: contingency and modes of practical reasoning.' *Journal of Risk Research 8*, 3, 253–272.

Horlick-Jones, T. (2005b) 'On "risk work": professional discourse, accountability and everyday action.' *Health, Risk and Society 7*, 3, 293–307.

Houston, S. and Griffiths, H. (2000) 'Reflections on risk in child protection: is it time for a shift in paradigms?' *Child and Family Social Work 5*, 1, 1–10.

Hudson J. (2002) 'Digitising the structure of government: the UK's information age government agenda.' *Policy and Politics 30*, 4, 515–531.

Ives, B. and Olson, M.H. (1984) 'User involvement and MIS success: a review of research.' *Management Science 30*, 5, 586–603.

Kemp, A.M., Kemp, K.W., Evans, R., Murray, L., *et al.* (1998) 'Diagnosing physical abuse using Bayes' theorem: a preliminary study.' *Child Abuse Review 7*, 3, 178–188.

Kemshall, H. (2000a) 'Researching risk in probation practice.' *Social Policy and Administration 34*, 4, 465–477.

Kemshall, H. (2000b) 'Conflicting knowledges on risk: the case of risk knowledge in the probation service.' *Health, Risk and Society 2*, 2, 143–158.

Kemshall, H. (2001) *Risk Assessment and Management of Known Sexual and Dangerous Offenders.* Paper 140. London: Home Office, Policing and Reducing Crime Unit.

Kemshall, H. and Maguire, M. (2001) 'Public protection, partnership and risk penality: the multi-agency risk management of sexual and violent offenders.' *Punishment and Society 3*, 2, 237–264.

Kemshall, H., Parton, N., Walsh, M. and Waterson, J. (1997) 'Concepts of risk in relation to organizational structure and functioning within the personal social services and probation.' *Social Policy and Administration 31*, 3, 213–232.

Laming, Lord (2003) *The Victoria Climbié Inquiry: Report of an Inquiry by Lord Laming.* Cmnd 5730. Norwich: The Stationery Office.

Laming, Lord (2009) *The Protection of Children in England: A Progress Report.* HC330. London: The Stationery Office.

Lipsky, M. (1980) *Street-level Bureaucracy: Dilemmas of the Individual in Public Services.* New York: Russell Sage Foundation.

Littlechild, B. (2008) 'Child protection social work: risks of fears and fears of risks – impossible tasks from impossible goals.' *Social Policy and Administration 42*, 6, 662–675.

Little, J. and Rixon, A. (1998) 'Computer learning and risk assessment in child protection.' *Child Abuse Review 7*, 3, 165–177.

Maguire, M., Kemshall, H., Noaks, L. and Wincup, E. (2001) *Risk Management of Sexual and Violent Offenders: The Work of Public Protection Panels.* Police Research Series Paper 139. London: Home Office.

Mattison, M. (2000) 'Ethical decision making: the person in process.' *Social Work 45*, 3, 201–212.

Munro, E. (1999) 'Common errors of reasoning in child protection work.' *Child Abuse and Neglect 23*, 8, 745–758.

Munro, E. (2004) 'A simpler way to understand the results of risk assessment instruments.' *Child and Youth Services Review 26*, 9, 873–883.

Munro, E. (2005) 'What tools do we need to improve identification of child abuse?' *Child Abuse Review 14*, 6, 374–388.

Munro, E. (2008) *Effective Child Protection.* London: Sage Publications.

Norman, D.A. (1998) *The Design of Everyday Things.* Cambridge, MA: MIT Press.

Parton, N. (1998) 'Risk, advanced liberalism and child welfare: the need to rediscover uncertainty and ambiguity.' *British Journal of Social Work 28*, 1, 5–27.

Parton, N. (2008) 'Changes in the form of knowledge in social work: from the "social" to the "informational"?' *British Journal of Social Work 38*, 2, 275–277.

Parton, N., Thorpe, D. and Wattam, C. (1997) *Child Protection: Risk and the Moral Order.* Basingstoke: Macmillan.

Reder, P. and Duncan, S. (1999) *Lost Innocents: A Follow-up Study of Fatal Child Abuse.* London: Routledge.

Reder, P. and Duncan, S. (2004) 'Making the most of the Victoria Climbié Inquiry.' *Child Abuse Review 13*, 2, 95–114.

Reder, P., Duncan, S. and Gray, M. (1993) *Beyond Blame: Child Abuse Tragedies Revisited.* London: Routledge.

Richards, L. (2004) *'Getting Away With It': A Strategic Overview of Domestic Violence Sexual Assault and 'Serious' Incident Analysis.* London: Metropolitan Police Service.

Ruch, G. (2005) 'Relationship-based practice and reflective practice: holistic approaches to contemporary child care social work.' *Child and Family Social Work 10*, 2, 111–123.

Shlonsky, A. and Wagner, D (2005) 'The next step: integrating actuarial risk assessment and clinical judgement into an evidence-based practice framework in CPS case management.' *Children and Youth Services Review 27*, 4, 409–427.

Stalker, K. (2003) 'Managing risk and uncertainty in social work: a literature review.' *Journal of Social Work 3*, 2, 211–233.

Wald, M.S. and Woolverton, M. (1990) 'Risk assessment: the emperor's new clothes?' *Child Welfare LX1X*, 483–511.

Wastell, D. White, S., Broadhurst, K., Peckover, S. and Pithouse, A. (2010) 'Children's services in the iron cage of performance management: street-level bureaucracy and the spectre of Švejkism.' *International Journal of Social Welfare 19*, 3, 310–320.

Webb, S.A. (2007) *Social Work in a Risk Society: Social and Political Perspectives.* Basingstoke: Palgrave Macmillan.

White, S., Hall, C. and Peckover, S. (2009a) 'The descriptive tyranny of the Common Assessment Framework: technology, child welfare and professional practice.' *British Journal of Social Work 39*, 7, 1197–1217.

White, S., Pithouse, A. and Wastell, D. (2009b) *Error, Blame and Responsibility in Child Welfare: Problematics of Governance in an Invisible Trade: Full Research Report.* ESRC end of award report, RES–166–25–0048-A. Swindon: Economic and Social Research Council. Available at www.esrcsocietytoday.ac.uk, accessed on 18 July 2010.

CHAPTER 6

MENTAL HEALTH AND RISK

TONY MADEN

INTRODUCTION

Risk assessment has assumed increasing if not central importance in UK mental health services over the last two or three decades. The three main risks, in descending order of media profile and public concern are violence; suicide; and self-neglect. This chapter is concerned with violence risk.

The emphasis on violence is justified partly by the level of public interest but mainly because there is more to say about it. Suicide and self-neglect are relatively straightforward because we can all agree that they are important; bad; and often avoidable by improving care and treatment.

Violence risk on the other hand is controversial and politicised. Homicides by the mentally ill sometimes attract intense media attention. In 1994, the Department of Health mandated that 'in cases of homicide, it will always be necessary to hold an inquiry which is independent of the providers involved' (NHS Executive 1994). Concerns about safety have continued to grow, leading to a steady flow of legislation and guidance aimed at improving risk management. Although life-threatening violence against staff is rare, mental health services continue to have high rates of assaults despite the NHS's zero tolerance policy.

The opposing argument presented mainly by user groups and some professionals is that violence risk is overstated; violence by the mentally ill accounts for a tiny proportion of all violence in the community; it is difficult if not impossible to predict or prevent; and we should concentrate on making services better and more attractive to users as a long-term strategy for violence reduction. It is argued that excessive concern with violence serves only to increase stigma, discourages users from contacting services and thus tends to increase the risk (e.g. Dawson and Szmukler 2006; Munro and Rumgay 2000).

Both sides make valid points and one may have expected compromise and unity around the general principle that violence to others is a bad thing and all reasonable steps should be taken to stop it happening. Instead the debate has been surprisingly bitter. It reached its maximum level of hysteria during arguments over the 2007 revision of the Mental Health Act. Opponents of the new legislation sometimes talked as though the new law represented the final sweeping away of all rights belonging to those with mental ill health.

Why is there such polarisation? There is no simple answer, but the question deserves further exploration because attitudes have an impact on the effectiveness of risk management. In this chapter, I argue that the technical aspects of risk assessment and management are well understood. Refinements will continue but, unless we discover new and more effective treatments for mental illness, there will be no quantum leap. Progress will depend largely on dissemination and implementation of existing knowledge. It follows that, along with training, motivation and commitment are of critical importance. Why do people feel so strongly about violence and mental health?

WHY DO WE WORRY ABOUT VIOLENCE RISK?

There are two ways of answering the question. The first deals with the scientific evidence concerning the links between violence and mental disorder. The second concerns attitudes and values.

The science

There is a vast and growing literature on the epidemiology of violence and mental disorder so a full review is beyond the scope of this chapter. The field is big but recent. It was only in the late 1980s and early 1990s that large-scale community studies were able to provide good evidence.

One of the most widely quoted is Swanson et al.'s (1990) finding of a 12-month incidence of self-reported violence in 8 per cent of people with a diagnosis of schizophrenia compared to only 2 per cent of those without a psychiatric diagnosis. Figures are even higher for anti-social personality disorder; drug or alcohol misuse; or any combination of these conditions with or without mental illness.

There have been many similar findings since, for example, Shaw et al. (2006) found schizophrenia in 5 per cent of men remanded on a charge of homicide compared with approximately 1 per cent in the general population. Even though we would prefer it to be otherwise, it is an established fact that a diagnosis of schizophrenia is statistically associated with an increased risk of violence, and the association is even stronger for substance misuse or anti-social personality disorder (Mullen 2006).

The science is therefore straightforward but it is possible to complicate it if you wish. Many words have been generated using different comparison groups; so, if schizophrenia is compared with diagnoses with even higher statistical associations with violence, it looks as though it has a low risk. It is all, of course, relative.

If we accept the evidence that some common mental disorders are statistically associated with increased violence risk, then we must also accept management of that risk as a legitimate task for mental health services.

It is worth mentioning that this evidence comes from group comparisons; people with diagnoses were compared with those without. Less researched but more enlightening is intra-individual comparison. Practitioners routinely deal with clients who are not violent when well but present a much higher risk of violence when they relapse – irrespective of whether the relapse is an episode of schizophrenia or intoxication with drugs or alcohol. That is why risk management matters: treatment can make a difference.

Attitudes and values

Many pressures have led to a greater concern with risk and most are not specific to mental health. Society is generally more risk averse than it was and there is particular concern about crime and violence. We are more aware of victims and their rights, which leads inevitably and rightly to greater emphasis on protection and prevention. These are not abstract considerations, and clinicians or employers may face criminal or civil legal action if their acts or omissions cause injury.

One product of these changes is the National Patient Safety Agency (NPSA), which among its other activities commissions the National Confidential Inquiry into Suicide and Homicide by People with Mental Illness (NCISH, Appleby *et al.* 1999, 2001). Both reflect the wider impact of consumerism on health services. They focus on patient experience and in particular on outcome.

Doctors have been slow to measure outcome and mental health professionals have good reason to be defensive. Until the late 1980s, the orthodox teaching in psychiatry was that there was no statistical association between mental illness and violence (Monahan 1992) and there was little research. Suicide was also a minority interest and largely neglected by researchers.

Violence presents problems over and above other outcome measures because it is a rare example of medicine being concerned primarily with third-party risk. Doctors often manage chronic diseases in order to reduce the risk of complications – for example, the risk of stroke in hypertension. Violence risk in psychiatry is different because the risk is not to the patient but to a third party and therefore introduces obligations that do not apply to most health practitioners.

Although rare, third-party risk in medicine is not limited to violence and mental health. Examples of doctors acting on behalf of others rather than the patient include certification of sickness absence; regulation of fitness to drive; control of infectious diseases; and child care proceedings or indeed any health concerns that affect children in contact with an adult patient. All are examples of practitioners balancing the rights of the patient against those of third parties.

These examples show that third-party risk in medicine is unusual but, when it exists, the expectation is that doctors will intervene readily to safeguard others. Society has a low tolerance for third-party risks and medical risks are no different. We accept the risks we face if we are unlucky enough to develop a disease, but we do not readily accept risks associated with somebody else's disease.

Some mental health practitioners have been slow to accept that they have obligations rarely encountered in other branches of medicine. They feel nostalgia for a golden age when the doctor–patient relationship was all, and the consulting room more akin to the confessional than an outpost of the Multi-Agency Public Protection Arrangements (MAPPA). All practitioners know of the need to manage violence risk but for some it retains a whiff of the unethical or underhand so they do it without enthusiasm or belief.

Ethics and violence

The ethical concerns about violence risk management are exaggerated. They usually involve concerns about stigma, unnecessary labelling, confidentiality and excessively restrictive treatment.

A diagnosis of mental illness carries enormous stigma, which we should work to reduce (Thornicroft 2006), but it does not follow that talk of violence risk is inevitably stigmatising. We do not know how to reduce stigma and well-publicised anti-stigma campaigns have achieved little. In the absence of better evidence from the field of mental health, it is reasonable to follow the strategy used for cancer by showing that effective treatments are available and outcomes are improving. Mental health services can be proud of their contribution to falling suicide rates. The most reassuring message to the public would be that there is a similar determination to reduce rates of violence through better treatment.

Risk assessment is not only or even primarily about attaching negative labels that lead to detention or other adverse consequences.

The other side of risk is safety and any useful assessment must indicate low as well as high risk. Good risk management avoids unnecessary treatment or monitoring so resources are used where they can be of most benefit. Nobody can object to an assessment that indicates a safe management plan. Once we accept the principle, we must also accept that in other patients the assessment will identify risk factors that need further intervention.

Risk management has been demonised by opponents as a process of locking up people who have not done anything. Neither part of the criticism is valid. Most risk management is about reducing the risk of re-offending and an individual who has 'not done anything' is unlikely to be identified as high risk (see later). When risks are identified the aim is always safe management in the least restrictive circumstances and the vast majority of interventions are small changes in the treatment of voluntary patients.

Violence risk management inevitably involves tensions between different values. We value patient autonomy while also recognising the rights of others to live safely. The conflict of values is real and cannot be avoided by loudly trumpeting only one side of the argument. Guidance on the limits to medical confidentiality attempts to reconcile these conflicting pressures.

User groups sometimes behave as though the mentally ill form an enlightened minority besieged by a hostile and ignorant public. In reality, mental illness is common and can affect anyone. Patients are also members of the public. It is similarly misleading to pretend those with mental ill health form a homogeneous group. There may be little in common between a person with mild to moderate depression and another who is acutely psychotic.

In fact, one of the defining features of mental illness is that there may be little in common between different mental states in the same individual. So it can be hard to believe that the man in the consulting room, calmly complaining about the side-effects of anti-psychotic medication, is the same person who a few weeks earlier was psychotic and insightless in a seclusion room following an attempt to kill his partner. In these circumstances, it is understandable if doctor and patient prefer to stay with the present. Yet it is essential for risk management that they also discuss the man in the seclusion room despite the fear, anger and humiliation that went with the experience. The danger of taking anti-stigma pressure too far is that we collude with this natural squeamishness and we attempt to sanitise mental health. Good risk management requires open discussion of the most serious and frightening forms of illness as well as acknowledgement of what can go wrong when serious illness is not properly managed.

THE MECHANICS OF RISK ASSESSMENT AND MANAGEMENT

Assuming the ethical and philosophical obstacles can be overcome, how should practitioners go about the task? What are the techniques, and are they effective?

There is a bewildering array of risk assessment instruments to choose from and new ones appear constantly. Practitioners must feel as though they are in the cereal aisle of an American hypermarket faced with a vast and confusing array of products that have a lot of similarities while each claims superiority over the others.

In fact, the choice is less daunting than it appears. As in the cereal aisle, there may be strong personal preferences but in the broader scheme of things there is often little to choose between the different brands. To understand why this is so, we need to consider the principles of risk assessment and the predictive accuracy of risk instruments.

Principles of risk assessment

The first basic assumption is that the past is the best guide to the future. Assessment therefore begins with a description of previous violence and the internal or external factors associated with it. We assume that when similar circumstances arise again there will be high risk of violence and we look for factors we can change in order to reduce the risk.

The importance of this principle is partly because it is so obvious to anybody conducting an inquiry after the event. There may be sympathy for practitioners when violence occurs in unforeseen circumstances, but there is much less sympathy when the violence amounts to repetition. It follows logically that, although rarely stated explicitly, the main priority in risk management is to prevent a repetition of violence. Expectations are lower in relation to a first act of violence by an individual. It is almost impossible for a patient to be rated as presenting a high risk of violence without a history of actual or threatened violence. An efficient risk management system prioritises cases in which there has been previous violence.

Of course the past is not a perfect guide to the future. People change and develop. Surprises happen. Younger people have a shorter history and therefore less of a basis for prediction. In these circumstances, we have to rely on general indicators of violence risk.

Fortunately the range of indicators of risk is fairly short. In addition to the individual's history of violence, they include negative attitudes; non-compliance with treatment; relapse; lack of insight; intoxication; psychopathy; and other personality disorders. The themes running through the list are psychopathy or anti-social personality disorder;

drug or alcohol misuse; and difficulties in treatment. All are associated with increased risk.

The relatively small number of general risk factors is reflected in the design of standardised instruments. The Historical Clinical Risk 20 (HCR-20) (Webster *et al.* 1997) of course has 20 items and the Violence Risk Appraisal Guide (VRAG, Harris, Rice and Quinsey 1993) has 12. Measures of sexual offending risk also concentrate on a handful of variables including psychopathy; non-sexual offending; victims unknown to the perpetrator; paraphilia; male victims; and inability to establish stable relationships.

A short list of variables therefore goes a long way towards summarising the general risks of violence associated with a case. A couple of these factors deserve further comment.

PSYCHOPATHY

Psychopathy as measured by the Psychopathy Checklist-Revised (PCL-R, Hare 1991) has a strong positive association with violence risk whether alone or in combination with other disorders. For our purposes, it can be considered a more severe form of anti-social personality disorder. Many risk instruments incorporate items related directly or indirectly to psychopathy.

It is perhaps no surprise that features such as lack of empathy, callousness, impulsivity and irresponsibility increase violence risk whether they derive from schizophrenia, autism or a personality disorder. Psychopathy also has the added advantage of requiring a careful recording of the range and extent of previous anti-social behaviour, so it ensures that a thorough history is taken.

MENTAL ILLNESS

While features of psychopathy are associated with increased risk, it is a serious mistake to assume their absence necessarily means a low risk of violence. The mistake is most often made when dealing with mental illnesses such as schizophrenia. Psychoses such as schizophrenia can cause high violence risk even in the absence of general risk factors. While risk factors interact, they are not additive in a simple way: one may trump the absence of all the others and dictate management of a case.

Hence risk instruments that rely heavily on indicators of psychopathy can be misleading in those with mental ill health. They are not, however, irrelevant, because psychopathy increases the risk of violence in schizophrenia; the essential point to remember is that the converse is not true, so the absence of psychopathy does not equate to low risk in mental illness.

If I appear to labour the point, it is because it illustrates why treatment is so important. Mental illness alone can elevate an individual rapidly from the lowest to the highest level of risk in a way that few other things can.

Predictive accuracy

As noted earlier, a small number of variables crop up again and again in violence risk assessment instruments. They are combined in different ways and may be supplemented by other data. The crucial question remains how accurate they are in measuring violence risk.

The widely used measure of accuracy of prediction in health care is the Receiver Operator Characteristic (ROC) curve, which plots the true positive rate against the false positive rate. True positives are those people predicted as likely to be violent who actually go on to behave violently. False positives are people predicted to be violent who do not in fact behave violently. Tossing a coin (i.e. chance) would produce a diagonal, straight line plot.

The statistic used to summarise the graph is the area under the curve (AUC). In the straight line produced by chance the AUC is 0.5, whereas a perfect predictive instrument would have an AUC of 1. The statistics can get complicated and Mossman (1994) explains why AUC is the most appropriate statistic. For present purposes it is sufficient to note that we strive for an AUC of 1 while knowing we can never attain it; and anything higher than 0.5 is an improvement on chance.

The National Institute for Health and Clinical Excellence (NICE 2009) evaluated several risk assessment instruments as part of its guideline on the treatment of anti-social personality disorder. AUCs were typically in the range 0.6–0.8. The conclusion was that all appeared to predict risk moderately well and there was no clear evidence to distinguish between them in terms of accuracy. Similar comments apply to their use in mental illness (Webster and Hucker 2007).

In summary, a relatively small number of variables account for much of the variance in risk of violence. There is often overlap between the items used in different standardised measures. Once the basic list of variables is covered, little added value results from extending the list. All established instruments tend to have similar predictive accuracy, which is reliably better than chance but moderate rather than outstanding. The results are a corrective to more pessimistic views (e.g. Munro and Rumgay 2000) but they also serve as a warning against unrealistic expectations.

In terms of overall accuracy one instrument has no advantage over another. Prediction can probably be improved further in an individual case by knowing reference to idiosyncratic risk factors that would be difficult to include in any standardised measure. It follows that it is wrong to assume that any standardised list is all one needs to know about the case. It is also pointless to imagine that by administering a large number of instruments the predictive accuracy will be further improved. It is far better to expend the effort on a structured clinical/professional assessment (see later).

In the next section we consider how these conclusions are reflected in different approaches to assessment. First we need to consider what the output of an assessment should be. The simplistic division into high and low risk, as used in evaluation of instruments, is an over-simplification.

THE MULTI-DIMENSIONAL NATURE OF VIOLENCE RISK

Violence risk cannot be reduced to a score on a single dimension. A full account includes qualitative and descriptive factors. One should also be suspicious of claims for absolute rather than relative measurements. It is safer to rely on statements that say how different factors will have an impact on the risk, or how an individual stands in relation to his peers.

The facets of violence risk include nature, severity, immediacy and likely victims. These dimensions interact in complex ways. A moderate probability of minor assault may be acceptable whereas even a low probability of life-threatening violence may be unacceptable.

Risk is not an inherent property of the individual but depends also on circumstances and contingencies. For example, intoxication with alcohol or drugs usually increases violence risk and may be more important in risk management than the underlying mental disorder. Non-compliance with treatment is a major risk factor for violence in schizophrenia.

A comprehensive risk assessment therefore leads readily to risk management because it includes a detailed description of risks and the factors likely to increase or reduce them. It follows that the quality of a risk assessment cannot be judged simply on predictive ability, especially as they are all much the same in this respect. For practitioners, the critical factor is the extent to which the assessment aids risk management. Unfortunately that quality is much more difficult to measure than predictive ability.

THREE METHODS OF RISK ASSESSMENT

The three approaches are:

1. Unstructured clinical assessment.

2. Actuarial risk assessment.

3. Structured clinical judgement.

In line with the principles discussed earlier, the preferred method is structured clinical judgement (also known as 'structured professional judgement' or 'SPJ') so the other two are given only brief consideration. See Maden (2007a) for more details.

Unstructured clinical assessment

The only rules are those of good clinical practice. Until recently it was the most common method of assessing violence risk in the UK. It is widely used, flexible and can be adapted to any case.

The downside is wide variation in individual practice. Standards vary widely according to the skill and experience of the practitioner. Different clinicians may have different ways of talking about risk so communication is difficult. There is a lack of transparency and accountability. It is difficult to defend decisions in the face of criticism. It is also difficult to challenge the opinion of the expert or to understand how conclusions were reached. The process is open to bias.

In fact it can be argued that pure unstructured assessment no longer exists because clinical practice is now so highly regulated and subject to guidelines national and local. Most NHS trusts will insist on a checklist of risk factors to be considered.

A more structured approach is inevitable and can be justified solely because it improves transparency, helps to reduce discriminatory practice and improves communication.

Actuarial risk assessment

The term derives from the insurance industry. A small number of facts are combined according to a strict formula to estimate the level of risk. Actuarial assessment is therefore at the opposite end of the spectrum from the unstructured clinical method. There are fixed rules about the data to be used and how they must be interpreted.

The strengths are that it is systematic and eliminates variation between individual practitioners as well as excluding bias. Statistical evaluation shows it to be reliably better than chance in predicting violence.

The weakness is that statistical evaluations are done on populations whereas clinical risk management deals with individuals. Individuals cannot be treated as identical members of a group to which they may belong. So a group of a thousand people may be estimated accurately to have a 30 per cent chance of violence within a given period, but it would be quite wrong to assume any individual from that group has a 30 per cent chance of behaving violently.

The inflexibility of the actuarial method is also a problem because an individual may present a high risk of violence because of a single problem such as untreated psychosis. If there are no other generic risk factors, an actuarial assessment would be seriously misleading.

The Violence Risk Appraisal Guide (or VRAG, Quinsey *et al.* 1998) is a widely used actuarial scale whose authors have said it could and should supplant clinical estimation of risk (Quinsey *et al.* 1998, p.171).

The VRAG was developed on adult male patients followed up after release from a high-security hospital with violent re-offending as the outcome measure. Twelve items were found to predict re-offending. Total scores on the instrument are divided into nine 'bins', each with an attached probability of violence expressed in percentage terms and relating to a 7-year time frame.

The VRAG amounts to a detailed description of which factors were associated with violent re-offending in the population used to develop it. In that sense it is a history lesson. According to our first principle of risk assessment, it is a reasonable basis for prediction so long as it is used on patients similar to those used in the design. In population terms it fares as well as any other instrument in suitable settings.

For clinical use it has too many associated problems. One of its oddities is the negative effect on risk of a diagnosis of schizophrenia. The anomaly arises because the psychopathic patients in the original group presented even higher risks. The research literature would not support downgrading of risk because the diagnosis is schizophrenia.

Incidentally, none of these objections matters in large groups where the oddities cancel each other out. Actuarial measures such as the VRAG are useful and valid for commissioners, planners and researchers who wish to compare or evaluate services. The clinician should use them with caution and only as part of a comprehensive assessment of the individual.

Structured clinical judgment

The structured clinical method combines the best aspects of actuarial assessment and the unstructured clinical method. It requires the collection of standard data about the individual but allows flexibility to collect additional data and in its use to draw conclusions and formulate plans. There are no rules about how risk is judged once the data have been assembled.

The best known example of structured clinical judgement is the HCR-20 (Hart, Cox and Hare 1995). It requires the collection of 20 data items: ten are historical and refer to the past; five are clinical and relate to present state; and five risk items relate to the future.

Each item is scored as definitely present (2), probably or partially present (1), or absent (0). The definitions for each item are included in Webster *et al.* (1997). They are not operational but provide examples of behaviour that may be scored, thereby allowing further exercise of discretion.

With the basic data plus any idiosyncratic variables in place, the clinician describes the risks with complete freedom to interpret the data as seems appropriate. Ideally the work is carried out by the clinical team. The next stage is to formulate feared scenarios of violence along with protective and aggravating factors, and from those to develop a risk management plan.

The number of scenarios is potentially infinite but in practice the same few recur frequently and relate to situations such as non-compliance, substance misuse, relapse and stressors.

EVALUATION OF THE HCR-20

The HCR-20 is popular because it helps clinicians without telling them what to do. It informs and can improve clinical judgement without attempting to abolish it. As a result it has become the de facto standard for risk assessment in UK forensic mental health services (Khiroya, Weaver and Maden 2009).

Maybe its strength is also its weakness. The final decisions and judgements remain with the practitioners. There is a message here for planners in a world awash with guidelines. Violence risk management involves complex choices in which conflicting values have to be balanced against each other. There is almost always a range of right answers rather than one. No standard formula can come up with the right answer because no single right answer exists. There is no escape from this reality. The system relies on competent and well-trained practitioners who can use their judgement.

The HCR-20 was one of the tools evaluated by NICE in its guidelines on anti-social personality disorder (ASPD) (see earlier) and for those purposes it was treated as an actuarial instrument by adding up scores on its 20 items. It did as well as any other instrument.

It is interesting to reflect on how it could be better evaluated. Idiosyncratic variables by definition apply only to the individual so cannot be included in a statistical analysis. In clinical use it requires the use of discretion, which is not easy to measure.

As the aim is to formulate a good risk management plan, it should be judged by that standard rather than its predictive accuracy. Unfortunately there are no such measures. The challenge to practitioners must be to develop them so we can progress beyond a preoccupation with prediction.

THE LIMITS OF PREDICTION

The most important general point to emerge from this survey of risk assessment is that there is a limit to the accuracy of violence risk prediction. Also, assuming we make use of state-of-the-art methods, we have reached the limit. There is little to distinguish between the accuracy of the best instruments, and it is most unlikely anything better is going to come along. There is too much randomness or noise in the system.

People have not stopped trying to develop better instruments. The MacArthur Violence Risk Assessment Study (Monahan *et al.* 2001) has attempted a sophisticated Iterative Classification Tree (Monahan *et al.* 2005) but it encounters the problem common to all actuarial instruments that the more precisely it describes the original population, the less likely it is to generalise to a new population that has different idiosyncrasies. Note that this is a theoretical and absolute limit to the actuarial method; it is not soluble by better statistics.

If prediction has reached its limits we are left with the following responses:

1. Maximising prevention.

2. Dealing with uncertainty.

3. Managing negative outcomes.

Maximising prevention

Prevention does not depend on specific prediction. As Munro and Rumgay (2000) noted, it was much more common for homicide inquiries to conclude that homicides could have been prevented than that they could have been predicted. For example, violence in florid psychotic states is often impulsive. Prediction is possible to the extent of saying that a person who has been violent during previous psychotic states is likely to be violent during future psychotic states. It is not possible to predict precisely when or how the violence will occur during the episode, and there is no point in trying. Prevention therefore depends on using early intervention to minimise the time a person spends in a psychotic state.

It was established long ago that the Mental Health Act (1983) allows early intervention in such circumstances (e.g. Blom-Cooper, Hally and Murphy 1995). Yet it is still acceptable, if not common practice, to delay treatment until the psychosis becomes florid. In most cases no great harm results (if no good either) but in a small percentage of cases there will be a negative outcome such as violence or suicide. It is an example of unnecessary gambling.

Prevention also depends on making full use of existing methods of risk management. Guidance has been issued by the Department of Health (2007) and the Royal College of Psychiatrists (2008).

Dealing with uncertainty

Precise and accurate prediction of individual behaviour is never possible and we can never eliminate violence risk entirely. Therefore we have to deal with uncertainty.

The first step is to clarify one's responsibilities. Risk assessment and management can be considered as a three-stage process that addresses the following questions (Maden 2005):

1. What are the risks associated with treatment?

2. How can the risks be reduced?

3. Are the residual risks acceptable?

Mental health practitioners have expertise to contribute when answering the first two but not the third question. Questions about the acceptability of risk are moral, social or philosophical considerations rather than matters of clinical or technical expertise. If we stray too readily into this area, we take on unnecessary responsibility and are likely to be blamed when things go wrong.

The solution is to allow wider consideration of the acceptability of risk, as happens in the case of a restricted hospital order where the clinicians may propose but the tribunal or the Home Secretary decides on the acceptability of risk.

The principle of risk sharing should be applied whenever possible and appropriate. Relations and carers should be involved in decisions. The views of other members of the multidisciplinary team should always be sought. When dealing with mentally disordered offenders, there may be collaboration with probation or a Multi-Agency Public Protection Panel (MAPPP). In addition to the sharing of responsibility, the introduction of other perspectives is likely to improve the quality of decisions in areas where there is a lot of uncertainty.

When there is no clear right or wrong answer, a second opinion is an invaluable resource. It is another example of risk sharing. Forensic services should be used to assist general services by endorsing treatment plans if they have no improvements to suggest. A homicide inquiry is effectively a second opinion delivered with the luxury of hindsight. It is much better to have the benefit of others' wisdom before the event.

Managing negative outcomes

It is inevitable that things will sometimes go wrong and planning for a bad outcome is part of risk management. There should of course be support and advice for staff involved. There is also a need to offer or to arrange care for the victim's relatives. Health services are often uncomfortable with the role and sometimes ignore secondary victims or hide behind confidentiality, leaving them feeling neglected or excluded from the process.

Services need to learn from negative outcomes and homicide inquiries are part of that process. The standard is variable and their value is often reduced by long delays between the incident and publication of the report. If several years have elapsed, it is likely that practice will already have changed, either because the service took steps to change it or because NHS policy changes so rapidly anyway. Several reviews are available (e.g. Maden 2007b; Munro and Rumgay 2000; Petch and Bradley 1997).

The future of inquiries is uncertain. They are expensive and their conclusions sometimes repetitive. The National Confidential Inquiry (Appleby et al. 1999, 2001) may be a better way of learning from these tragedies.

Although there is scope for reducing the number of homicides, it is inevitable that tragedies will happen occasionally. Some are unavoidable even with the best treatment. It is an inescapable corollary of a socially inclusive service that it treats people who may be anti-social and violent for reasons unrelated to their mental disorder.

In these circumstances, managers and politicians need to support their staff and not assume that violence necessarily indicates a failure of treatment. Until we achieve that goal, the management of violence risk will remain a stressful process.

KEY POINTS

1. Violence risk assessment always requires a detailed history of previous violence and the circumstances in which it occurred.

2. Violence risk is multidimensional, so a comprehensive assessment can never be reduced to a number or percentage on a single measure.

3. Structured risk assessment enhances but can never replace clinical judgement.

4. The best risk assessments are relative rather than absolute. They facilitate risk management by describing factors that will increase or decrease risk.

5. Clinical and non-clinical factors contribute to violence risk. Multi-agency working allows for better management and appropriate sharing of risk.

6. Decisions on the acceptability of risk are social and political rather than medical. High-risk cases often involve courts and tribunals. Clinicians should take all reasonable steps to involve relatives and carers.

7. Violence risk can never be eliminated, so comprehensive risk management includes planning for a negative outcome.

8. There are few absolutes in risk management. There is usually a spectrum of reasonable decisions rather than a single right answer. In doubtful or high-risk cases, the best protection is a second opinion.

REFERENCES

Appleby, L., Shaw, J., Amos, T., McDonnell, R., et al. (1999) Safer Services. Report of the National Confidential Inquiry into Suicide and Homicide by People with Mental Illness. London: The Stationery Office.

Appleby, L., Shaw, J., Sherratt, J., Amos, T., et al. (2001) Safety First. Report of the National Confidential Inquiry into Suicide and Homicide by People with Mental Illness. London: The Stationery Office.

Blom-Cooper, L., Hally, H. and Murphy, E. (1995) The Falling Shadow. One Patient's Mental Health Care. London: Duckworth.

Dawson, J. and Szmukler, G. (2006) 'Fusion of mental health and incapacity legislation.' British Journal of Psychiatry 188, 504–509.

Department of Health (DH) (2007) Best Practice in Managing Risk. London: DH.

Hare, R.D. (1991) The Psychopathy Checklist Revised. Toronto: Multi-Health Systems.

Harris, G.T., Rice, M.E. and Quinsey, V.L. (1993) 'Violent recidivism of mentally disordered offenders: the development of a statistical prediction instrument.' *Criminal Justice and Behaviour 20*, 315–335.

Hart, S.D., Cox, D.N. and Hare, R.D. (1995) *The Hare Psychopathy Checklist: Screening Version.* Toronto: Multi-Health Systems.

Khiroya, R., Weaver, T. and Maden, A. (2009) 'The use and perceived utility of structured violence risk assessments in English medium secure forensic units.' *Psychiatric Bulletin 33*, 129–132.

Maden, A. (2005) 'Violence risk assessment: the question is not whether to do it but how.' *Psychiatric Bulletin 29*, 121–122.

Maden, A. (2007a) *Treating Violence: A Guide to Risk Management in Mental Health.* Oxford: Oxford University Press.

Maden, A. (2007b) 'A New Look at Homicides by the Mentally Ill.' In A. Maden, *Treating Violence: A Guide to Risk Management in Mental Health.* Oxford: Oxford University Press. 121–156.

Monahan, J. (1992) 'Mental disorder and violent behaviour: perceptions and evidence.' *American Psychologist,* April, 511–521.

Monahan, J., Steadman, H.J., Silver, E., Appelbaum, P.S., *et al.* (2001) *Rethinking Risk Assessment. The MacArthur Study of Mental Disorder and Violence.* Oxford: University Press.

Monahan, J., Steadman, H.J., Robbins, P.C., Appelbaum, P.S., *et al.* (2005) 'An actuarial model of violence risk assessment for persons with mental disorders.' *Psychiatric Services 56*, 810–815.

Mossman, B.T. (1994) 'Assessing predictions of violence: being accurate about accuracy.' *Journal of Consulting and Clinical Psychology 62*, 4, 783–793.

Mullen, P.E. (2006) 'Schizophrenia and violence: from correlations to preventative strategies.' *Advances in Psychiatric Treatment 12*, 239–248.

Munro, E. and Rumgay, J. (2000) 'The role of risk assessment in reducing homicides by people with mental illness.' *British Journal of Psychiatry 176*, 2, 116–120.

National Institute for Health and Clinical Excellence (NICE) (2009) 'Risk Assessment and Management.' *Antisocial Personality Disorder: Treatment, Management and Prevention.* NICE Clinical Guideline 77. London: NICE. 143–168.

NHS Executive (1994) *Guidance on the Discharge of Mentally Disordered People and their Continuing Care in the Community.* HSG (94)27. London: Department of Health.

Petch, E. and Bradley, C. (1997) 'Learning the lessons from homicide inquiries: adding insult to injury?' *Journal of Forensic Psychiatry 8*, 161–184.

Quinsey, V., Harris, G., Rice, M. and Cormier, C. (1998) *Violent Offenders: Appraising and Managing Risk.* Washington DC: American Psychological Association.

Royal College of Psychiatrists (2008) *Rethinking Risk to Others in Mental Health Services. College Report CR150.* London: Royal College of Psychiatrists.

Shaw, J., Hunt, I.M., Flynn, S., Meehan, J., *et al.* (2006) 'Rates of mental disorder in people convicted of homicide: a national clinical survey.' *British Journal of Psychiatry 188*, 143–147.

Steadman, H., Monahan, J., Appelbaum, P. *et al.* (1996) 'Designing a New Generation of Risk Assessment Research.' In J. Monahan and H. Steadman (eds) *Violence and Mental Disorder.* Chicago, IL: University of Chicago Press.

Swanson, J.W., Holzer, C.E., Ganju, V.K. and Jonjo, R.T. (1990) 'Violence and psychiatric disorder in the community: evidence from the epidemiologic catchment area surveys.' *Hospital and Community Psychiatry 41*, 761–770.

Thornicroft, G. (2006) *Shunned: Discrimination against People with Mental Illness.* Oxford: Oxford University Press.

Webster, C.D. and Hucker, S.J. (2007) *Violence Risk: Assessment and Management.* London: Wiley-Blackwell.

Webster, C.D., Douglas, K.S., Eaves, D. and Hart, S.D. (1997) *HCR-20. Assessing Risk for Violence, Version 2.* Vancouver: University, Mental Health, Law and Policy Institute.

CHAPTER 7

RISK AND INTIMATE PARTNER VIOLENCE

AMANDA L. ROBINSON

INTRODUCTION

Beginning with Jacqueline Campbell's risk assessment tool (Campbell 1986), there has been increased interest in assessing and measuring risk associated with intimate partner violence (IPV) – both for continued abuse and for homicide. A proliferation of risk assessment tools and practices has emerged on both sides of the Atlantic in a context of increased attention to IPV, and a more concerted effort to reduce its overall incidence. It is hoped that, by identifying victims at higher risk of repeat victimisation and then intervening, the likelihood of violence may be reduced. This work coincides with other important, progressive developments over the past 20 years that have been initiated in many countries, such as the implementation of police pro-arrest policies, dedicated training for police and prosecutors, specialist courts, and expanded and professionalised advocacy services for victims (see Robinson 2010 for an overview). The common motivation behind these various efforts is to minimise the more horrific tragedies that can result from the unchecked escalation of violence over time.

'Risk' is a concept that has intuitive meaning for those front-line practitioners coming into contact with victims and perpetrators, and the idea of being able to identify, assess and manage (reduce) risk is now embedded into the working practices and occupational cultures of many agencies involved in this field, particularly those in the criminal justice system. Perhaps unlike other areas of risk assessment and management, in the context of IPV it is the victim rather than the perpetrator who is the focus of most risk-based work, although others are involved in the risk assessment of perpetrators. This chapter will chart the emergence of this victim-oriented phenomenon and explore both the utility and limitations of risk-based practices for IPV. The current UK approach – in total less than 2 years old – is briefly described as follows:

- There is a common risk assessment tool and accompanying guidance for all police forces in England and Wales, known as DASH (Domestic Abuse, Stalking and Harassment and Honour-based Violence).

- Independent domestic violence advisors (IDVAs) are trained support workers who use a version of the same risk tool when providing support to victims.

- Risk assessment is linked to the provision of services for victims; those identified as 'very high risk' are referred to MARACs (Multi-Agency Risk Assessment Conferences). Police and IDVAs make the majority of referrals to MARACs.

- MARACs are operational in most areas of the UK (they are now being run across England, Wales, Scotland and Northern Ireland).

- Assessing and responding to risk are considered key elements of Parliament's approach to domestic violence (DV).

TERMINOLOGY
Risk and IPV
Traditionally, violence risk assessment has been based on a clinical approach to prediction of the risks posed by particular offenders. In the contemporary British context for IPV, victims at risk of re-victimisation rather than offenders at risk of re-offending are the main 'targets' of risk-based activities. Although risk assessment of perpetrators does take place, this represents only a fraction of the total number of incidents, being confined to convicted perpetrators. In contrast, risk work with victims, undertaken by a range of professionals, is not limited to those victims who have cases going through the criminal justice system. Of course, the behaviour of perpetrators is what poses a risk to victims. Gaining information from victims about perpetrators, rather than asking perpetrators themselves, is what makes the current approach unique.

Drawing on the definition used by the prison and probation services, risk of serious harm refers to:

> ...a risk which is life-threatening and/or traumatic, and from which recovery, whether physical or psychological, can be expected to be difficult or impossible. (as cited in Richards, Letchford and Stratton 2008, p.112)

As applied to IPV practice with victims, risk refers to the increased likelihood that a victim may experience additional *violence of any type*, future *severe violence or injury*, or *homicide*. The inclusion of many different outcomes contributes to the term's ambiguity. This has problematic implications for the practitioners who are relying on risk assessment to clarify and guide their professional judgement in deciding how to help a particular victim achieve safety. This particular challenge for risk assessment will be discussed in more detail later in the chapter.

The risk assessment process

As knowledge of – and involvement with – risk assessment has grown, so has the number of associated terms and their meanings. Risk assessment is now viewed as a three-stage process. Importantly, this is not an endeavour to gather information for its own sake, but rather to provide relevant information for multi-agency safety plans and police investigations. For example, guidance issued by the National Policing Improvement Agency (NPIA) in 2008 on the investigation of IPV explains the process in the following way:

- Risk identification is used to refer to the identification of established risk factors in a specific case. This process can be undertaken by any police officer or other trained practitioner, and should be based upon an awareness of established risk factors. Risk identification does not include assessment.

- Risk assessment is the process of estimating and regularly reviewing the likelihood and nature of a risk posed by an offender to a particular victim, any children or others. Only appropriately trained staff (e.g. specialist domestic violence officers or IDVAs) should carry out risk assessments that result in the categorisation of risk (e.g. 'high risk').

- Risk management is the process of monitoring a case to ensure that risk of further harm is minimised, by using a multi-agency approach that is based on appropriate information sharing, and the development and implementation of multi-agency interventions (e.g. MARACs).

The main benefits and challenges for practitioners undertaking this process are discussed in later sections. First, however, it is worth mentioning the specific factors that provide the foundation for the risk assessment process and, once identified, cause concern for those involved.

Established risk factors

Many studies have assessed the factors predictive of violence recidivism among offenders, resulting in a well-established group of empirically based risk factors (for a review, see Hilton and Harris 2005). Risk factors are usually grouped into factors associated with the perpetrator's behaviour (e.g. criminal history, previous violent incidents), characteristics of the current incident (e.g. weapons used, escalation of violence) and contextual factors to the case (e.g. relationship separation, victim's social isolation). The Spousal Assault Risk Assessment (SARA) Guide is one example of a tool that includes many of these factors (Kropp and Hart 2000; Kropp et al. 1999). Research has also documented the importance of victims' levels of fear, because their intuition about the potential for future violence has been shown to accurately predict re-victimisation (Robinson 2007; Weisz, Tolman and Saunders 2000).

In the largest study of its kind to date, data from more than 2500 victims accessing IDVA services in eight projects in England and Wales provide a good overview of the prevalence of the more well-known risk factors in a recent sample of British victims. Table 7.1 displays the findings, and also provides a good representation of most of the risk factors included in the DASH 2009 risk assessment tool (Howarth et al. 2009).[1] Many of the risk factors listed are derived from tools used with offenders (e.g. SARA) and thus focus on the behaviour of perpetrators from the victims' perspective.[2]

In considering these findings, it is important to acknowledge that little is known in a systematic way about the risks facing other groups of victims (e.g. those who did not access IDVA services, those who have never contacted the police, etc.). Further analyses are needed to establish the relative importance of each factor, while holding constant the effects of other factors. Understanding whether some factors could be combined would also be useful. Analytical work to identify which risk factors correlate with re-victimisation for different types of victims (using their socio-demographic characteristics), for different types of violence (physical, sexual, psychological, harassment) and levels of violence (moderate versus extreme) is currently being undertaken (see Robinson and Howarth, 2010).

1   There are some differences between the risk factors listed in Table 7.1 and those found in DASH 2009, reflecting the fact that the IDVA research began earlier than the development of DASH. The notable differences are that DASH includes additional items on honour-based violence, abuse of pets and violations of bail conditions/injunctions. Other differences are mostly semantic.

2   It should be noted that other sources of information, particularly those available to the police, such as criminal history records, are used to validate and/or supplement the information provided by victims.

Table 7.1: Prevalence of risk factors in a sample of 2567 accessing IDVA services		
Risk factor	**Frequency of victims (N = 2567)**	**Percentage of victims (N = 2567)**
Current incident resulted in injuries	1309	51
Use of weapons	567	22
Jealous and controlling behaviour	2333	91
Stalking	790	31
Sexual abuse	729	28
Victim has been strangled/choked	1559	61
Escalation of abuse	1874	73
Perpetrator has threatened to kill the victim	1582	62
Perpetrator has threatened to kill other partner	241	9
Perpetrator has threatened to kill others	536	21
Victim is frightened	2070	81
Victim is afraid of further injury	2136	83
Victim is afraid of being killed	1122	44
Perpetrator has a criminal record	1296	50
Perpetrator has a criminal record for DV	669	26
Perpetrator has financial problems	1151	45
Perpetrator abuses alcohol	1374	54
Perpetrator abuses drugs	989	39
Perpetrator has mental health issues	713	28
Perpetrator has threatened suicide	904	35

Table 7.1: Prevalence of risk factors in a sample of 2567 accessing IDVA services		
Risk factor	Frequency of victims (N = 2567)	Percentage of victims (N = 2567)
Victim and perpetrator have separated	2137	83
Victim is pregnant	158	6
Victim has threatened suicide	589	23
Conflict around child contact*	725	41
Perpetrator has threatened to kill children*	199	11
Victim is afraid of harm to children*	476	27

Source: Howarth et al. (2009).
Note: * Figures refer to the 1774 victims with children.

PRACTICE OF RISK ASSESSMENT IN THE UK

Various models of risk assessment have emerged in England, Wales, Scotland, Australia and the US. As stated previously, in most areas of the UK there is now a model of intervention for all cases reported to the police. This follows a process of risk identification, in order to assess those at highest risk, so that a specialist multi-agency approach may be undertaken on behalf of victims. This process was developed as the MARACs in Cardiff in 2003 and has now been adopted in more than 200 jurisdictions across the UK.[3]

A common risk tool – the emergence of DASH

The Association of Chief Police Officers (ACPO) Risk Management Expert Panel (of which the author was a member) was convened in 2008 and included representation from the police, National Policing Improvement Agency (NPIA), academics and Co-ordinated Action Against Domestic Abuse (CAADA, the charity responsible for training and accrediting IDVAs). The panel created the new risk assessment tool named DASH following consultation with police, academics and victim groups over an approximate 18-month period. Drawing on the development and implementation of existing tools by the South Wales Police (the FSU9, see Robinson 2004) and the London Metropolitan Police Service (SPECCs, see Richards 2003), this process also included reviews of relevant research and evidence derived from intimate partner homicide cases. The panel piloted DASH and then produced accompanying guidance detailing the recommended processes for risk identification, assessment and management. Shortly after endorsement by the ACPO Council in March 2009, DASH was made available to all forces and their community partners. The corresponding version for use by IDVAs, along with specialist guidance, was published by CAADA at the same time.

Thus, within a decade, the response to IPV moved from one where few, if any, practitioner decisions were guided by structured risk assessment, to the appearance of many different (although similar) tools used sporadically by a both the police and community-based

3   MARACs are for very high-risk victims of domestic violence and their children (see Robinson, 2004, 2006a; Robinson and Tregidga, 2007). They are a central component of the Home Office's National Domestic Violence Strategy (2006), as well as featuring centrally in the government's Tackling Violence Action Plan (2008) (Home Office 2008). Co-ordinated Action Against Domestic Abuse (CAADA), the charity that provides training and accreditation of IDVAs, has published many useful resources on MARACs (see www.caada.org), in addition to running a MARAC quality assurance programme on behalf of the Home Office.

projects, to one where national leadership and local commitment have forged a single risk assessment tool and – importantly – a common risk management process, intended for use by all police and multi-agency partners.[4]

A structured judgement approach

Risk assessment in cases of IPV is most often undertaken by police or IDVAs, who use the 'structured professional judgement' approach. This method of assessing risk attempts to bridge the gap between 'unstructured clinical assessment', where decisions are made without any constraints or guidelines, and 'actuarial assessment', where discretion is completely removed with the use of highly structured tools that attempt to predict the likelihood of certain behaviours occurring. In contrast, the use of 'structured professional judgement' allows practitioners to rely on guidelines such as a minimum set of risk factors to consider in every case, but empowers them to employ their judgement in reaching conclusions about who is at higher or lower risk of violence (Kropp 2004).

Unlike other areas of research and practice in violence risk assessment, which draw upon clinical psychologists' use of structured tools in health care settings, British risk assessment with the victims of IPV is undertaken by front-line professionals in contact with victims often at the time of, or shortly after, the violent incident. Their aim is to gather information in order to develop a safety plan and to aid in the investigation of the case. For police, this approach developed to structure the discretion employed by officers as they responded to 'domestics', in order to ensure they gathered a consistent level of information to aid investigation and more robust and defensible decision making in cases that were subject to increasing scrutiny from both supervisors and the public. The notion of completely removing officers' discretion could never have been 'sold' to the forces, even if this were a realistic option. NPIA (2008) guidance endorses the use of 'professional judgement while conducting the assessment' and Association of Chief Police Officers (2009) guidance states that risk assessment 'structures and informs decisions that are already being made by you'.

Victim-oriented practitioners – IDVAs – have emerged only in the past few years, and their work has always been closely aligned with

4   At the time of writing, MARACs have been established in more than 200 areas in England and Wales. In Northern Ireland, 14 MARACs have been operational since January 2010. Some areas of Scotland have been running MARAC-type arrangements for several years (most notably Glasgow), although the approach is not as consistent or established in this nation.

risk assessment (Robinson 2004, 2006a, 2009; Howarth *et al.* 2009). Recent developments have reinforced, and made more visible to those working in other agencies, this central aspect of IDVAs' work. Guidance from CAADA to IDVAs is consistent with the structured judgement approach endorsed for police. Evidence from research and practice-based experience indicated that the 'number of ticks' on the risk tool and an IDVA's assessment of a victim's risk level were not always a 'perfect match', indicating the need for IDVAs to use their professional judgement (Co-ordinated Action Against Domestic Abuse 2010; Robinson 2006b). This is recognised as good practice because:

> There will be situations where a victim either refuses to answer questions or answers only a very few but it is the professional's judgment that they are at high risk of harm. (Co-ordinated Action Against Domestic Abuse 2010)

Risk assessment directly linked to risk management

As Kropp (2004) noted, 'Properly applied, risk assessment can serve as a language for communicating our concerns about danger and *the recommended steps for preventing violence*' (p. 693, emphasis added). The use of a common tool among multi-agency partners allows information to be shared in an efficient and consistent way, enabling the kind of discussion necessary to achieve the shared goal of violence prevention. As indicated previously, in the UK the MARACs have become the established forums for these risk management activities and the scale of their use is noteworthy, with over 33,000 adult victim cases and over 46,000 associated child cases discussed in the 12-month period ending in September 2009 in England and Wales alone (Co-ordinated Action Against Domestic Abuse 2009).

Risk assessment is directly linked to risk management in the contemporary British approach. It is not a 'paper exercise' but has practical significance contributing to the amount of resources and attention afforded to victims by involved agencies. As a practitioner in one area explained:

> Yes, I mean the 'high' and the 'very high' get everything and the 'standard' and the 'medium' although they get the letter and sometimes a phone call, that's all they get whereas I think they are looking at getting somebody to contact these people, then perhaps they can prevent them from becoming 'high risk'... (quoted in Robinson 2009)

While it is necessary to target limited resources at the most vulnerable victims, in practice this causes difficulties. Although a valuable guide for action, risk assessment does not provide complete predictive accuracy and many of the mental processes used by practitioners to reach determinations about risk levels remain hidden. Furthermore, as the quote from Robinson (2009) attests, the current arrangements preclude much preventative work with those at lower levels of risk. Even among experienced IDVAs, risk assessment is considered to be a highly skilled practice in need of constant maintenance:

> My job is to look at the risk assessments they're completing...and check are there gaps in the risk assessments, are there questions that I'm thinking 'are you struggling to ask this?', and approaching each IDVA individually in a supervision capacity... Also in [group] discussions, we learnt a lot from each other, we learnt the techniques that each of us are using, and I think it kind of reinvigorates the IDVAs to see new ways of approaching [risk assessment]. (Robinson 2009)

BENEFITS OF RISK ASSESSMENT
Benefits to victims

It would be worrying if all the innovations described thus far had no discernible impact on those they were designed to assist – the victims themselves. The key aspiration is increased victim safety (or decreased rates of re-victimisation). The difficulty is establishing the specific impact of risk *assessment* processes. The small amount of empirical work in this area has focused on establishing a link between risk *management* processes (MARACs), which of course rely on risk assessment techniques, and victim safety. Direct benefits to victims are more confidently attributable on the basis of existing research to risk management rather than risk assessment practices.

Risk assessment and risk management are, however, mutually dependent and interconnected, and implementing tailored plans to increase victim safety has had a measurable impact on victim safety. The evaluation of the first MARACs in Cardiff found that 6 in 10 high-risk victims did not experience repeat victimisation after six months of monitoring; this decreased to 4 in 10 after 12 months (Robinson 2006a; Robinson and Tregidga 2007). More recent data from 217 MARACs support these initial findings, showing lower than expected rates of repeat victimisation (Co-ordinated Action Against Domestic Abuse 2009).

Understanding how victim safety is achieved via these practices is illustrated by research on the working practices of IDVAs who use risk assessment tools to gather detailed and relevant information from victims (Howarth *et al.* 2009; Robinson 2009). Advocates use the information gained by risk assessment as a foundation for safety planning – for example, by understanding their needs and establishing risk reduction strategies to address those needs (e.g. re-housing, removal of the perpetrator through bail conditions, high-level probation, etc.). This information can assist IDVAs in determining which victims will require more intensive advocacy and support and, when shared with other agencies, can help provide better services because victims' specific needs are identified.

There are psychological benefits to victims from participating in the type of discussion that is required for IDVAs to complete a risk assessment, although research specific to this issue is scant. Advocates must engage with women to encourage them to understand that their own perceptions of risk are vital: if they are fearful of further harm, they should not ignore that fear (Campbell 2004). When an IDVA sits down with a victim and discusses the detail of the abuse, her experiences and perceptions of it, and the implications of these issues for her and her children where relevant, this process – although difficult – can be viewed positively (Armitti and Robinson 2008). The valuing of the victims' opinions and perceptions by trained and empathetic professionals can be empowering:

> She stated that the risk assessment was extremely helpful to her because it challenged her mind and allowed her to admit the fact that the perpetrator was a danger to her. (Howarth et al. 2009, p.34)

Finally, victims' positive experiences with risk assessment may translate into their increased satisfaction with involved agencies and systems, although there is currently no empirical evidence to demonstrate this potential benefit.

Benefits to front-line practice

Risk assessment is meant to inform police decision making and action, including effective investigation and evidence gathering, by yielding more detailed and relevant information about incidents more consistently. This is not to imply that all risk assessments are completed to the same high standard, but that relative to the discretionary and unstructured approach of yesteryear it is reasonable to suppose that police are now gathering more useful information, which may also be used in efforts to 'bring offenders to justice'.

Risk assessment also shapes the content and detail of the police input into multi-agency meetings such as local child safeguarding boards, MARACs and MAPPA (Multi-Agency Public Protection Arrangements) processes. As the police are key contributors to these meetings, it is vital that they provide information that is relevant to the case, in an efficient and consistent way that is understood by their multi-agency partners. Sharing a common framework for risk identification, assessment and management makes this more likely to occur.

There are other potential benefits such as increased reporting and public confidence as a result of the adoption of this new approach, although these have yet to be empirically substantiated. A more professional and standardised response by police and other front-line staff in these cases should be viewed by most as an important achievement in its own right.

Benefits to multi-agency working

When embedded within multi-agency frameworks, risk assessment improves agencies' awareness of the most persistent and dangerous offenders, helping to keep practitioners safe. Typically, police – and to a lesser extent probation – would be the only agencies privy to this information. By sharing information, it is possible to ensure that health visitors and other integrated specialists are aware of households where they, as visitors, could be at higher risk of harm (e.g. because weapons are known to be present). Practitioners acknowledged that using common systems helped increase their understanding of the nature of IPV, and made the specific risks to victims and to the practitioners with whom offenders come into contact more readily apparent (Robinson 2004).

Risk assessment helps inform criminal justice decision making, because many decisions rely upon information provided by the police in the public interest. For example, a properly conducted risk assessment helps to provide an enhanced 'paper trail' of evidence should the victim choose not to go forward with the case, enabling prosecutors to make more informed decisions as to whether to proceed with cases when victims retract. It can also contribute to the prevention of further offences and/or lead to new evidence or avenues of investigation in a particular case. For example, the behaviour of a serial perpetrator was identified and brought to the attention of multi-agency partners as a result of the risk assessment process:

> Last month I referred a case [to MARAC]...as [the risk assessment revealed that] he was a perpetrator who was linked with three other women that we've worked with, and so that needed to be discussed in a multi-agency forum, the fact that he was a perpetrator who was violent against four women in this area let alone... (Robinson 2009)

Finally, risk assessment can conserve scarce criminal justice resources by helping to identify those victims who require more intensive assistance. It is hoped that expending more resources 'up-front' for such victims will prove effective in terms of preventing future incidents, because it is well known that incidents of domestic violence tend to escalate in severity over time. These actions may also translate into increased public confidence in the criminal justice system, although research on this issue has not yet been conducted.

CHALLENGES FOR RISK ASSESSMENT
Evidence-based challenges

Despite recent progress, there is still ambiguity around the term 'risk'. As indicated previously, 'risk' for IPV might include future violence, severe injury, threats, emotional harm, suicide or homicide. Furthermore, the risk is usually towards the victim but might also encompass children, family members or others (and these other potential victims are catered for in tools such as DASH). Risk assessment is a comprehensive effort to gather any information that has the potential to be relevant in the long term, rather than an attempt to be selective at the outset, perhaps before a full understanding of the situation is possible. Although commendable, the following type of obfuscation is likely:

> Most studies on spousal violence risk and recidivism appear to define risk in terms of the likelihood that some form of violence will take place sometime in the future...[but] an offender could be at risk for imminent, minor, physical violence against his spouse, such as pushing or shoving, but not at risk for long-term, frequent, sexual violence. (Kropp 2004, p.678)

These different scenarios present very different implications for the victim, offender and any practitioners with whom they come into contact; however, the distinctions between different types and levels of IPV are rarely made either in practice or in research (Howarth *et al.* 2009). A degree of ambiguity in the risk assessment process remains so long as the specific type of risk posed by the offender is not explicitly known. Extant research cannot specify whether correlates for IPV are actually correlates of physical, psychological, sexual or financial factors, or some combination of these, nor is it clear whether they correlate with mild or severe levels of each or all of these types. Even if the risk factors are similar for the various forms of IPV (a very big 'if'), the relative importance of the risk factors might vary, but this remains unclear (Kropp 2004). The lack of an agreed operational definition of risk continues to hamper efforts to establish an evidence base using measures that are directly comparable.

A second evidence-based challenge relates to the degree of measurement error within commonly used risk factors. Hoyle (2007) argued that 'risk assessment models for domestic violence are not as scientifically rigorous as those using them might presume' because the risk factors utilised draw upon research on homicide and the findings from homicide reviews (p.330), rather than from other forms of IPV. Others also have argued that it is unwise to deduce that a risk factor for homicide will likewise be a risk factor for other (lesser) types of IPV, because homicides are statistically rare events (Hilton and Harris 2005). An additional problem is that gathering information about these events retrospectively (e.g. in the form of homicide reviews) is more likely to result in recall bias as well as making assessments of the context and circumstances of the homicide much less accurate (Dobash *et al.* 2002). The types of evidence used to establish the reliability and validity of certain risk factors are not equal across all the tools currently in use, such as DASH. Some factors have been consistently identified as correlates of future harm (e.g. criminal record) while others have had less empirical scrutiny (e.g. abuse of pets). All these problems make it likely that there is a significant degree of error in the construction and application of existing risk factors, although at present we are unable to even measure the extent of this error in a scientific way.

Additionally, several of the risk factors seem to be so commonly experienced that they cannot differentiate victims very well. In other words, the lack of variability in some factors makes it difficult to distinguish victims who go on to experience further victimisation from those who do not. For example, in 91 per cent of cases victims reported jealous or controlling behaviour from the perpetrator, and in 81 per cent of cases the victim expressed being very frightened (Howarth *et al.* 2009). Perhaps re-phrasing these to capture a less common experience would be useful, although further research is necessary.

Tools include both static risk factors and those amenable to change (dynamic). Both are important for prediction and judging the intensity of concern, although only the latter guide the content of risk management. At present both are weighted equally, giving a total risk score that might reflect mostly static factors for one victim, but mostly dynamic factors for another. Adding to the challenge is the considerable interplay between static and dynamic risk factors that is possible, although 'little [has been] published about about how best to measure and incorporate these changeable factors into the risk assessment process' (Mills 2005, p.238). In short, more research that focuses on the relationship between dynamic risk factors and the likelihood of violence is required.

A new methodological approach is needed when risk assessment is used for prevention, in order to demonstrate a relationship between professional decisions based on chosen risk factors and violence, rather than the risk factors themselves and violence as in the actuarial context

(Kropp 2004). The empirical focus would be determining how accurate professionals are at assessing those at lower and higher risk of violence. While 'we do not want persons identified as high risk to become violent, as that would mean we failed to prevent violence' (Kropp 2004, p.692), we can learn from those cases where violence ensued after the risk assessment was conducted. Likewise, studying the risk factors in cases where violence was prevented would be illuminating.

In conclusion, further research is necessary to determine (a) whether risk factors are correlated with different types and levels of IPV to the same extent, (b) the potential of risk management to alter dynamic risk factors, and (c) the effect of these efforts on violence prevention.

Practitioner-based challenges

The worth of any risk-based process ultimately relies on the people using it. Failures of risk assessment will sometimes be attributable to 'poor workmanship' rather than 'faulty tools'. Previous research has highlighted a number of challenges facing practitioners charged with implementing risk-based practice, including:

- a lack of understanding of the risk concepts in the instrument

- no minimum qualifications or consistent training programme

- failure to collect the required information accurately

- the misguided belief that risk assessment detracts from individual professional skills and judgement

- a lack of systematic methods to evaluate and monitor assessments. (Borum 1996; Kropp 2004; Perez Trujillo and Ross 2008)

Some of these issues are more pertinent to the current British approach than others. Not all police officers using risk assessment tools have received adequate training in their use. Reassuringly, it is stated in the ACPO guidance that training for all officers is recommended, and that only specialist domestic violence officers (DVOs) should be making the actual determination of risk level (i.e. risk assessment rather than risk identification). The quality and level of information collected during risk assessments has been shown to vary according to specialist expertise held. This may affect the information victims choose to disclose during the risk assessment process, as this officer explained:

...if they've not had specialist DV training, the way that they [officers] ask the questions can sometimes affect the way the victims answer them… It's because they don't want to ask the questions enough, you know… So it's really difficult. (Robinson 2009)

All IDVAs have been trained in risk assessment as part of their accreditation (although there only several hundred IDVAs compared to more than one hundred thousand police officers in England and Wales). Research has indicated that IDVAs are perceived to be more successful at obtaining 'full disclosure' of pertinent information, because victims are willing to provide a more comprehensive account of the abuse, including sharing sensitive details (e.g. sexual abuse) (Armitti and Robinson 2008; Howarth *et al.* 2009; Robinson 2009). Likely reasons for this include IDVAs' specialist training and experience, conducting risk assessments in a safe environment some time after the initial offence, and possibly victims' willingness to disclose to a female rather than a male practitioner. For example:

> With the sexual question on the police risk assessment…95 per cent of the time they answer 'No', and you can go back, and I don't know the percent but an awful lot of the time [victims] say 'Well actually he did make me do this, or this did happen…' and obviously they've got a male police officer asking them that, and it may be more difficult for them to disclose that, especially if there's just been a crisis… (Robinson 2009)

If IDVAs obtain fuller disclosure, then they will identify proportionally higher levels of 'high-risk' victims than will police, because more comprehensive information about the details of the abuse is available to them. This poses a challenge for effective multi-agency practice.

The lack of understanding of the process by which practitioners (whether police or IDVAs) translate information about risk factors into a risk level is also a concern, because this is an area practically devoid of empirical scrutiny. Until this 'black box' of interpretive mental processes is fully understood, there will be potentially indefensible variability in how risk assessments are made across the UK.

Process-based challenges

One noteworthy challenge facing risk assessment is to what extent victims' perceptions should inform practitioners' judgements about risk. When do victims know what is best for them and their children, and when are they minimising potentially fatal abuse? How can their views be incorporated into the risk assessment process, especially when these views may be difficult for the victims to express? Some authors have promoted the idea that predictions made by victims about their own risk of re-victimisation must be the most accurate because they have more contact, knowledge and history of the abuser than anyone else (de Becker 1997; Hart 1994; Walker 1984). The cycle of violence that many victims experience over time means that they could be especially attuned to the 'warning signs' of impending violence. On the other hand, psychological abuse and trauma may make them desensitised to the actual danger they face (Campbell 2004). The very nature of abuse means that victims are faced with degrading attacks that can affect their self-esteem and lead to doubts about their own judgement.

There is empirical support for the idea that victims' perceptions can be accurate predictors of future violence (Robinson 2007; Weisz *et al.* 2000), and it appears that practitioners are more willing to incorporate victims' perceptions into risk-based practice. Perez Trujillo and Ross (2008) found that the victim's level of fear, along with the escalation of violence over time, were the two most influential factors in determination of risk level. Recent research showed that IDVAs were significantly more likely to facilitate access to support or services when the victim disclosed that she was very frightened of further abuse (Howarth *et al.* 2009). DASH and its guidance highlights the importance of collecting information about the victim's fear, and concerns over her own safety and that of her children and/or any other family members. However, as one practitioner noted, fundamentally the quality of the risk assessment process depends on the information provided by the victim, and victims are not infallible:

> ...if they're not going to disclose that he's tried to choke her, or that she's pregnant, you know, you can't work with that if she's going to lie on the risk assessment... Obviously those women are a huge worry. (Robinson 2009)

A second challenge is whether generic models of risk assessment will be found to be equally useful for different types of victims (e.g. women, men, gay, heterosexual). The current three-stage risk assessment process has emerged primarily from work with female victims driven by theoretical notions of 'power and control' that has greatly informed our understanding of violence perpetrated within heterosexual relationships. Thus, risk assessment, as currently practised, is based on gendered notions of IPV with a more developed understanding of how risks to female victims are manifested. In a British study comparing risk assessments across male and female victims, Robinson and Rowlands (2009) found that the perpetrator's being jealous or controlling affected nearly six times as many female as male victims (72% compared with 13%). In other words, female perpetrators were far less likely to have one of the hallmark characteristics of a 'domestic perpetrator'.

This begs the question of how applicable current processes will be across a diverse array of victim experiences. Research has identified unique risk factors exhibited by members of the lesbian, gay, bisexual and transgendered communities (Allen and Leventhal 1999), including help-seeking behaviour and therefore whether they will access a service utilising risk assessment (Turell and Cornell-Swanson 2005). What is lacking is a tool that might equip practitioners outside specialist services readily to assess the risks faced by men (especially gay men) in the same manner that research to date has identified the risks facing heterosexual women (Hilton and Harris 2005). As one practitioner working with male victims of IPV explained:

> Safety and risk for male victims are the same priorities as for female victims, but long-term counselling implications may be different for gay men. Men also may need a different risk assessment, [with] slightly different questions (as with the BME (black and minority ethnic) community) because any group concerned about prejudice is going to require additional questions and concern. (Robinson and Rowlands 2006, p.55)

Likewise, although specific questions have been added about so-called 'honour'-based violence to the DASH tool, it is unclear whether adding questions to a generic tool is sufficient or whether separate tools should be developed. The danger is that the existence of a generic tool might preclude the careful formulation of other more specialised tools, especially when there is no robust evidence base to guide their development.

CONCLUSION

Risk identification, assessment and management processes for IPV have become mainstream practice among practitioners working in the UK, particularly police officers and IDVAs. A common tool has been endorsed recently, which should help practice become more consistent and professional within multi-agency partnerships, thereby improving their efficiency. This should support a more skilled and tailored response provision to victims, increasing the likelihood that appropriate risk reduction strategies are put into place to help them achieve safety.

Challenges that remain include ambiguity in risk concepts and their measurement, uneven training and expertise with regard to the practice of risk assessment, and the extent to which a process that has been developed largely from data on female victims of violence from their heterosexual male partners can be successfully extended to other types of victims and other types of gender-based violence. The fact that each year tens of thousands of victims and their children are considered by trained professionals to be faced with extremely serious, potentially life-threatening risks to their safety means that a more sophisticated and robust analysis of the processes designed to help them is essential.

REFERENCES

Allen, C. and Leventhal, B. (1999) 'History, Culture, and Identity: What Makes GLBT Battering Different?' In B. Leventhal and S. Lundy (eds) *Same-Sex Domestic Violence: Strategies for Change.* Thousand Oaks, CA, Sage Publications. 73–83.

Armitti, L. and Robinson, A.L. (2007) 'Risky judgments? Understanding how practitioners and victims conceptualise "risk".' *SAFE – The Domestic Abuse Quarterly,* 24.

Association of Chief Police Officers (ACPO) (2009) *DASH: Domestic Abuse Risk Assessment Guidance for Police Staff.* London: ACPO.

Borum, R. (1996) 'Improving the clinical practice of violence risk assessment: technology, guidelines and training.' *American Psychologist 51,* 945–956.

Co-ordinated Action Against Domestic Abuse (2009) *Facts and Statistics.* Available at www.caada.org.uk/News/factsandstats.htm, accessed on 9 March 2010.

Co-ordinated Action Against Domestic Abuse (CAADA) (2010) *The CAADA MARAC Guide: From Principles to Practice.* Available at www.caada.org.uk, accessed on 18 July 2010.

Campbell, J.C. (1986) 'Nursing assessment for risk of homicide with battered women.' *Advances in Nursing Science 8,* 36–51.

Campbell, J.C. (2004) 'Helping women understand their risk in situations of intimate partner violence.' *Journal of Interpersonal Violence 19,* 12, 1464–1477.

de Becker, G. (1997) *The Gift of Fear: Survival Signals that Protect us from Violence.* Boston, MA: Little, Brown.

Dobash, R.P., Dobash, R.E., Cavanagh, K. and Lewis, R. (2002) *Homicide in Britain: Risk Factors, Situational Contexts and Lethal Intentions.* ESRC end of award report. Swindon: Economic and Social Research Council.

Hart, B. (1994) 'Lethality and dangerousness assessments.' *Violence Update 4,* 10, 7–8.

Hilton, N.Z. and Harris, G.T. (2005) 'Predicting wife assault: a critical review and implications for policy and practice.' *Trauma, Violence and Abuse 6,* 1, 3–23.

Home Office (2008) *Saving Lives. Reducing Harm. Protecting the Public: An Action Plan for Tackling Violence 2008–11.* London: Home Office.

Howarth, E., Stimpson, L., Barran, D. and Robinson, A.L. (2009) *Safety in Numbers: A Multi-site Evaluation of Independent Domestic Violence Advisor Services.* London: The Henry Smith Charity. Available at www.drop.io/safetyinnumbers, accessed on 18 July 2010.

Hoyle, C. (2007) 'Will she be safe? A critical analysis of risk assessment in domestic violence cases.' *Children and Youth Services Review 30,* 323–337.

Kropp, P.R. (2004) 'Some questions regarding spousal assault risk assessment.' *Violence Against Women 10,* 6, 676–697.

Kropp, P.R. and Hart, S.D. (2000) 'The Spousal Assault Risk Assessment (SARA) Guide: reliability and validity in adult male offenders.' *Law and Human Behavior 24,* 1, 101–118.

Kropp, P.R., Hart, S.D., Webster, C.D. and Eaves, D. (1999) *Spousal Assault Risk Assessment Guide (SARA): An Assessment of the Likelihood of Domestic Violence.* Harlow: Pearson Education Ltd.

Mills, J.F. (2005) 'Advances in the assessment and prediction of interpersonal violence.' *Journal of Interpersonal Violence 20,* 2, 236–241.

National Policing Improvement Agency (NPIA) (2008) *Guidance on Investigating Domestic Abuse.* Bedfordshire: NPIA.

Perez Trujillo, M. and Ross, S. (2008) 'Police response to domestic violence. Making decisions about risk and risk management.' *Journal of Interpersonal Violence 23,* 4, 454–473.

Richards, L. (2003) *MPS Domestic Violence Risk Assessment Model.* London: Metropolitan Police Service.

Richards, L., Letchford, S. and Stratton, S. (2008) *Policing Domestic Violence: Blackstone's Practical Policing.* Oxford: Oxford University Press.

Robinson, A.L. (2004) *Domestic Violence MARACs (Multi-Agency Risk Assessment Conferences) for Very High-Risk Victims in Cardiff: A Process and Outcome Evaluation.* Cardiff: Cardiff University, School of Social Sciences.

Robinson A.L. (2006a) 'Reducing repeat victimisation among high-risk victims of domestic violence: the benefits of a coordinated community response in Cardiff, Wales.' *Violence Against Women: An International and Interdisciplinary Journal 12*, 8, 761–788.

Robinson A.L. (2006b) *Advice, Support, Safety and Information Services Together (ASSIST): The Benefits of Providing Assistance to Victims of Domestic Abuse in Glasgow.* Cardiff: Cardiff University, School of Social Sciences.

Robinson A.L. (2007) 'Risk assessment and the importance of victim intuition.' *Safe – The Domestic Abuse Quarterly 21*, 18–21.

Robinson, A.L. (2009) *Independent Domestic Violence Advisors: A Multisite Process Evaluation Funded by the Home Office.* Cardiff: Cardiff University, School of Social Sciences.

Robinson, A.L. (2010) 'Domestic Violence.' In F. Brookman, M. Maguire, H. Pierpoint and T. Bennett (eds) *Handbook of Crime.* Cullompton: Willan.

Robinson, A.L. and Howarth, E. (2010). 'Understanding how risk judgments are made in cases of domestic violence' [under review].

Robinson, A.L. and Rowlands, J. (2006) *The Dyn Project: Supporting Male Victims of Domestic Abuse.* Cardiff: Cardiff University, School of Social Sciences.

Robinson, A.L. and Rowlands, J. (2009) 'Assessing and managing risk amongst different victims of domestic abuse: limits of a generic model of risk assessment?' *Security Journal 22*, 3, 190–204.

Robinson, A.L. and Tregidga, J. (2007) 'The perceptions of high-risk victims of domestic violence to a coordinated community response in Cardiff, Wales.' *Violence Against Women: An International and Interdisciplinary Journal 13*, 11, 1130–1148.

Turell, S.C. and Cornell-Swanson, L.A. (2005) 'Not all alike: within-group differences in seeking help for same-sex relationship abuses.' *Journal of Gay and Lesbian Social Services 18*, 1, 71–88.

Walker, L. (1984) *The Battered Woman Syndrome.* New York: Springer.

Weisz, A.N., Tolman, R. and Saunders, D.G. (2000) 'Assessing the risk of severe domestic violence: the importance of survivors' predictions.' *Journal of Interpersonal Violence 15*, 75–90.

CHAPTER 8

GOOD LIVES AND RISK ASSESSMENT: COLLABORATIVE APPROACHES TO RISK ASSESSMENT WITH SEXUAL OFFENDERS

GEORGIA D. BARNETT AND RUTH E. MANN

Individuals do not have to abandon those things that are important to them – only to acquire them differently. (Ward and Maruna 2007, p.108)

INTRODUCTION

The traditional purpose of forensic risk assessment is to decide how likely an offender is to reoffend. More recently, notions of risk assessment have expanded to include processes that identify the factors that make an offender likely to reoffend, so that they can be translated into treatment targets, and to include an assessment of the likely level of harm that would result from a reoffence. The risk assessment of serious offenders serving custodial sentences is viewed by some, particularly perhaps the offender involved, as a fundamentally adversarial process, in which the offender tries to disguise risk to reduce the level of restriction placed on him or her, while the risk assessor engages in various tactics to expose the risk the offender is attempting to hide. However, over the last ten years, attitudes and approaches to risk assessment with sexual offenders have started to change as both academics and clinicians alike search for ways in which to maximise the success of risk assessment, while valuing the autonomy and dignity of the offenders they work with.

In this chapter, we propose that rather than a purely deficit-led approach to risk assessment, which focuses only on those factors that could raise an individual's risk, an examination of strengths should be included within the risk assessment to make it a more collaborative, and therefore arguably a more productive, endeavour. The Good Lives

Model (GLM) (Ward 2002; Ward and Brown 2004; Ward and Marshall 2004; Ward and Stewart 2003) is one such approach that can be used to underpin risk assessment by asking the risk assessor to consider the individual's values and strengths, so that we consider not only what could aggravate risk, but also what could protect against it. We start with a brief history of risk assessment, and then explain how the GLM can be used to make risk assessment a more balanced, ethical and collaborative process.

HISTORY OF RISK ASSESSMENT WITH SEXUAL OFFENDERS

Most literature on risk assessment with offenders, including sexual offenders, has identified that our understanding of how to assess risk has developed in stages (Bonta 1996; Mann, Hanson and Thornton 2010a; Rice 2008). Originally, 'first-generation' risk assessment involved subjective clinical judgement; generally, assessors would report on what they considered to be relevant to an individual's risk, based on their experience, and would make a judgement on the level of risk posed. However, such subjective judgements, even when performed by experienced professional assessors, appeared to lead to high rates of error (Grove et al. 2000). The next phase involved the production of 'second-generation' assessment instruments – statistically derived tools that asked assessors to code and combine specific information about an offender, such as age and number of previous convictions, to produce a risk rating, or a risk group, that the individual could be assigned to. The items included in these scales were selected purely on the basis of how well they predicted reconviction in large datasets, without regard for theoretical or clinical value.

Examples of second-generation scales developed for the assessment of sexual offending risk include the Risk Matrix 2000 (Thornton et al. 2003), used widely in the UK, and the Static-99 (Hanson and Thornton 2000), used widely elsewhere in the world. Second-generation instruments like these have been honed and tested across numerous studies, and it is clear that they outperform clinical judgement and sometimes demonstrate an impressive level of accuracy in discriminating between those who reoffend and those who do not. This supports the identification of those who will respond most to rehabilitative treatment. The 'risk principle' of offender rehabilitation (Andrews and Bonta 2006) indicates that higher risk offenders respond best to psychological treatment, a finding that has been replicated recently with sexual offenders (Hanson et al. 2009). Second-generation tools were used by researchers to establish this pattern and, because of its systematic replication across studies, should be used to inform treatment allocation decisions (Mann, Ware and Fernandez 2010b).

However, second-generation instruments are often dissatisfying to treatment practitioners (as well as to offenders) because they do not provide any direction about what to address in treatment, and they do not offer any opportunity to re-evaluate risk in the light of treatment progress. The third generation of risk assessment tools, therefore, aimed to identify potentially changeable factors that have a scientifically evidenced relationship with recidivism. Some tools of this nature are now well established among those who practise with sexual offenders, such as the Structured Risk Assessment (Thornton 2002) and its close derivative, the Structured Assessment of Risk and Need (SARN) (Webster *et al.* 2006), or the Stable Assessment Tool (Hanson *et al.* 2007). These tools have demonstrated the ability, although to a limited extent, to improve the risk prediction of second-generation tools. More certainly, they enable the systematic assessment of psychologically meaningful, causal, risk factors, which can be used to direct the content of treatment to ensure that only those factors that contribute to risk of reoffending are targeted. Mann *et al.* (2010) have set out some straightforward lists of psychological factors that have been studied in relation to sexual recidivism, categorised according to the strength of the existing evidence base for each risk factor.

To date, however, third-generation tools have had only preliminary testing in terms of their ability to measure meaningful changes in risk. As Rice (2008) sets out, it is a real challenge to demonstrate that a changed score on a risk tool predicts recidivism significantly better than the unchanged score, as well as adding to second-generation risk assessments. Mann *et al.* (2010a) concluded that research has yet to establish reliable ways to identify and quantify when someone has changed enough, so that their risk can be said to be reduced. This is the question to which research effort must now turn, and which will, it is hoped, eventually result in sophisticated, fourth-generation tools.

The current state of thinking about risk assessment, then, inextricably links risk assessment procedures with treatment approaches. The Risk-Need-Responsivity (RNR) Model sets out the key characteristics of effective offender rehabilitation, and states that treatment works best if it is directed at higher risk offenders (the risk principle) and if it targets issues that have been empirically demonstrated to raise risk (the need principle). To operationalise these principles requires that offenders' risk and needs are systematically assessed, and this in turn requires the use of validated second- and third-generation risk tools.

While all this sounds straightforward and uncontroversial, less has been written about the actual methods available to an assessor to identify which psychologically meaningful factors are present in an offender. At the simplest level of analysis, there are two approaches: to ask the offender (and thus rely on self-report), or to attempt to ascertain what factors are present through more objective means, which do not necessarily require the offender's cooperation. Within each of these two approaches are a number of possible methods for obtaining evidence. For instance, self-report could take the form of psychometric measures (generally in the form of questionnaires measuring attitudes or behavioural patterns), or could involve the analysis and scoring of the offender's responses to an interview, or in a treatment session.

Both these options have been reported in the risk assessment literature, and each has both advantages and disadvantages. While psychometric testing has the advantage of being cheap and easy to administer (for instance, offenders can be tested in groups, thus reducing staff costs), and interview data are easy to gather during routine supervision appointments with offenders, it appears that the information produced only tells us something meaningful about their risk of reoffending when, somewhat counterproductively, it is not gathered for the purpose of risk assessment (Mann *et al.* 2010b). When offenders believe their risk is being evaluated and consequently view the testing situation as potentially adversarial, it appears that their responses are less valid, presumably because they want to present themselves in as favourable a light as possible. However, when potential risk factors are measured as part of intake for treatment, and no risk-related outcome is perceived to be present, the information that offenders provide about their attitudes does seem to have a relationship with subsequent risk of reconviction.

This finding makes sense, but it presents a challenge to jurisdictions charged with both treating and assessing sexual offenders. An assessment for treatment, if the information will not be used for risk assessment, produces information that is relevant to risk. However, if the information is gathered for the purpose of risk assessment, it will not be valid. How can this conundrum be overcome? It would not, of course, be ethical to mislead offenders about the uses to which information will be put. Therefore, either new ways of gathering valid information must be sought, or evaluators must seek to reduce the adversarial context of a risk assessment setting. In short, we need to find ways of making information-gathering for risk assessment purposes a more collaborative endeavour. This chapter will now turn to considering how the latter challenge may be met by considering not only the offender's deficits, but their strengths as well.

GOOD LIVES MODEL

The predominant model of offender rehabilitation, Andrews and Bonta's (2006) RNR, has been criticised for leading to an almost exclusive focus on avoidance strategies for managing risk (Ward and Stewart 2003). Birgden (2004) argues that, while the RNR is primarily concerned with prevention of further reoffending, the GLM is concerned with both prevention and protection.

The GLM is a strength–capabilities approach to offender rehabilitation. According to this model, offenders are viewed holistically, as people with different values, motivations and strengths, but who possess characteristics, or exist in environments that serve to frustrate their ability to find value and meaning in their lives through pro-social avenues. While the GLM is not an aetiological theory of sexual offending, and therefore does not seek to explain its causes, this approach conceptualises offending as an attempt to achieve value, meaning or personal satisfaction through inappropriate means (Ward and Marshall 2004). Indeed, the GLM views all meaningful human action as an attempt to achieve needs that are reflective of a person's individual values and priorities, because humans are perceived to be goal-directed agents who seek to achieve primary human goods.

Primary goods are those things that are, in of themselves, beneficial to humans, and can refer to:

- characteristics (e.g. creativity)

- states of mind (e.g. happiness, sense of belonging or relatedness, inner peace, spirituality)

- actions (e.g. keeping fit, engaging in meaningful activity to achieve physical and mental health)

- states of affairs (e.g. being in a secure, stable environment in which you have autonomy or agency)

- experiences (e.g. mastery of certain skills, gaining knowledge and achieving). (Ward 2002; Ward and Stewart 2003)

According to the GLM, primary goods are common to all humans (certainly in western culture) because they relate to basic human needs, but the ways in which these are sought (referred to as secondary goods) differ depending on an individual's characteristics and circumstances. For example, the primary good of experiencing mastery could be achieved by pursuing the secondary good of teaching, or by excelling in a sport or in the arts. How and through which means an individual chooses to experience mastery will depend on their abilities and strengths, but also on the opportunities open to them and the values held by those around them. Secondary goods are therefore very much influenced by the context in which an individual lives. Therefore, when applying the GLM to understanding someone's offending, this model places the offender and the offence in context, considering both the internal characteristics such as the individual's values and priorities, and external factors such as their environment and support systems, which contributed to their behaviour.

This model not only has implications for the way in which we understand an offender's risk, but also for how we go about managing it. According to the GLM, criminogenic needs (factors that have a causal relationship with offending) are simply obstacles to the pursuit of legitimate goals and needs. As a result, risk management becomes less about eradicating or avoiding those factors and more about finding alternative ways of attaining the primary good that offending was being used to attempt to achieve. The GLM suggests that, by equipping offenders with the opportunities, capabilities and skills to live a satisfying and fulfilling life in pro-social ways, the risk of harming themselves or others will be reduced. This approach suggests that as well as focusing on prevention of further offences by avoiding risk-increasing situations, thoughts or behaviours, risk management should be equally concerned with protection against such risk, through a focus on building on strengths and creating an alternative life that is incompatible with offending (Birgden 2004).

Understanding offending and good lives

Ward and Mann (2004) proposed that the achievement of particular primary goods – namely, agency, relatedness and inner peace – could be frustrated by the traditional psychological deficits associated with risk of sexual reoffending; see Hanson and Morton-Bourgon (2004, 2005) and Mann et al. (2010a) for a review of these criminogenic factors. For example, someone who has an emotional congruence with children is likely to have difficulties in achieving a sense of relatedness with other adults, while someone who has an actively hostile, suspicious view of the world could struggle to find inner peace that is freedom from emotional stress. The pursuit of a sense of control over life or agency could be more difficult for those who are impulsive, or have poor emotional control. In fact, each of the factors that research has indicated have a reliable relationship with sexual reoffending can be construed as an obstacle to achievement of at least one of the primary goods. By using the 'good lives' framework, a risk assessor could arrive at an understanding of the main causes of someone's offending by focusing on identification of the primary goods that the offender was directly, or indirectly, pursuing through offending, and, concomitantly, which of the criminogenic risk factors frustrated the offender's ability to achieve these through pro-social means.

Ward and Maruna (2007) suggest six phases to understanding offending using the GLM:

- Phase 1 identifies the problems an offender presents with, and which criminogenic needs are evident.

- Phase 2 establishes the primary good that the offending served to achieve, and discusses which of the goods the offender values most to gain an idea of his/her personal identity and those things to which he/she is fundamentally committed. The GLM proposes that personal identity is defined by the things an individual values and, more specifically, by the relative priorities he/she assigns to the primary goods.

- Phase 3 involves identifying the offender's strengths: those things that will help him/her to achieve identified and valued outcomes in pro-social ways.

- Phase 4 involves identifying ways of achieving the goods in pro-social ways that are meaningful and realistic for the offender; this is essentially identifying secondary goods.

- Phase 5 considers the external factors that the offender will be subject to when restrictions are removed – the conditions under and environment in which he/she will be living, which will have an impact on the opportunities and means available through and with which to realise secondary goods.

- Phase 6 is the creation of a 'good lives' plan based on the first five phases. This should outline what measures and steps need to be taken to enable the offender to realise his/her goals. The 'good lives' plan will be based on information about existing criminogenic factors that could frustrate achievement of the plan, strengths, resources, support and environment, and, crucially, what the offender values and wants from life.

There is some evidence to suggest that incorporating the good lives approach into risk management plans can be beneficial. Grace and Willis (2008) examined the resettlement plans of a sample of child molesters, 39 of whom were recidivists and 42 of whom were non-recidivists, matched on static risk level and time at risk. As well as finding that the more deviant offenders in the sample (as measured using psychometric measures of dynamic risk factors for sexual offending) tended to have poorer reintegration planning, they found that non-recidivists were more likely than the recidivists to have included specific approach goals relating to secondary goods in their resettlement plans. Relatedness was the most common good addressed in resettlement plans, and there were no differences in the goods addressed in the plans of recidivists and non-recidivists. Grace and Willis (2008) also reported that the presence of goals relating to GLM secondary goods was still significantly higher in the non-recidivist group, even when IQ and deviance level were controlled for, a finding that they suggested means GLM secondary goods could be a protective factor against recidivism. For risk assessors, this highlights the importance of using a more balanced approach to risk assessment, which can be achieved by considering protective, as well as criminogenic, factors.

PROTECTIVE FACTORS

The most commonly used risk assessment procedures for sexual offenders are entirely 'deficit-focused' (Maruna and LeBel 2003). Offenders often voice their frustration with being on the receiving end of risk assessment because of the deficit-focused nature of the process, uttering statements such as 'it's just pure negative that people look at, not the positives' (Attrill and Liell 2007). It appears that this focus is due to nothing more than tradition: there is no academic reason why the study of protective factors – defined here as factors that enable desistance from offending, in those who have previously offended – would not be as fruitful, or even more so, than the study of risk factors. It is therefore perhaps surprising that so little attention has been paid to identifying and validating protective factors for sexual offending. What work has taken place in this area is mainly published in the criminological, desistance literature rather than in the psychological, risk assessment literature. The exception to this is the Dutch research group who have developed a tool to measure protective factors in violent (non-sexual) offenders (de Vogel *et al.* 2009). It also seems that researchers are more comfortable with the examination of protective factors in relation to adolescent sexual abusers, who are arguably a less stigmatised category than the highly vilified adult abusers.

There is some early, limited, but indicative evidence that identification of protective factors will improve upon a wholly deficit-focused procedure. The AIM2 framework (Griffin *et al.* 2008), a revision of the AIM framework, was designed to assess adolescents who had sexually abused others. It incorporates both *static* and *dynamic concerns*, criminogenic risk factors that are either historical factors that cannot be changed through intervention (static), or psychological characteristics that could potentially be addressed through treatment (dynamic). However, this framework also assesses *dynamic strengths*, psychological and external factors that are protective for reoffending. Griffin *et al.* (2008) reported that eight strengths factors differentiated recidivists from non-recidivists, and that, when summed, the strengths items made an independent contribution to the prediction of recidivism. Indeed, even when someone had a high score on the criminogenic items, high scores on the strengths items were (inversely) predictive of recidivism. While the small number of recidivists in the sample ($N = 7$) makes it difficult to draw firm conclusions from these findings, it does suggest that there is merit in pursuing examination of the seemingly predictive relationship between strengths and reoffending.

Protective factors are more than just the opposite of risk factors. In one of the few studies of apparently desisting sexual offenders, Farmer and Beech (2007) found them to have an enhanced sense of personal agency and a stronger internal locus of control, to be consistently more able to find positive outcomes from negative events, to identify treatment as having provided them with a turning point, and, most strikingly, to have seemingly found a place within a social group or network (the desisters described belonging to three particular types of social groups or communities: family, friends and church). It is therefore likely that, as with risk factors, desistance factors will encompass not only psychological characteristics but also the nature of the social environment in which the offender is located.

Until researchers and practitioners make a commitment to understanding and researching protective factors for sexual offending, it is quite possible that progress will halt, with risk assessment tools reaching a validity ceiling. It is also likely, if the deficit-focused approach persists, that offenders will increasingly detach themselves from risk assessment activities, perceiving them as both adversarial and inherently biased toward a negative assessment. In our view, it is crucial to pay more attention to an assessment of strengths within the overall risk assessment. The GLM offers an obvious model to underpin such a broadening of direction.

COLLABORATIVE RISK ASSESSMENT

It is easy to see why, for both the offender and the assessor, risk assessment can be experienced as an adversarial activity. Risk assessment is rarely something requested by an offender; more often it is something imposed on offenders by authorities for whom the offender's interests are secondary to those of public protection. Furthermore, the process is entirely deficit-focused and therefore the evaluator often shows little interest in what the offender perceives to be his/her strengths and achievements. As a result, it would be entirely reasonable for an offender to feel that risk assessment is something that is done to him/her for the benefit of everyone else, with little regard for his/her interests and with a predetermined emphasis on finding fault rather than favour. Mann and Shingler (2006) argued that risk assessment should be a collaborative process in which the needs and goals of the assessor and the offender are reconciled. They described ways in which this could be achieved, including reframing risk assessment as *need* assessment; a process through which the assessors and offender work together to identify the offender's problems and to establish ways in which to work towards addressing them. They argued that by increasing transparency, considering an individual's strengths and values, working respectfully and in the spirit of collaborative inquiry, risk assessment could become a more motivational and ultimately more productive exercise for both offender and assessor.

Birgden (2004) proposed that therapeutic jurisprudence (TJ), a framework for the study of law, can be combined with GLM to encourage a more collaborative approach to any forensic work with offenders. TJ is a legal theory that uses psychological knowledge to determine ways in which the law and reforms can be used to increase well-being; the law and those who work in legal systems are viewed as potential therapeutic agents (Birgden 2004). Birgden (2002) combined TJ with GLM to produce a framework for offender rehabilitation, arguing that these approaches are both fundamentally humanistic and aim to enhance well-being. One of the principles of this framework is that autonomous decision making is necessary in rehabilitation and risk reduction. The assumption is that, if decisions to change and address risk are made voluntarily in a non-coercive context, positive expectations, motivation and chance of success are maximised. Birgden (2004) argued that this means that rehabilitation is more likely to be successful if it is preceded by informed decision making, and that the right to refuse intervention is in itself therapeutic. Clearly there are numerous issues relating to voluntariness in a correctional environment, which is intrinsically coercive and which can (and does) impair an individual's autonomy in many ways. However, using this model, as therapeutic agents of change, those working within this environment could maximise the chances of an offenders' success in leading an offence-free life by protecting their autonomy, in part facilitated by ensuring that they have the capacity and resources required to make informed decisions about the services they receive. By working more collaboratively with offenders during risk assessment, we as practitioners can, as much as possible, involve offenders in decisions about the interventions or restrictions that will help to reduce or manage the risk they present in the future.

Arguably the 'good lives' approach lends itself more easily to collaboration between the practitioner and the client than does the RNR, because of the former's focus on an individual's values and strengths, as well as the future, and its use of approach goals. Approach goals are related to achievement, require action and their success can be measured (e.g. I will eat five pieces of fruit or a day), while avoidance goals involve both the inhibition of certain behaviours and avoidant behaviour such as ceasing an activity (e.g. I will not eat fatty foods) (Ward *et al.* 2006). A risk assessor using the RNR framework alone will focus primarily on establishing which criminogenic factors led to and/or maintained the offender's criminal behaviour, and subsequently on what sort of conditions would increase risk of reoffending. The aim is to establish the exact nature of risk so that it is known, can be monitored and managed. A risk management plan is constructed that specifies the restrictions, usually in the form of avoidance goals that should be placed on the offender to minimise the chance of entering into a situation that could make offending more likely. Such consideration of protective factors and positive action, such as skills-building interventions, aims to minimise risk, rather than maximising the quality of the offender's life. Conversely, a risk assessor using the GLM as a framework for understanding and creating plans for managing risk will take account of those things offenders strive for in life, as well as their individual values, and will try to find out which criminogenic factors present obstacles to the achievement of these valued outcomes. They will also assess offenders' strengths, and those aspects of their lives that could be built upon to create appropriate opportunities for achievement of the things they value. The risk management plans will focus on building the skills and creating the conditions necessary for them to live fulfilling lives in a pro-social way.

While both approaches to risk assessment involve consideration of criminogenic and protective factors, the difference in their aims – risk reducing versus maximising opportunities to live a fulfilling but offence-free life – are likely to result in very meaningful differences in the way in which risk assessment is experienced by the offender. Indeed, the aims of the two approaches arguably point to fundamental differences in the way in which offenders, their potential contribution to society and their individual rights, are viewed by their assessors.

ETHICAL ISSUES

The past few years have seen renewed debate about offenders' rights. Ward and colleagues challenged those in the field to question their fundamental views of offenders and risk, asking whether they view offenders primarily as bearers of risk, whose rights are secondary to the protection of the public, or whether they view offenders as inherently valuable to society, and as people who should be managed in such a way that minimises the risk they pose to others, while maximising their potential to contribute to society (Ward, Gannon and Birgden 2007). This seems particularly pertinent for sexual offenders, whose rights are threatened more often than most offender groups, because of the nature of the risk posed and public and political feeling. Ward and Connolly (2008) argued that human rights protect the values of individuals and allow them to pursue their 'good lives' conceptions without unjustified intervention from others. As risk assessors, we have the challenge of making a judgement about what intervention is justified for the sake of public protection, and what will unjustifiably impede on an offender's ability to create a satisfactory life for him/herself. However, it has been argued that over recent years the balance has shifted overwhelmingly in favour of public protection with little regard for the rights of offenders (Snacken 2006). While the right to safety and protection from those who pose a threat to the public is a hugely important concern, this does not mean the rights of offenders have to be ignored. As Erooga (2008) argued, the two are not mutually exclusive, and by attending to the rights of offenders we are likely to be more effective in our attempts to reduce reoffending, thereby more successfully protecting the public.

Ward and Connolly (2008) argued that the fundamental values and interests of individuals should be protected, and that everyone, regardless of their past behaviour, should have the opportunity to pursue their conception of a good life so long as it does not violate the rights of others. This is in keeping with the ethical principle that all human beings should respect the rights and interests of others, and should themselves be afforded the basic rights of freedom and well-being. Freedom refers not just to freedom of movement, which is of course restricted for those in custody, but includes freedom of speech and freedom to pursue personally meaningful goals. Ward and colleagues have argued that practitioners should use a human rights-based framework in risk management to help offenders develop the skills and capabilities required to realise their 'good lives' conceptions, while endorsing the need to act in a way that demonstrates the value of the rights and interests of others (Ward and Birgden 2007; Ward and Connolly 2008; Ward et al. 2007). In practice, this means that those responsible for risk assessment and management have to make a conscious effort to examine the rights and needs of the offenders they are working with, alongside the rights and needs of victims and the wider public, and to consider all these issues when making decisions about restrictive and constructive intervention.

Ward and Connolly (2008) presented a normative rights-based framework, the Offender Practice Framework (OPF), which can be used to incorporate offender rights into risk assessment and management. The OPF consists of three strands: the justice and accountability perspective, the offender-focused perspective and the strengths and evidence-based perspective.

- The justice and accountability perspective requires practitioners to engage in collaborative inquiry with an offender to establish the problems that need addressing, while ensuring that the offender understands the processes he/she is subject to and the rights that he/she has in that situation. Transparency of practice is therefore essential to this perspective. External factors that could support or interfere with the achievement of the offender's 'good lives' conceptions should also be identified and considered when creating a risk management plan.

- The offender-focused perspective requires the practitioner to consider the offender's interests and priorities and, crucially, to identify pro-social ways in which the offender's 'good lives' conceptions could be achieved. The plans should encourage the development of a sense of agency, and a feeling of responsibility for, and control over, the success of his/her life plans.

- Finally, the strengths and evidence-based perspective asks the practitioner to incorporate the offender's strengths, and to identify (using reliable, valid and ethically sound risk assessment instruments) relevant criminogenic factors that could interfere with the realisation of the 'good lives' plan. Any interventions recommended should adhere to the principles of effective treatment, and relevant risk monitoring strategies should be in place, which should activate the revision of the management plans if circumstances change. The focus is on conducting an ethically and scientifically rigorous assessment of risk that considers both the public's and the offender's needs. This should result in the production of a risk management plan that maximises the chances that the individual will valuably contribute to society while minimising the chances of harm coming to others.

Birgden (2004) suggested that correctional staff working with offenders need to create external conditions that support change by endorsing the belief that change is possible, and by being motivational when interacting with offenders. The GLM offers a framework within which practitioners can work to achieve a more collaborative, responsive, motivational and ethically sound risk assessment with offenders. By valuing individual autonomy and personal identity, and working with them to create plans that help them to realise their life goals in pro-social and personally fulfilling ways, we as risk assessors not only motivate and support them to change, but, importantly, deliver the message that we expect that they can and will be valuable members of society. We argue that, by following the principles of the GLM, while retaining a strong focus on risk reduction, we can maximise the effectiveness of risk assessment and management, thereby better serving the public and the offenders we work for.

There is some tentative evidence to suggest that incorporating a 'good lives' approach into practice with sexual offenders can increase motivation to change. Marshall and colleagues recently reported the results of a preliminary appraisal of a Canadian preparatory programme for sexual offenders in custody, whose design was informed, in part, by the GLM. Compared to a matched control group, those who attended this programme had significantly higher scores on a measure of treatment readiness, while programme participants reported feeling significantly more positive about their ability to change and to have control over their lives by the end of treatment (Marshall *et al.* 2008). Mann and colleagues conducted a similarly small-scale study in which sexual offenders attending an avoidance-based relapse prevention (RP) intervention were compared to a group of those attending a more positively oriented RP programme. Those who attended the more positively focused intervention were more engaged in treatment, as measured by compliance with between-session work and willingness to report lapses. Therapists also rated those in the approach-focused interventions as more motivated to live an offence-free life than those in the avoidance-oriented programme (Mann *et al.* 2004).

CONCLUSION

The science of risk assessment of sexual offenders has progressed rapidly through three generations of approaches, from the unstructured approach favoured in the 1980s and early 1990s, to the more sophisticated combination of historic and psychologically meaningful factors found in today's third-generation tools. Progress is now slowing, as researchers face the obstacle of measuring change, and practitioners face the obstacle of overcoming disengagement and resistance by offenders. In this chapter, we have suggested that an understanding of the GLM may assist those who evaluate sexual offenders in overcoming these obstacles. We have argued that when sexual offenders are engaged with the process of risk assessment, when they find it accessible and meaningful rather than adversarial and oppressive, and when they feel that risk assessment offers them hope rather than doom, the twin goals of public protection and offender rehabilitation can best be realised. While this chapter has focused on sexual offenders, the message that risk assessment can and should be more collaborative and motivational is relevant to anyone working with offenders. Through use of a strengths-based approach to risk assessment, practitioners can better serve not only their offender clients but the public too, making risk assessment a more worthwhile endeavour for all involved.

REFERENCES

Andrews, D.A. and Bonta, J. (2006) *The Psychology of Criminal Conduct* (4th edition). Newark, NJ: LexisNexis/Matthew Bender.

Attrill, G. and Liell, G. (2007) 'Offenders' Views of Risk Assessment.' In N. Padfield (ed.) *Who to Release? Parole, Fairness and Criminal Justice.* Cullompton: Willan. 191–201.

Birgden, A. (2002) 'Therapeutic jurisprudence and "good lives": a rehabilitation framework for corrections.' *Australian Psychologist 37*, 180–186.

Birgden, A. (2004) 'Therapeutic jurisprudence and responsivity: finding the will and the way in offender rehabilitation.' *Psychology, Crime and Law 10*, 3, 283–295.

Bonta, J. (1996) 'Risk-needs Assessment and Treatment.' In A.T. Harland (ed.) *Choosing Correctional Options that Work: Defining the Demand and Evaluating the Supply.* Thousand Oaks, CA: Sage Publications. 18–32.

de Vogel, V., de Ruiter, C., Bouman, Y. and de Vries Robbe, M. (2009) *SAPROF: Structured Assessment of Protective Factors for Violence Risk.* Utrecht, Netherlands: Forum Educatief.

Erooga, M. (2008) 'A human rights-based approach to sex offender management: the key to effective public protection?' *Journal of Sexual Aggression 14*, 3, 171–183.

Farmer, M. and Beech, A. (2007) 'Assessing desistance in child sexual abusers: a qualitative study.' Unpublished manuscript.

Grace, G.M and Willis, R.C. (2008) 'The quality of community reintegration planning for child molesters.' *Sexual Abuse: A Journal of Research and Treatment 20*, 2, 218–240.

Griffin, H.L., Beech, A., Print, B., Bradshaw, H. and Quayle, J. (2008) 'The development and initial testing of the AIM2 framework to assess risk and strengths in young people who sexually offend.' *Journal of Sexual Aggression 14*, 3, 211–225.

Grove, W.M., Zald, D.H. Lebow, B.S., Snitz, B.E. and Nelson, C. (2000) 'Clinical versus mechanical prediction: a meta-analysis.' *Psychological Assessment 12*, 19–30.

Hanson, R.K. and Morton-Bourgon, K.E. (2004) *Predictors of Sexual Recidivism: An Updated Meta-analysis.* Ottawa: Public Safety and Emergency Preparedness Canada.

Hanson, R.K. and Morton-Bourgon, K.E. (2005) 'The characteristics of persistent sexual offenders: a meta-analysis of recidivism studies.' *Journal of Consulting and Clinical Psychology 73*, 1154–1163.

Hanson, R.K. and Thornton, D. (2000) 'Improving risk assessment for sexual offenders: a comparison of three actuarial scales.' *Law and Human Behavior 24*, 119–136.

Hanson, R.K., Bourgon, G., Helmus, L. and Hodgson, S. (2009) 'The principles of effective correctional treatment also apply to sexual offenders: a meta-analysis.' *Criminal Justice and Behavior 36*, 865–891.

Hanson, R.K., Harris, A.J.R., Scott, T.-L. and Helmus, L. (2007) *Assessing the Risk of Sexual Offenders on Community Supervision: The Dynamic Supervision Project.* Ottawa: Public Safety Canada.

Mann, R.E. and Shingler, J. (2006) 'Collaboration in Clinical Work with Sexual Offenders: Treatment and Risk Assessment.' In W.L. Marshall, Y.M. Fernandez, L.E. Marshall and G.A. Serran (eds) *Sexual Offender Treatment: Controversial Issues*. Chichester: John Wiley.

Mann, R.E., Hanson, R.K. and Thornton, D. (2010a) 'Assessing risk for sexual recidivism: some proposals on the nature of psychologically meaningful risk factors.' *Sexual Abuse: A Journal of Research and Treatment 22*, 172–190.

Mann, R.E., Ware, J. and Fernandez, Y.M. (2010b) 'Managing Sex Offender Treatment Programs.' In D. Boer, L.A. Craig, R. Eher, M.H. Miner and F. Pffafflin (eds) *International Perspectives on the Assessment and Treatment of Sexual Offenders: Theory, Practice and Research* Oxford: Wiley.

Mann, R.E., Webster, S.D., Schofield, C. and Marshall, W.L. (2004) 'Approach versus avoidance goals in relapse prevention with sexual offenders.' *Sexual Abuse: A Journal of Research and Treatment 16*, 1, 65–75.

Marshall, L.E., Marshall, W.L., Fernandez, Y.M., Malcolm, P.B. and Moulden, H.M. (2008) 'The Rockwood preparatory program for sexual offenders: description and preliminary appraisal.' *Sexual Abuse: A Journal of Research and Treatment 20*, 1, 25–42.

Maruna, S. and LeBel, T. (2003) 'Welcome home? Examining the Re-entry Court concept from a strengths-based perspective.' *Western Criminology Review 4*, 91–107.

Rice, M.E. (2008) 'Current Status of Violence Risk Assessment: Is There a Role for Clinical Judgement?' In G. Bourgon, R.K. Hanson, J.D. Pozzulo, K.E. Morton-Bourgon and C.T. Tanasichuk (eds) *Proceedings of the 2007 North American Correctional and Criminal Justice Psychology Conference*. Available from www.publicsafetycanada.gc.ca, accessed on 21 July 2010. 20–23

Snacken, S. (2006) 'A reductionist penal policy and European human rights standards.' *European Journal of Criminal Policy research 12*, 143–164.

Thornton, D. (2002) 'Constructing and testing a framework for dynamic risk assessment.' *Sexual Abuse: A Journal of Research and Treatment 14*, 137–151.

Thornton, D., Mann, R., Webster, S., Blud, L., et al. (2003) 'Distinguishing and combining risks for sexual and violent recidivism.' *Annals of the New York Academy of Sciences 989*, 225–235.

Ward, T. (2002) 'Good lives and the rehabilitation of offenders: promises and problems.' *Aggression and Violent Behavior 7*, 513–528.

Ward, T. and Birgden, A. (2007) 'Human rights and correctional clinical practice.' *Aggression and Violent Behavior 12*, 628–643.

Ward, T. and Brown, M. (2004) 'The Good Lives Model and conceptual issues in offender rehabilitation.' *Psychology, Crime and Law 10*, 243–257.

Ward, T. and Connolly, M. (2008) 'A human rights-based practice framework for sexual offenders.' *Journal of Sexual Aggression 14*, 2, 87–98.

Ward, T. and Mann, R.E. (2004) 'Good Lives and Rehabilitation of Sex Offenders: A Positive Approach to Treatment.' In A. Linley and S. Joseph (eds) *Positive Psychology in Practice*. New York: John Wiley.

Ward, T. and Marshall, W.L. (2004) 'Good lives, aetiology and the rehabilitation of sex offenders: a bridging theory.' *Journal of Sexual Aggression 10*, 2, 153–169.

Ward, T. and Maruna, S. (2007) *Rehabilitation*. Abingdon: Routledge.

Ward, T. and Stewart, C.A. (2003) 'The treatment of sex offenders: risk management and good lives.' *Professional Psychology: Research and Practice 34*, 353–360.

Ward, T., Gannon, T. and Birgden, A. (2007) 'Human rights and the treatment of sex offenders.' *Sexual Abuse: A Journal of Research and Treatment 19*, 195–216.

Ward, T., Vess, J., Collie, R.M. and Gannon, T. (2006) 'Risk management or goods promotion: the relationship between approach and avoidance goals in treatment for sex offenders.' *Aggression and Violent Behavior 11*, 378–393.

Webster, S.D., Mann, R.E., Carter, A.J., Long, J., et al. (2006) 'Inter-rater reliability of dynamic risk assessment with sexual offenders.' *Psychology, Crime and Law 12*, 439–452.

CHAPTER 9

RISK AND PERSONALISATION

ROSEMARY LITTLECHILD AND JON GLASBY, WITH LOUISE NIBLETT AND TINA COOPER

INTRODUCTION

Direct payments, personal budgets and self-directed support are key mechanisms for implementing the current personalisation agenda. This approach to social care, based on 'prevention, early intervention, enablement and high-quality personally tailored services' (HM Government 2007, p.2), was founded on the principle that people have the right to control the budget and support they need to live fulfilling lives (for a full discussion of the history and introduction of direct payments and personal budgets in the UK, see Glasby and Littlechild 2009). However, of all the challenges raised by personalisation, the issues of risk and protection are paramount. While few people would disagree that people should exercise choice and control over their lives and receive services which are flexible and responsive, some are concerned that new ways of working may lead to a situation in which already vulnerable people may be exposed to even greater risks.

Against this background, this chapter identifies some of the arguments involved in the debate about risk and protection in the implementation of personalisation, with particular reference to direct payments and personal budgets. The chapter considers how these issues are addressed and balanced from a local authority perspective and also includes the views of Louise, a direct payments recipient, and Tina, a carer whose son, James, receives an individual budget, all of whom offer their own 'top tips' for future practice. While all the contributors are largely in support of these innovative ways of working, the chapter enables people from different standpoints in the system to express their own views about potential issues of risk involved in these new arrangements. The chapter concludes with the emerging themes from their various perspectives, highlighting ways forward for future policy and practice development.

SETTING THE CONTEXT

Vigorous lobbying by service users and their allies ensured that the Community Care (Direct Payments) Act 1996 allowed *all* adult service users aged under 65 to receive direct payments (followed by other groups in 2000 and 2001), despite ambivalence in the attitudes of staff:

> I am very worried about direct payments – vulnerable people managing their own services. (Social worker in a multidisciplinary team)
>
> Can I risk [direct payments]...on behalf of clients? (Adults' team social worker) (quoted in Fruin 2000, p.17)

Other campaigners, including the National Centre for Independent Living (NCIL), insisted that 'Disabled people must be given the same rights to take risks as all citizens' (National Centre for Independent Living 1999, p.8), and that direct payments may in fact *reduce* risks by enabling people to be more in control of their lives.

Central to the initial direct payments policy was that people should be 'willing and able' to receive direct payments and that, regardless of support they received to manage direct payments, *the recipients* were ultimately responsible for them. However, the Health and Social Care Act 2008 extended the range of people eligible to receive direct payments and local authorities are now able to appoint a 'suitable person' to receive direct payments on behalf of someone who lacks the capacity to direct their own care.

Professional opinion has remained divided. An online survey of 600 social workers by *Community Care* in October 2008 found that 96 per cent of front-line staff thought personalisation would make service users more vulnerable (Mickel 2008). Similarly, the pressure group, Action on Elder Abuse, claims that the government has given little explicit attention to the potential risks for people in more vulnerable situations (Mickel 2008). In contrast, In Control, an advocate of self-directed support, claims that 'personalisation makes people safer' because it focuses on people's abilities, strengthens the concept of citizenship and communities, and facilitates a person-centred risk assessment process that enables a more robust risk management system (Duffy and Gillespie 2009, p.1). Such was the strength of the government's commitment to self-directed support that the Department of Health stated that by April 2011 at least 30 per cent of users and carers should be receiving a personal budget (Improvement and Development

Agency, Association of Directors of Adult Social Services and Local Government Association 2009, p.6).

In 2009, the government (Department of Health 2009a) completed a consultation exercise reviewing the 2000 *No Secrets* guidance on adult protection (Department of Health 2000). Respondents to the consultation concluded that a satisfactory balance between risk and choice had yet to be established, although some local authorities had begun effectively to integrate issues of safeguarding within the personalisation agenda (Department of Health 2009a). However, in the evaluation of the 13 Department of Health sites piloting individual budgets (known as the IBSEN study), 13 adult protection leads reported that they had not been actively involved in their implementation. Furthermore, at that very early stage of individual budget implementation, they felt that the two policies of choice and safeguarding vulnerable people were on separate and parallel tracks (Manthorpe *et al.* 2009).

RAISING THE ISSUES

What, then, are the issues raised in the debate about risk in the implementation of the personalisation agenda?

Respondents to the Department of Health review (Department of Health 2009a), and other earlier work on direct payments (e.g. Fruin 2000), identified a key area of concern as risk of abuse from paid carers, especially those who are directly employed as personal assistants (PAs) by service users. This may be physical abuse or more subtle – for example, carers behaving in an inappropriate way, such as expecting use of the service user's car or computer, or to be fed while at work.

Henwood and Hudson (2007), in their review of self-directed support schemes, also identified concern about financial exploitation, because paid carers or family members may have greater access to a service user's money. However, as Duffy and Gillespie (2009 p.14) point out, institutions are not necessarily safe places to be and the incidence of abuse of older people is higher in residential care than in people's own homes. Furthermore. recent research, conducted for Skills for Care on the perceptions of both employers and PAs, showed a *reduction* in the number of people reporting any kind of abuse from PAs, compared to staff employed by the local authority, from 18 per cent to 10 per cent (IFF Research 2008 p.34).

The risks associated with paying friends and family members have been well documented in both UK and international literature with concerns about how and whether it will change the relationship between family members and lead to a 'commodification of care'

(Glendinning *et al.* 2008; Manthorpe *et al.* 2009; Ungerson 2006). Equally well documented, however, are the benefits that people now report since the restrictions on employing family members have been relaxed (e.g. Stuart 2006; Vick *et al.* 2006).

Critics of the personalisation agenda claim that some forms of self-directed support are likely to change the face of British welfare provision, transferring risk from the state to the individual and diminishing disabled people's opportunities to have a 'collective voice' in the planning and development of services (e.g. Ferguson 2007; Scourfield 2007). Advocates of self-directed support would argue that, far from isolating individuals, this approach is largely empowering and offers the opportunity to share risk between the individual and the system, and as well as being more likely to contribute to services that better meet people's needs (Glasby and Littlechild 2009).

Finally, there is concern about the risk to PAs as employees, and the potential for them to experience poor conditions of service, including lower pay than their counterparts in home care services and exploitation by their employers (Leece 2010; Social Care Institute for Excellence 2008). While the limited research on the experiences of PAs, conducted for Skills for Care, does highlight the lack of training opportunities and concern about low pay (IFF Research 2008), it also provides evidence that the vast majority of PAs are happy in their roles and feel appreciated most of the time (IFF Research 2008; Leece 2006).

HOW ARE RISKS CURRENTLY MANAGED?

Early research shows that, in addressing issues of risk, some local authorities have responded with bureaucratic and restrictive reporting and accounting procedures that have had the effect of deterring people from accessing direct payments (Commission for Social Care Inspection 2004). The debate about managing risk as services change has focused largely on PAs and what degree of regulation and inspection they should be subject to. At present, the requirement for PAs to have a Criminal Record Bureau (CRB) check before taking up employment is entirely at the discretion of their employer. The Skills for Care research indicated that many of the people who employed PAs already knew them in advance, and a third had not checked references or conducted a CRB check (IFF Research 2008). The government resisted pressure to require PAs to register under the Independent Safeguarding Authority's vetting and barring scheme, introduced in October 2009 in England, Wales and Northern Ireland (Independent Safeguarding Authority 2009), although in Scotland existing legislation specifies that councils can withdraw direct payments from people if they employ PAs who have not had enhanced disclosure checks (Scottish Government

2009). Similarly, PAs are not currently workers whom the Care Quality Commission regulates or whom the General Social Care Council plans to include in its registration process.

As the personalisation agenda progresses throughout the UK, the workforce implications of more people employing PAs are considerable (Department of Health 2009b; IFF Research 2008; Social Care Institute for Excellence 2008). In Scotland, UNISON, the public sector union, many of whose members work as PAs, and SPAEN (Scottish Personal Assistant Employers Network), which is a user-led organisation representing PA employers, are working together to produce good practice guidelines to help establish an employment relationship that is legal, safe and beneficial for both parties (Scottish Personel Assistant Employers Network and UNISON Scotland 2009).

Self-directed support as a system of delivering social care can, in many ways, strengthen the local authority's management of risk in that, if people are involved in assessing their own needs and identifying solutions for meeting them, the whole process of risk management is more transparent and honest. Duffy and Gillespie (2009) identify six critical stages in the process of self-directed support from the first point of contact to the review of outcomes. At each point, risk should be openly discussed with service users or, in the case of people who lack capacity, someone who has been identified as a 'suitable person' to make decisions on their behalf (Duffy and Gillespie 2009, p.10). As part of the 'signing-off' and evaluating of possible support plans, some local authorities have set up Risk Enablement Panels as multidisciplinary forums where situations, which are complex and identified as particularly 'high risk' by practitioners, can be discussed and where perceptions can be challenged and debated. As a result, such panels aim to make shared decisions by a transparent process that involves balancing issues of risk and responsibility (for an example, see Department of Health Care Networks n.d.).

Since the initial introduction of direct payments, a recurrent theme of any research on self-directed support has been that adequate support systems for recipients of direct payments or individual budgets are a critical element in its effective implementation (for a summary, see Davey *et al.* 2007; Glendinning *et al.* 2008; Vick *et al.* 2006). Support may come in different forms, including advocacy and brokerage services, peer mentoring services or 'buddying' programmes, but as a minimum should cover accessible information about what self-directed support is and how it works, as well as support on employment issues, money management and about what to do and how to manage if things go wrong (Department of Health 2009a). Research evidence suggests that support to different user groups and in different parts of the country is variable both in volume and quality, but concludes that *inadequate* support systems may seriously undermine the ability of people to exert choice and control over their own care (Davey *et al.* 2007; Glendinning *et al.* 2008).

Finally, anecdotal evidence and the limited research on individuals working as PAs highlight the need for them to be able to access appropriate support to avoid isolation and help establish good working conditions (IFF 2008, Leece 2010, Mickel 2009). As the number of PAs grows as part of the social care workforce, attention must also be paid to their experiences as employees of private employers.

A LOCAL AUTHORITY'S PERSPECTIVE[1]

It's such a pity that there is a tendency to polarise these two issues of personalisation and safeguarding. It's making everyone rather anxious – of course, safeguarding is everyone's business but we've got to get it into perspective. Personalisation is about helping people to live ordinary lives and the more you get disabled people out, living and socialising in the community, the safer they're going to be. Of course there are risks; there were before, with directly provided services, but with self-directed support you're helping people identify those risks and supporting them to manage them. There are many points built into the process when you are assessing checking, reviewing, but the difference with self-directed support is that you're reviewing *whether the outcomes are being achieved*, not the services themselves.

We give people the opportunity to tell us themselves what they need through a self-assessment questionnaire and this guides the professional assessment. Throughout the process we are assessing risk and discussing it with the person. When the person is clear about what resources are available to them, they can take as much or as little control of the money as they want.

We help people make their support plan – sometimes it will be someone from the local authority, sometimes an independent agency or the person or their family will complete it. At that point we really give people the opportunity to voice what their concerns might be and talk about how together we can help them to manage them. We use 'a

1   Taken from an interview with staff who are implementing the personali-
     sation agenda.

person-centred approach to risk assessment' (see Table 9.1 for a model, used on Worcestershire County Council's individual budget pilot project 'Doing it your way'), which helps the person involved, their family and friends and the worker to quantify the risk, which enables them to make a more honest and responsible assessment of the situation.

Once a support plan has been worked out, the local authority has to approve it to ensure it is legal, safe, ethical and reasonable. If people decide to employ their own PAs, in many instances we find they want to employ people whom they know and trust already. That element of trust is, not surprisingly, absolutely critical. Certainly, you may find people occasionally who try to exploit the situation and employ a relative to do something you might reasonably expect within ordinary caring relationships – for example, would we enable an older man to employ his grand-daughter to take him down to the local coffee shop for a drink and a cake each week? Possibly not, but on the other hand we provided money for someone to pay their relative to give up work on the family farm in order to provide personal support to enable the person to remain living within the family on the farm. Otherwise, they would have had to leave to live in institutional care.

We give information to people about keeping safe and encourage them to take up the opportunity for us to undertake CRBs on people they want to employ. We'll pay for that, but currently, to be honest, less than 20 per cent of people take them up. But that's not the point, we give them all the information and, as long as people have capacity, we let them make the decision – they're in control.

In the past, reviews have been more about monitoring services than the outcomes the person wants to achieve. With self-directed support, it's our responsibility to keep checking how the plan is going – what has the money been used to achieve? – is the person feeling they are staying in control of their lives, is there anything they would like to change? Are there any new concerns which have been identified? It's an opportunity to check but not get in the way.

And social workers must remember, once they start to work with people to access self-directed support, they don't leave all their other knowledge and professional assessment skills behind. They don't forget all they knew about

Table 9.1: A person-centred approach to risk assessment

Name _____

Date _____

What is it ……… wants to do?	What are the benefits to the person in doing this?	What might go wrong?	What might happen if the person does not do this?	Can control measures reduce the risk?	With control measures, how likely is it to go wrong? (scale of 1–10)	If it goes wrong, how serious will it be? (scale of 1–10 × previous score) The higher the final score the greater the risk

Source: Adapted from a model used on Worcestershire County Council's individual budget pilot project 'Doing it your way'.

safeguarding. They continue to use their communication and assessment skills and exercise their professional judgement to enable people to stay safe, but in a way that does not prevent them having as full a life as possible. There are certainly some social workers who feel anxious about working in this very different way, but, if we are serious about offering choice and control, we have to enable people to take decisions about their lives that we may previously have considered 'too risky'. Provided we can show we have considered the risks and fully discussed them with the person or their family, recorded the decisions clearly and we continually monitor this, then we can feel we have done a good job and defend the decision we have made. This is a journey – we're not going to get there straight away. It will take some time to change the culture in which we work but we've got more chance if we ensure that different parts of the system work together and we stay focused on supporting people to take more control of their lives.

Top tips for practitioners

1. Make sure you know what your agency's policy is on personalisation and risk. Ensure senior management support for a positive approach to risk taking. Develop a policy statement that clearly sets out the approach.

2. It's crucial to work in partnership with other agencies – no-one can do it alone. Self-directed support is about people looking at their whole life, not little bits of it in isolation.

3. 'Risk assessment' is not a form – it is an ongoing process. Keep assessing risks with people as their situations change.

4. Document your decisions carefully. As long as you can show that you have talked with the person and their family, and you have supported them in making an informed decision in relation to identified risks, then you have acted appropriately and can justify your decision. If you judge there are serious risks that other people are not addressing, then you may have to take independent action and you *may* have to move to safeguarding procedures.

5. Continue to review the situation and discuss any concerns with the person and their family.

A SERVICE USER'S PERSPECTIVE – LOUISE'S STORY

I have been in receipt of direct payments for 13 years. I thought that the term 'at risk' didn't apply to me. I do not identify myself as 'disabled' and am quite able to take care of myself – I just employ a PA to be able to do so.

However, on closer examination, I see that the concept of risk does apply to me and the many others on direct payments – it is the risk of being able to withstand the stress and strain of managing a direct payment.

One has to be 'Jack of all trades and master of none'. For instance, one must learn management skills, such as how to be an employer, how to deal with conflict, how to recruit, how to run what is essentially a small business, all while being assisted by the people one is trying to manage.

One must learn professional distance. This is essential. Although particularly difficult where the assistant is providing support socially, it can have positives to be friends with a PA. However, a PA can easily 'overstep' or blur the line between their work and pleasure if not properly instructed or supervised. The employee may think of themselves as a member of the employer's extended family, accept invitations for when they are not at work and the person on direct payments may not know how to deal with them in that situation. This may cause conflict or a feeling of unease for the direct payments recipient.

PAs gain all employment rights. This is a must, rightly so, to protect the employer as well as the employee. The flipside of this is that when things go pear shaped (and believe me they do) and conflict arises, one cannot simply dismiss them, because of their rights under employment legislation. It makes no difference that the employer is a 'vulnerable adult' or what the employee has done to the employer or how small and insignificant 'it' makes the employer feel. There is still a process to be followed, and it is very, very stressful for the employer.

Recently there was a major, major breach of confidentiality within my home. So major that it can only have come from one person – my PA. I did not want her in my home or anywhere near ever again. Thus, I started the dismissal process, suspended her on full pay, but because of her statutory rights it is a process that took a long time. I held two disciplinary meetings, and was forced by a union representative to relive the whole affair twice. The Employment Tribunal eventually found in my favour but the whole process lasted for around 6 very stressful weeks.

If the PA had been working for an agency or the local authority, I would have reported the breach of confidentiality to them and they would have dealt with the employment regulations. As I employed her, it was left to me. The local authority employs an agency to support people on direct payments which is supposed to help with employment issues. The agency is very good at recruitment and initially setting the direct payment up but not at helping when things go 'pear shaped'. Therefore, I was left to battle my way through employment legislation and processes that I knew nothing about, without any support at all.

I have no choice but to trust someone. In the context of my life there will always have to be someone there to do the things that my disability dictates that I cannot. I feel really, really vulnerable because of this abuse of trust. Yet, I will have to trust again.

It would be very tempting to go back to 'in-house' care or agency care, but I remember the feelings of uncertainty, what time someone is going to come and the planning of my life around care. At least with direct payments I am in control.

If a PA is off sick or on holiday I must call on my 'contingency plan'. That is my partner and my elderly parents. In the past, I have experienced problems as I require 'intimate' personal care and not the kind of assistance that I would necessarily want to ask from a sexual partner or my parents. Yet I do and have no choice or control over this. On the other hand, neither do my partner or my parents. They do it from a sense of duty. I feel horrible.

My 'case' is reviewed every year by the local authority and it is always a worry. The 'goal posts' are always moving, the 'care' that they will pay for is getting less and less. I get the distinct impression that the social worker is trying to trick/bully me into saying that I am using the money for other purposes. I know the 'system'. The point I am making is that I shouldn't have to know how to 'stand up for myself' and not every person with a disability is as 'savvy' as me. It does alarm me when I hear of people with the incorrect care package that is allowing them to 'survive' not 'live'.

I have seen many changes in the direct payments scheme, over the past 13 years. For instance, I do not have to explain to social workers what a direct payment is any more but I do find that a lot of social workers are ignorant as to what they can be used for. However, for all of its faults, and this rather negative picture, for most of the time, personally, it is a really good 'thing' and is much better than 'in-house' care because I am in control. To be empowered in this way, to be able to say who, when, what time someone comes into my home is a basic human right.

I suppose the 'ideal' system would be to have a true 'mixed economy' of care where people with a disability have true choice and control, with an equally good 'in-house' system to respond to crisis situations.

Louise's top tips for service users

1. Think about a contingency plan. The time will come when it becomes essential.

2. Never forget that PAs become employees, so keep up with employment legislation. The time will come when it is essential.

3. Keep a diary of events and how PAs make you feel. Keep a record of the good times and the bad.

4. You can use a direct payment for anything, as long as it is meeting an assessed need. They are to make life easier. For example, I use mine to go swimming and to meetings because one of my assessed needs is not to be isolated in the community. You can be creative and flexible, as long as you are meeting a need. The direct payment scheme is all about choice and independence to maintain a lifestyle.

A CARER'S PERSPECTIVE – JAMES'S STORY, TOLD BY HIS MOTHER, TINA

Who says individual budgets are not suitable for people with complex needs? My son James is 27 years old – he has profound and multiple physical and mental disabilities – he can't speak or see well and is unable to walk or feed himself. But 17 months ago he moved out of the family home where he lived with me, his dad and his sister, and moved into a specially adapted bungalow, where he lives independently with 24-hour support.

Yes, of course there are risks, as a parent you never stop worrying, but then there always were. James lived with us for 25 years. Every morning, I got up at 5.30, James had to get up at 6.30 to be ready to leave on the bus at 7.45 for the day centre, 12 miles away. He was spending 3 hours on transport every day. There were risks then – he might have had an epileptic fit. If he did, they'd have to stop the bus. Then they'd have to get in touch with me.

We'd been caring for James for 25 years but we realised we couldn't do it forever. So we looked for somewhere closer to his day centre, found out about individual budgets and now he's in this shared ownership scheme, supported 24 hours a day. There are still risks, but they are different risks and we've found ways of managing them. For example, this bleep on my phone – that tells me when his support worker has left and James is on the way to the day centre.

When we first thought about James moving out we sat down with the support worker and set out in detail what James does, hour by hour, from day to day. And all the while we put in checks – for example, James wears a hip spiker which has to be put on right or he can't sit up straight in his wheelchair. If not, he gets pressure sores. I know that as soon as he gets to the day centre they will check his support worker has put it on OK – it's just another pair of eyes.

James receives support from a local agency but he was involved from the start about who should be employed. Usually you don't have any say in who is looking after you, it's just whoever is on duty, but with an individual budget you're in charge! Although he can't speak, he can tell you absolutely what he likes and doesn't like.

When the support workers first started I said, 'Include him, he may not be able to speak, but talk to him and involve him in everything.' So that means, they take him out to the pub and he's recognised and accepted there. He has become part of the community – he lives in a small cul-de-sac and he's begun to get known there. First it was, 'The young man in the wheelchair' and now it's 'James'. Someone came across the other day and said, 'Is James all right? We haven't seen him for a couple of days.' There is an old lady in the road with Alzheimer's disease, and every morning she gets up and dressed, just to stand and wave James off on the bus. It gives her a purpose – he's giving something back to the community. Far from being *more* isolated living in his own home, he now has a better network than when he was living with us. Then, people didn't bother because they knew he lived with his parents. Now they look out for him.

I've been appointed by the Court of Protection as James's official 'receiver' (now termed a 'deputy'). I am in overall control of how his individual budget will be spent and I know I must make decisions that are in his best interests. But these will be taken only after discussion with family, who know and love James, and with relevant professionals.

This has brought me into contact with lots of other parents in similar situations – I can advise them on the basis of our experience. Sometimes, you can't believe it will work – it just seems too good to be true and you think the risks will just be too great. But we've got to let go – it might not be so easy in 5 years' time. We've identified the risks, we've managed them and they are far outweighed by the quality of life James now has!

Tina's top tips for carers

1. Make sure the professionals look at the whole person – make them listen to you, parents, friends and anyone the person wants to support them.

2. Seek support from the professionals when it's right for you. At some points you may need very little support, but turn to them when you need to and don't be afraid or embarrassed about asking for help.

3. Be creative in your thinking – don't be constrained by thinking about existing services! There's so much you can do to make people's lives better and you're in a good position to know what that is!

4. Get together with other carers to talk about things – they can be a great support and source of knowledge and ideas about how best to do things. Spread the word – tell other people the good news stories!

WAYS FORWARD

This review of issues surrounding risk and personalisation illustrates that the introduction of self-directed support raises many complexities that need to be faced and addressed if the personalisation agenda is to be introduced effectively with proper attention to balancing identified risks. No social care system can ever guarantee to eliminate abuse and exploitation – there is always likely to be some degree of risk. Likewise, risk rarely remains static but fluctuates and changes over time. Some risks can be anticipated, others may arise completely unexpectedly. However, as people are enabled to exercise choice and control over their lives, some will need support in explicitly identifying and anticipating risks, and in making informed decisions about the kind of support that will best meet their needs. In principle, self-directed support offers a better framework for practitioners to more genuinely safeguard service users on the basis of *outcomes* achieved – focusing on what impact support has on people's lives, rather than on what exactly is provided and how it is delivered.

In this chapter, we have presented views from different standpoints on the issues of risk and personalisation, and, while there are differences in the local authority perspective and those of Louise and Tina, a number of common themes have emerged that point to ways forward and may help in establishing this framework:

- Louise and Tina's accounts of receiving care suggest that service users and carers may have a broader view of risk than the traditional focus of some practitioners on abuse and exploitation. They were equally concerned, for example, with the more subtle risks of a blurring of the relationship between the PA as employee and friend, the risk associated with not having robust contingency plans and risks to their own physical and mental health. Local authorities must ensure that their personalisation and risk policies encompass this wider perspective.

- Louise and Tina's accounts also demonstrate clearly that a relationship of trust is paramount between social care employees and the people they support. This is more likely to occur when employees are well recruited, trained and offered good conditions of service. To date, very little work has been done on establishing what are the rights and responsibilities within an employer/employee relationship in the self-directed support sector. Local authorities must support these new ways of working if the risks to both employers and employees are to be identified and minimised.

- The role of support services is critical in helping people to identify and assess the risks involved in trying to achieve the outcomes they want, and then to consider how they might address them. This worked particularly well for Tina who was able to share her detailed knowledge of her son with the support worker in order to devise an appropriate plan, having explicitly addressed the risks involved.

- Support includes clear, accessible information about different kinds of self-directed support, advice about becoming an employer and recruitment and employment issues, ongoing support over time and advice about what to do if things go wrong. Louise may have benefited from this advice at an early stage of setting up direct payments, but she felt isolated and abandoned when things did go wrong.

- All three perspectives emphasise the increased importance of reviewing outcomes within self-directed care, which is a further opportunity to assess and review risk. However, this is a change in emphasis from the old system of monitoring cases and, as Louise's account indicates, is a point at which people may need an independent advocate to help represent their views.

- Peer support seems to be particularly effective in both encouraging people to aim high in terms of their aspirations and yet to take a realistic approach to risk and to what is achievable. For Tina, a carer's forum has been an effective channel for sharing information.

- Local authorities must be clear about their policies towards risk and demonstrate political and senior management support for front-line workers. Effective risk management policies are essential to ensure a more consistent approach to managing complex cases, and to offer advice and support to staff in sharing responsibility for risk.

- Training for practitioners in understanding the principles and practice of self-directed support is essential if people are to be supported to achieve the aims of independent living and the opportunity to exercise more choice and control over their lives. Social work educators and trainers are well placed to ensure that students are informed about new forms of self-directed support, and they have the right value base and skills to make these aims a reality.

For all the complexities that personalisation raises, there is a growing body of research and practice evidence to suggest that enabling people to be in control of their own services and their own lives, and helping them to be visible in the community, is a better way of keeping people safe than previous approaches of separation and segregation. However, while the evidence about self-directed support is beginning to emerge, it is likely that any future negative publicity could lead to a rapid backlash and to the recreation of the old system under new language. As the personalisation agenda develops and services change accordingly, local authorities are grappling with the ways in which they balance their responsibilities of extending choice and control with those of keeping people safe. As the local authority perspective presented earlier suggests, rather than viewing personalisation and safeguarding as two discrete processes with different and separate processes and procedures, a more helpful way forward may be to identify ways of helping people focus on the outcomes they wish to achieve, identify the risks involved and help facilitate the means to achieve them in ways that are 'legal, safe, ethical and reasonable'. In that way, safeguarding becomes part of the personalisation process.

The final words of this chapter are from Tina:

> At first it seemed like a fairy tale; it didn't seem real. Here is young man who can do nothing, living by himself in his own home! It *is* still worrying, but we have safeguards and we still support him and I know as soon as I see him whether he is happy or not. He can let us know – he's in control!

ACKNOWLEDGEMENTS

Thanks to Christine Clarke, Annie Dickson and Deborah Redman from Worcestershire Council for sharing their experiences as we drafted this chapter.

REFERENCES

Commission for Social Care Inspection (CSCI) (2004) *Direct Payments. What are the Barriers?* London: CSCI.

Davey, V., Fernandez, J., Knapp, M., Vick, N. *et al.* (2007) *Direct Payments: A National Survey of Direct Payments Policy and Practice.* London: Personal Social Services Research Unit, London School of Economics and Political Science.

Department of Health (2000) *No Secrets: Guidance on Developing and Implementing Multi-agency Policies and Procedures to Protect Vulnerable Adults from Abuse.* London: The Stationary Office.

Department of Health (2009a) *Safeguarding Adults. Report on the Consultation on the Review of 'No Secrets.'* London: The Stationary Office.

Department of Health (2009b) *Working to Put People First: The Strategy for the Adult Social Care Workforce in England*. London: DH.

Department of Health Care Networks (n.d.) *London Borough of Newham Risk Enablement Panel*. Available at www.dhcarenetworks.org.uk/_library/Resources/Personalisation/Personalisation_advice/LBN_risk_enablement_panel.doc.

Duffy, S. and Gillespie, J. (2009) *Personalisation and Safeguarding*. Version 1.1. Discussion Paper. Available at www.in-control.org.uk, accessed on 9 November 2009.

Ferguson, I. (2007) 'Increasing user choice or privatising risk? The antimonies of personalization.' *British Journal of Social Work 37*, 387–403.

Fruin, D. (2000) *New Directions for Independent Living*. London: Department of Health.

Glasby, J. and Littlechild, R. (2009) *Direct Payments and Personal Budgets* (2nd edition). Bristol: The Policy Press.

Glendinning, C., Challis, D., Fernandez, J., Jacobs, S. *et al.* (2008) *Evaluation of the Individual Budgets Pilot Programme*. York: University of York, Social Policy Research Unit.

Henwood, M. and Hudson, B. (2007) *Here to Stay? Self-directed Support: Aspiration and Implementation (a Review for the Department of Health)*. Heathencote: Melanie Henwood Associates.

HM Government (2007) *Putting People First: A Shared Vision and Commitment to the Transformation of Adult Social Care*. London: HM Government.

IFF Research (2008) *Employment Aspects and Workforce Implications of Direct Payments*. London: IFF.

Improvement and Development Agency, Association of Directors of Adult Social Services and Local Government Association (2009) *Making Progress with Putting People First: Self-directed Support*. Available at www.dhcarenetworks.org.uk/_library/Resources/Personalisation/Personalisation_advice/Making_progress_with_PPF_-_self-directed_support_final.pdf, accessed on 7 December 2009.

Independent Safeguarding Authority (ISA) (2009) *ISA Referral Guidance*. Darlington: ISA. Available at www.isa-gov.org.uk, accessed on 7 December 2009.

Leece, J. (2006) '"It's Not Like Being at Work": A Study to Investigate Stress and Job Satisfaction in Employees of Direct Payment Users.' In J. Leece and J. Bornat (eds) *Developments in Direct Payments*. Bristol: The Policy Press.

Leece, J. (2010) 'Paying the piper and calling the tune: power and the direct payment relationship.' *British Journal of Social Work 40*, 1, 188–206.

Manthorpe, J., Stevens, M., Rapaport, J., Harris, J., *et al.* (2009) 'Safeguarding and system change: early perceptions of the implications for adult protection services of the English individual budgets pilots – a qualitative study.' *British Journal of Social Work 39*, 1465–1480.

Mickel, A. (2008) *Professionals Split Over Future of Adult Social Care*. Available at www.communitycare.co.uk/Articles/2008/10/22/109761/personalisation-exclusive-poll-of-social-workers-views.html, accessed on 14 October 2009.

Mickel, A. (2009) *Who is Responsible for Personal Assistants' Pay and Conditions?* Available at www.communitycare.co.uk/Articles/2009/07/06/112020/Who-is-responsible-for-personal-assistants39-pay-and.htm, accessed on 14 October 2009.

National Centre for Independent Living (NCIL) (1999) *Government White Paper: Modernising Social Services – Response by the British Council of Disabled People's National Centre for Independent Living*. London: NCIL.

Scottish Government (2009) *Protection of Vulnerable Groups (Scotland) Act 2007. Draft Guidance*. Available at www.scotland.gov.uk/Resource/Doc/290841/0089369.pdf, accessed on 7 December 2009.

Scottish Personal Assistant Employers Network (SPAEN) and UNISON Scotland (2009) *Creating and Supporting an Informed Employer and Employee Relationship within the Self-directed Support Sector*. Glasgow: UNISON Scotland and SPAEN. Available at www.unison-scotland.org.uk/socialwork/PAreportfinal.pdf, accessed on 7 December 2009.

Scourfield, P. (2007) 'Social care and the modern citizen: client, consumer, service user, mamager and entrepreneur.' *British Journal of Social Work 37*, 107–122.

Social Care Institute for Excellence (SCIE) (2008) *Personalisation: A Rough Guide.* London: SCIE.

Stuart, O. (2006) *Will Community-based Support Services make Direct Payments a Viable Option for Black and Minority Ethnic Service Users and Carers?* London: Social Care Institute Excellence.

Ungerson, C. (2006) 'Direct Payments and the Employment Relationship: Some Insights from Cross-national Research.' In J. Leece and J. Bornat (eds) *Developments in Direct Payments.* Bristol: The Policy Press.

Vick, N., Tobin, R., Swift, P., Spandler, H. *et al.* (2006) *An Evaluation of the Impact of the Social Care Modernisation Programme on the Implementation of Direct Payments.* London: Health and Social Care Advisory Service (with University of Central Lancashire and the Foundation for People with Learning Disabilities).

CHAPTER 10

PUBLIC HEALTH APPROACHES TO RISK ASSESSMENT AND RISK MANAGEMENT

JASON WOOD

INTRODUCTION

The responsibility for the risk assessment and management of sexual and violent offenders is predominately located with criminal justice agencies who have a range of powers and methods, designed to manage the 'critical few' offenders, who pose the highest risk to a community upon their release.

This dominant approach has been criticised in recent years for its failure to grapple with the nature and extent of sexual offending. While well resourced to manage those classified as high risk, it falls short in terms of a number of key areas required for the effective assessment and management of risk. There is some dispute in terms of the extent to which offenders are enabled to 'change' through these processes, with the current arrangements favouring the management of offenders and the reduction of potential harm. The extent to which these criminal justice policies involve 'the public' is also criticised and from a range of perspectives (see Kemshall 2008 for a full review). There are those, represented by sections of the popular press, who demand that the public should know where sex offenders live, in the mould of community notification schemes in the US. There are others who argue that only a small number of offenders (and offences) are being dealt with through existing arrangements, and that a new approach is required if the true extent of sexual and violent offences is likely to be tackled.

In this chapter, one alternative approach to the risk assessment and management of offenders is explored through a consideration of the Public Health Approach (PHA). The chapter reviews the key principles of such an approach before examining its application in one key contentious area of criminal justice: the management of child sex offenders.

THE COMMUNITY PROTECTION MODEL

The measures currently used to manage sex offender risk include the extensive deployment of restrictive conditions and controls that are designed to 'protect the public from serious harm' (Home Office 1990, p.2) through what has been termed a 'community protection model' (Connelly and Williamson 2000; Kemshall and Wood 2007). Offenders are subjected to post-custody licence and registration conditions that impose restrictions on movement, access to victims and living arrangements. Risk assessment tools are used to calculate the likelihood, imminence and seriousness of harm, and this in turn informs the deployment of risk management resources: the responsibility for which is vested in the organisations that come together under the Multi-Agency Public Protection Arrangements (MAPPA).

MAPPA was established by the Criminal Justice and Court Services Act 2000, which placed a duty on police and probation as 'responsible authorities' to 'establish arrangements for the purpose of assessing and managing risks' posed by sexual, violent and other offenders who may cause 'serious harm' to the public (see the Criminal Justice and Court Services Act 2000, Section 67[2]). The Criminal Justice Act 2003 extended the role of responsible authority to prisons and introduced a 'duty to cooperate' on a number of other agencies, notably housing, social services, health authorities and Youth Offending Teams (YOTs). While the principal responsibility for public protection from sexual and violent offences rests with criminal justice agencies, other agencies have an important contribution to make in terms of contributing to risk assessment and risk management.

There are two critiques of the dominance of the community protection model that are relevant to this chapter. The first concerns the focus on the intensive scrutiny and management of the 'critical few' – those very high-risk offenders deemed to require the most resources and levels of management under MAPPA. This represents a very small percentage of the overall number of registered sex offenders, and the potential for a wider pool of offenders to be identified as warranting high levels of management is a very real operational issue (Kemshall *et al.* 2005). Whatever the classification, MAPPA is concerned only with those who have already been convicted and in its present form can do very little to act as a preventative force. This is perhaps why there is a continuous disjuncture between the number of convicted sexual offenders and the true extent of the problem of sexual offending.

Studies that have explored the extent of child sexual abuse indicate that 1 in 6 children (with 1 in 4 in Northern Ireland) are victims (Cawson, Wattam and Kelly 2000). Only a small proportion of perpetrators and victims will therefore come into contact with the criminal justice system and the prevalence of child sexual abuse may not be addressed.

The second critique comes when exploring the relationship between the community protection model and the involvement of the 'public'. Given the extent of child sex abuse, there is potential for the public to contribute to the identification, assessment and management of risk if given the resources and support to do so (discussed later). However, the public are largely excluded from the formal arrangements designed to manage risk, viewing the 'public as a potential source of risk to expert-led risk management strategies' (Kemshall and Wood 2007, p.209). The assumptions that underpin this exclusion are that the public are likely to react in a negative way to the community management of offenders, resorting to vigilante action (as in the case of the responses to the *News of the World* 'Name and Shame' campaign – see Nash 2006). Consequently, public reactions are seen as a 'threat' to sex offender risk management policy (Kemshall and Wood 2007). The weak relationship between statutory arrangements and the public has itself, however, two negative effects.

- First, because of the lack of trust in experts and the nature of the risks, the exclusion of the public does not necessarily engender trust in the processes and may in fact heighten anxiety (Kemshall and Wood 2008). As a result, 'the methods for demonstrating accountability [of criminal justice provision] to the public are under-developed' (Wood and Kemshall 2008, p.149).

- Second, the arrangements do little to support members of the public in preventing child sexual abuse and contributing meaningfully to the reduction of child sex offences. It is to this problem that we now turn our attention.

WHAT IS THE PHA?

In parallel to the development of the community protection model, there has been the growth of several community and voluntary sector initiatives also concerned with how best to manage child sex offenders. One alternative initiative, usually based within voluntary sector organisations, faith-based communities and survivor groups, has been the adoption of the PHA.

The PHA to sexual offending is best articulated in the work of Richard Laws (1996, 2000). Laws argued that criminal justice responses to offending, characterised largely as reactive, had not proved effective in reducing the incidence of offences, nor increased public confidence or capacity to protect children. In fact, the perverse consequence of the traditional approaches was an inflation of public fears and rejection, particularly of sex offenders (Kemshall and Wood 2008; Laws 2000) and the exclusion of the public from tackling the problem (Kemshall and Wood 2007). Since the focus is on specific offenders found guilty of offences, there is little scope for traditional criminal justice approaches to 'deter sex offending generally' (Glaser 2009, p.252).

The PHA embodies a more preventative approach drawing from, as the name suggests, public health, which is concerned with the collective impacts of particular health concerns on groups of people in society. Examples of public health concerns are wide ranging. Smoking, for example, causes both individual and collective negative impacts and is subjected to a series of public health promotion measures including changes in legislation (the banning of smoking in confined public places), the promotion of better lifestyles (through positive messages about stopping smoking), messages about the dangers of smoking through to targeted interventions at smokers in order to help them change their behaviour (state-funded nicotine replacement therapy).

The transferability of public health to criminal justice problems is usually framed by advocates as a response to the psychological and physical impacts on victims of sexual or violent harm. Rosenberg and Mercy argue that the traditional response to violent crime has 'focused prevention on deterrence and incapacitation' (1991, p.4). Rosenberg and Mercy instead frame violence as a public health problem by examining its associated morbidity and mortality. As they argue:

> Although the data on nonfatal outcomes of violence are scarce and inadequate, there is overwhelming evidence that morbidity associated with violence represents a tremendous cost to society and the victims… which include physical and psychological injuries. (Rosenberg and Mercy 1991, p.4)

Negative health outcomes for victims of child sexual abuse abound. Finkelhor (1991) states that children who have been sexually abused experience an extensive array of mental health problems including longer-term effects that persist into adulthood. Violence and sexual abuse therefore herald negative health outcomes and proponents subsequently argue that applying the PHA to violence provides the opportunity to make a significant contribution to its prevention (Rutherford et al. 2007).

In the context of managing sexual offenders, the PHA is located at three levels:

- Primary level: the goal is prevention of sexually deviant behaviour before it starts, for example: the identification and prevention of sexually deviant behaviour in children and the long-term prevention of adults in engaging in sexual abuse.

- Secondary level: the goal is prevention of first time offenders from progressing, or the opportunistic and 'specific offence' offender from becoming a generalist.

- Tertiary level: the goal is effective work with persistent and more serious offenders. Goals are usually effective treatment and relapse prevention programmes (Laws 2000, p.31).

It could be argued that to some extent these levels are already addressed in existing criminal justice programmes, certainly at the tertiary level. However, Laws argues that increased effort should be targeted at the primary and secondary level, with a focus on 'prevention goals':

- Public awareness and responsibility: this involves informing the public of the characteristics and extent of sexual offending including the key message that sex offenders are part of a community and that adults have a responsibility for responding to sex offending.

- Public education: this involves challenging the myth that all sex offenders are monsters or demons, and that they are incapable of change. The main message here is that something can be done and that treatment is worth investing in. (Laws 2000, pp. 31–22).

The prevention goals guide work with offenders and potential offenders, with victims and, crucially, with the wider public. The key principles set out by the PHA are as follows:

- Sexual offending is more prevalent than current criminal justice approaches allow for.

- Sexual offending has profound negative psychological and physical health outcomes, and should therefore be seen as a public health problem.

- Sex offenders can be anybody: they are most likely to be friends, family members or other associates and less likely to be strangers.

- Most sex offenders can change behaviours if provided with the effective means to do so.

- The responsibility for detecting and responding to child sexual abuse should be vested in adults, not children.

- Members of the public can make a contribution to the risk assessment and management of sexual offending, and can do so in a rational way.

In order to explore the practical application of a PHA, this chapter now discusses two constituent groups where this approach can be used effectively: 'the public' and offenders (including potential offenders).

WORKING WITH THE PUBLIC

As stated earlier, the public have largely been excluded from the regulation of sex offender risks. Yet, given the statistics on prevalence and the problems of the limits of the community protection model, the public potentially have a very important role to play.

A preventative approach requires not only greater levels of public awareness but also strategies and support for the public to take the necessary action to promote risk management. As Craven, Brown and Gilchrist note:

> The public need to be made aware of how a potential offender would groom adults, children and the environment. It is important, however, that this is managed in a way whereby appropriate help and intervention is sought. Increasing awareness of sexual grooming without increasing awareness of appropriate interventions...is likely to result in vigilante culture and potential offenders going 'underground'. (2007, p.69)

Working with the public does present particular challenges, however. The public are largely excluded from arrangements designed to manage sex offenders and are often characterised as irrational in responses to the risks this particular group of offenders poses (Kemshall and Wood 2007). It is often assumed that the public will resort to vigilante action when presented with information about sex offenders living in their local areas (Kemshall and Wood 2007), a stance somewhat evidenced by public disorder in response to the *News of the World* 'Name and Shame' campaign in the early part of the last decade (*News of the World* 2000a, 2000b, 2001; see Nash 2006 for a full discussion).

However, there is evidence to indicate that the public are not as punitive towards sex offenders as is often assumed, although there are feelings of insecurity about exactly how such offenders are managed in the community (Brown, Spencer and Deakin 2007). Additionally, public perceptions are more complex and related to sex offence type, with rapists and paedophiles seen as more morally reprehensible and untreatable than other types (see Brown 2009 for a full review), and those in higher socio-economic groups as more supportive of treatment, although why this should be so is not fully explored (Brown 1999).

There is therefore a key role for criminal justice agencies in reducing uncertainty, and one mechanism is through increased partnership work with local communities and through effectively managed disclosures. For example, when public disclosure is managed effectively and supported by professionals engaged in risk management, evidence suggests that the public are capable of taking concrete actions to safeguard children and can act responsibly in relation to the confidential information that they receive about offenders (Kemshall and Wood et al. 2010).

Perhaps one of the biggest barriers to attempts to increase public awareness is the media's framing of child sexual abuse (Critcher 2003; Kitzinger 2004). The print media in particular has emphasised 'stranger danger' with salacious stories about the number and nature of predatory paedophiles at the expense of more reasoned debate about the role of the public in protecting children (Craven, Brown and Gilchrist 2006; Craven et al. 2007; Kemshall and Wood 2008). Despite the range of victims, offenders and varying types of offences, the media focus on strangers 'supersede(s) discussion around, for example, the high proportion of sexual offences that occur within the family' (Kemshall and Wood 2008, p.614). However, some of these common replications of sex offender risk can be challenged when there is a sustained attempt to influence public information. For example, the Stop it Now! campaign sought to emphasise key child protection messages in local and national media reportage. Analysis of the media responses to this campaign suggested that the key messages were often replicated in news stories (Kemshall, Mackenzie and Wood 2004). And while Craven et al. (2007) are right in claiming that the media must take responsibility for fuelling moral panic and fear of crime, it is also true that seeing the media as solely influencing public opinion is not borne out by research.

The traditional 'hypodermic' model (i.e. where audiences are passive and the media is pervasive in its influence) overlooks the way in which media messages are filtered, mediated and amended by recipients, often in discussion and debate within their immediate social networks and milieux. In effect, we need to understand the importance of the public's involvement in shaping their own views and responses to risk (Hughes, Kitzinger and Murdock 2006). Kitzinger (2004), for example, in an important study of public perceptions and responses to media coverage of paedophilia, found that local networks and associations are critical to how risk information is sought, received and acted upon, and are particularly crucial in the formation of local vigilante responses to paedophiles. Risk information is either negated, minimised or inflated by such networks, and it is important that local and national risk communicators understand and, if possible, influence these key processes. For example, if communities already feel 'under siege' and over-exposed to risk(s), particularly on under-resourced and under-policed housing estates, then trust in local criminal justice professionals to adequately manage sex offender risks is diminished and 'direct action' is more likely (Kitzinger 2004, p.151).

Finally, what we mean by 'the public' can be hotly debated. The public include you, me, our families, neighbours, colleagues, victims and offenders, and is divisible by gender, class, 'race' and a whole host of other socio-economic factors. The diversity of the public can be under-appreciated in child protection campaigns if campaigners fail to recognise cultural and language barriers in terms of key safeguarding messages. Also, risks are inequitably distributed with 'some communities less equipped to manage them' (Kemshall and Wood 2007, p.218) in a context of poor-quality social housing, poor health, minimal access to good education and a range of other risks. Any attempt to address public engagement must therefore consider a number of 'publics' as opposed to one unified 'public'.

STRATEGIES FOR WORKING WITH THE PUBLIC

As we have established, the PHA is primarily targeted at members of the public: it seeks to rebalance the responsibility for risk management from criminal justice agencies to individuals concerned about the behaviour of others or themselves. Using educational, information and awareness-raising strategies, practitioners can play an important role in equipping members of the public to play a part in keeping children safe. Public education campaigns are designed to attend to the primary level of the PHA in that the goal is preventative (Laws 2000). This is realised through a number of strategies including demystifying sexual offending; helping people to identify grooming and other potentially harmful behaviours; and supporting people to raise concerns by equipping people with strategies to manage risk. Such an approach could take the form of three stages, as outlined in Figure 10.1 and discussed after.

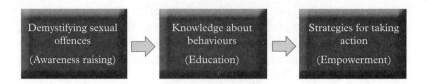

Figure 10.1: Three-stage approach to public education

Demystifying sexual offences (awareness raising)

An effective public-education campaign should seek first to address any misconceptions about the topic of concern. This means that prior to providing education about the behaviours that cause concern, members of the public need to have information that can counteract the dominant media messages about sex offenders and help them to locate the issue within their own lives. To draw on a parallel example, the first task of health promotion campaigns around smoking was to challenge the myths that smoking was good for health, not proven to be addictive and somehow a necessary fashion accessory, as previous commercial advertising had argued. Challenging these myths was done prior to providing education about how to change addictive behaviours and habits (Naidoo and Wills 2000).

Transferring this is difficult in terms of sexual offending, not least because it is a 'taboo' risk with no common language and diminished opportunities for informed public debate (Kemshall and Wood 2008). However, there are common myths that need challenging. Some of the key messages that Stop it Now! seeks to communicate are as follows:

- People who sexually abuse children aren't monsters; you can't pick them out in a crowd.

- Abusers are men, women, young people and children. They can be family members, friends or professionals known to the children concerned.

- They might also be complete strangers, but instances of a stranger abusing a child are very, very rare compared to the vast majority of cases of child sexual abuse.

- Abusers are people we know and people we care about.

- An abuser can be from any class, culture and background. Race, creed or religion make no difference – abuse happens!

- An abuser can be any sexual orientation: heterosexual or homosexual, bi-sexual or transgender.[1]

The methods used to raise awareness are similar to those used in any other public health campaigns. Stop it Now! uses a range of websites, videos, posters and leaflets to promote its key messages and is notable for disseminating its information in accessible and user-friendly ways. However, this approach assumes that the audience will receive messages, interpret them as intended and be able to be more informed as a result (Kemshall 2008). It also assumes that the public health messages will counteract more dominant messages: a difficulty in the continuing media focus on 'stranger danger'. Where approaches have been more effective is in the coupling of 'information' with professional advice targeted at a local level. For example, local Stop it Now! initiatives targeting professional groups such as teachers and local community group leaders were more effective (Kemshall *et al.* 2004). The subsequent evaluation recommended a more formalised and systematic approach to public-awareness campaigning, with an emphasis upon using existing networks and community groups, and by targeting local opinion formers for information and awareness raising:

> where the partner agency can carry the message into key user and key audience groups. This avoids 'wasting' the message, enables strong follow up and evaluation within more tightly bounded groups and enables a clearer cost-benefit analysis to be applied to dissemination. (Kemshall *et al.* 2004, p.12)

In addition, the authors concluded that communication needs to be: 'considered as a strategic issue within which cost-benefit is considered rather than viewing communication as a matter of pragmatism or opportunism' (Kemshall *et al.* 2004, p.13).

A more recent initiative under the Home Office Child Sex Offender Review (CSOR) involved a pilot of a public-awareness campaign by the Lucy Faithfull Foundation with the conclusion that such campaigns have to be intensive, long term and part of a broader awareness strategy (Collins 2009). However, the pilot events were not well attended, illustrating that the public find this an 'emotionally aversive' topic (Sanderson 2005). In the Lucy Faithfull pilots, 'hard to reach' groups and minority ethnic groups also proved challenging to engage.[2]

Despite the fact that 'participatory and communicative mechanisms for debating risks with the public are limited' (Kemshall and Wood

---

1   See www.educate2protect.co.uk/who.html, accessed on 20 July 2010.
2   For further information on the two pilots, contact Stop it Now! at office@stopitnow.org.uk

2007, p.218), there is scope to develop creative approaches to helping members of the public engage in a dialogue about sex offender risks. In addition to the traditional media and public education campaign approaches set out earlier, forums and debates can support people in thinking about and discussing the myths and realities with one another. One such approach was tested in the rather controlled environment of the British Festival of Science in 2006 where Kemshall and Wood encouraged members of the public to engage in a series of exercises designed to challenge myths about sex offenders and sexual offences. The exercises relied on using a series of statements about sexual offending to stimulate discussion. Participants were asked to signal their agreement or disagreement with myth and fact-based statements to encourage discussion. The approach was effective insofar as some participants reported having their misconceptions challenged. Such approaches must be carefully executed though not least in recognising that, given the high prevalence of child sexual abuse, there is a high chance that a member of the group can have been either a victim or perpetrator of abuse. Acknowledging this at the start of any discussion sessions is critical.

Knowledge about behaviours (education)

Craven *et al.* (2007) note that public awareness of what constitutes 'grooming behaviour' is limited – a reflection of poor definitions in law. There can also be difficulties in identifying behaviour in children that may be of concern. Useful public education campaigns need to address:

- clear definitions of child sexual abuse

- how child sexual abuse occurs, including the grooming strategies used by perpetrators

- behaviours of concern in children

- strategies for taking preventative action.

Leaflets produced by Stop it Now! support parents and carers in determining the difference between types of behaviour that are cause for concern and what might be classified as normal behaviour, particularly between children. In one leaflet, *What we all Need to Know to Protect our Children*,[3] the charity sets out a number of touching and non-touching activities that constitute child sexual abuse, and describes the grooming strategies used by offenders. The leaflet provides this

3   Available at: www.stopitnow.org.uk/help--advice/publications.aspx, accessed on 20 July 2010.

information in clear, jargon-free language and uses terminology that members of the public will understand. The clarity of information is essential here: it can enable individuals to make sound judgements about behaviour without negatively reacting to normal behaviour and, in turn, becoming too risk averse.

Strategies for taking action (empowerment)

What kind of action can be taken in response to the risks posed by sex offenders that avoids vigilantism and potential public disorder? Alternative approaches can be delivered in partnership with the public, but they should be executed in consort with the education and awareness-raising strategies set out earlier. A strategy that has recently been tested has the potential to enhance a parent's or carer's capacity to protect individual children through disclosure.

During the course of the development of MAPPA, there was an increasing expectation that panels would routinely consider the disclosure of information about sex offenders to 'third parties', including parents and carers, where it was deemed to enhance public protection. The Criminal Justice Act 2003 placed a duty on each MAPPA authority to consider disclosing a MAPPA-managed offender's convictions for child sexual offences to members of the public.[4] The legislation created a presumption that information will be disclosed where there is reason to believe that a child sexual offender poses a risk of serious harm to a particular child or children, and the disclosure to a particular member of the public is necessary to protect that child or children from serious harm caused by that offender (Kemshall and Wood et al. 2010). It is common, therefore, for disclosure to be used as part of the overall risk management of registered sex offenders and this often involves the cooperation of the offender (Wood and Kemshall 2007).

In June 2007, the government published the *Review of the Protection of Children from Sex Offenders* (Home Office 2007). This review considered the way in which the risks presented by child sex offenders in the community are managed, including the amount of information about child sex offenders that is disclosed to the public. The review set out 20 actions to strengthen efforts to keep children safe. Action 4 committed the government to:

> Pilot a process where members of the public can register their child protection interest in a named individual. Where this individual has convictions for child sex offences and is considered a risk, there will be

4   As a result of Section 140 of the Criminal Justice and Immigration Act 2008.

a presumption that this information will be disclosed to the relevant member of the public. (Home Office 2007, p.11)

In response, the government tested an approach in 2009 that provided members of the public with the opportunity to initiate an enquiry about someone they were concerned about. The managed approach to disclosure is based on the identification of key recipients (on a 'need to know' basis) either initiated by the MAPPA, or by individual members of the public making requests for information. Information that is disclosed is selective insofar as only those details that are pertinent to the protection of an identified child are disclosed. Following a year-long pilot, it was announced in March 2010 that these pilots would be extended throughout England and Wales. At the time of writing, a similar pilot scheme is underway in Scotland.

While the number of applicants using the scheme was small, there was evidence that it did have some impact upon the capacity of individuals to protect their children. As the evaluation of the scheme noted:

> Most applicants [interviewed], including those who had not received a disclosure, had felt enabled to safeguard the children concerned, and most applicants thought that the pilot could contribute to general levels of alertness about risks to children. (Kemshall and Wood et al. 2010, p.14)

Community notification schemes have been resisted on the grounds that they could result in public disorder and vigilantism, a position often strongly espoused by the major children's charities (see Fitch 2006 for the NSPCC). Evidence from the evaluation of this managed disclosure scheme suggested that, while some applicants struggled with 'not being able to pass information on', there was 'no evidence to suggest any serious or damaging breach of confidentiality' (Kemshall and Wood et al. 2010, p.13). What then enables members of the public to safeguard children and keep sensitive information confidential? The key lesson from this study appears to be the extent to which police (and other criminal justice agencies) supported applicants through the process and how this ensured a distinction between 'managed' disclosure and 'community notification'.

GOOD PRACTICE IN WORKING WITH THE PUBLIC

The effective engagement of the public in the risk assessment and management of sexual offenders can provide benefits. Indeed, a more informed public may be able to make better and more lasting contributions to existing community protection approaches that will continue to manage offenders. However, as this chapter has identified, such work also brings challenges. Good practice points have emerged from several key evaluations that seek to strengthen public engagement, and some of these ideas have been discussed within the chapter. In summary, good practice in working with the public involves:

- Understanding the diversity of 'the public': recognising that there are different groups that require information and education in different formats. Accessible, plain language is important for discussing taboo subjects and a range of good practice materials (such as those published by Stop it Now!) may offer guidance. Practitioners also need to take into account that some communities and therefore some 'publics' are already more at risk and will be more resistant to risk management messages.

- Providing information at a local level and targeting key networks: Kemshall et al. (2004) found that disseminating child protection information in a user-friendly way through key community groups and opinion formers was likely to yield better results than opportunistic attempts at reaching the public. Targeting teachers, doctors and local community groups is likely to lead to better advice or support accompanying the distribution of leaflets or other health promotion messages.

- Repeating key messages in different forms and in different locations: evidence from Kitzinger's (2004) work suggests that individuals hear, mediate and decode media messages in very different ways, and key messages need constant repetition if they are to be successful. Relying solely on occasional health promotion media campaigns at the expense of embedding clear and consistent child protection messages is likely to fail.

- Controlled and limited disclosure when accompanied by professional support does work: where information about offenders is disclosed to parents, carers or other targeted members of the public, there is evidence to suggest that safeguarding action can be taken (see Kemshall and Wood et al. 2010). However, this needs to be accompanied by criminal justice personnel who can build confidence and trust in order to support members of the public to take appropriate action.

WORK WITH OFFENDERS AND POTENTIAL PERPETRATORS

While the primary concern of this chapter was to explore how the public may be engaged in risk assessment and risk management, there is also evidence that aspects of the PHA can be adopted in strengthening work with sex offenders and potential perpetrators. This section of the chapter briefly explores how effective supervision can be underpinned by a 'preventative' paradigm that moves beyond merely monitoring offenders.

Child sex offenders engender particular feelings of distrust and rejection not only from the public but also among practitioners. In addition, they are regulated differently from other offenders with seemingly ever-extending community management requirements that are enacted beyond the period of an individual's sentence. Upon release from custody, offenders are subjected to close scrutiny under the MAPPA and are required to adhere to numerous restrictive licence conditions. Registration extends beyond the period of licence with many offenders subject to ongoing supervision by police for the rest of their lives. Working effectively and in a meaningful way with this group can therefore present its own challenges because at least some of the offenders are likely to be highly distrustful of criminal justice agencies. However, a key goal of criminal justice practitioners is to protect the public, and in doing so there needs to be a preventative element that will stop offenders from progressing or re-offending (in line with the secondary and tertiary levels of the PHA).

In addition, there are the challenges of working with people who are concerned about their own behaviour, *prior* to committing an offence. These 'potential offenders' are most likely to be less forthcoming about their own concerns in a climate of generalised hostility towards sex offenders. Working effectively with this group is critical to ensuring that the primary level of the PHA is made possible in practice: the prevention of sexually deviant behaviour.

Aspects of the PHA can be adopted in both work with offenders and with those concerned about their own behaviours prior to an offence. There are two key practice points to draw out here. The first example looks at work with offenders already subject to community management, where positive approaches have been adopted to strengthen individual or self-risk management. The second examines an approach that encourages members of the public to report concerns about their own behaviour and seek advice.

Strengthening self-risk management

Public health strategies place great emphasis on an individual's capacity to change behaviours as a result of receiving appropriate information and support. In the example of smoking, we can see the deployment of 'external' controls through legislative regulation of smoking in public spaces and the development of an individual's own 'internal' controls by encouraging people to take responsibility for their own smoking behaviour. The same approach is adopted in the management of sex offenders where practitioners not only instigate restrictive (external) conditions but also seek to support offenders to identify and manage their own risky behaviours and develop their own internal controls. The effective management of high-risk offenders therefore requires a blended approach between community protection and rehabilitative work, what Kemshall (2008) terms 'protective reintegration'.

The practical application of this approach is often found in practitioners promoting 'pro-social modelling' in their work, underpinned by a belief that offenders can/will change their behaviours and can/will take responsibility for managing their own risks. There was evidence of these approaches in the author's most recent evaluation of MAPPA (Wood and Kemshall *et al.* 2007), where successful supervision relationships were supported by an 'assumption that offenders, if given opportunities to engage effectively, *can* and *will* change behaviours in most cases' (Wood and Kemshall 2007, p.11). The approach was underpinned by a number of good practice points. Supervisors:

- emphasised support and encouragement

- were clear about the extent and limitations of their role, the boundaries and authority they possessed

- adopted a pro-social modelling approach to their engagement with offenders, including setting clear expectations of required behaviour using rewards and challenges

- showed a genuine interest in the well-being of offenders and encouraged them by showing attention to their personal and social problems. (see Wood and Kemshall 2007, pp.11–12)

Where these principles were applied, offenders reported a positive engagement in problem solving and felt a loyalty, commitment and accountability to their offender managers.

Later developments include the adoption of the 'Good Lives Model' (GLM) that proposes constructive and holistic ways of engaging with offenders, 'focusing less on individual offender deficits and more on the personal, inter-personal and social contexts required to enable offenders to live and sustain a "good life"' (McCulloch and Kelly 2007, p.15). This approach is underpinned by a number of assumptions, notably that meaningful work with offenders needs to provide positive and legitimate goals coupled with techniques and strategies for enabling an individual to avoid causing harm (see Barnett and Mann, this volume).

Providing support and advice to those who are concerned

In keeping with the themes of 'prevention' and 'responsibility' that underpin the PHA, services have sought to strengthen the availability of information, advice and treatment to those concerned about their behaviours prior to entering the criminal justice system. One such example is the Stop it Now! helpline, set up to provide information and advice to 'adults...concerned about their own behaviour or the behaviour of someone they know' (Kemshall 2008, p.79). The helpline seeks to enable people to discuss their concerns and, through specialist input from treatment professionals, challenge and change their own behaviour through prompts to take action. Helpline operators will also notify callers that, should a child protection risk become apparent, then the appropriate authorities will be notified as a result of the call and confidentiality is not guaranteed. Evaluations of the helpline have identified that most calls are from abusers or potential abusers (Eldridge *et al.* 2007; Kemshall *et al.* 2004).

GOOD PRACTICE IN WORKING WITH OFFENDERS

Both the approaches reviewed earlier provide valuable lessons for developing good practice in public health approaches to work with potential and actual offenders. In summary, good practice in working with offenders and potential perpetrators involves the following:

- *The adoption of supervision practices that seek to nurture a climate of individual responsibility for self-risk management:* this means supporting offenders to identify and prevent their own risky behaviour from escalating. Practitioners in our 2007 study of MAPPA reported using individual behavioural contracts, and being available and accessible by phone should an offender encounter any difficulties (Wood and Kemshall 2007). The end goal of this work is to strengthen an offender's internal controls so that they are strengthened in their own capacity to manage risk. Barnett and Mann (this volume) suggest that approaches to assessment drawing on the GLM can support a collaborative approach between offenders and practitioners.

- *Pro-social modelling:* there is some evidence to suggest that the ways in which supervisors model desired behaviour with offenders can have an impact upon engagement and risk management. In our studies, there was a clear link between pro-social modelling and the extent to which offenders reported their compliance with supervision. There was also evidence of higher levels of trust where supervisors adopted these principles.

- *The provision of information that helps people to identify problematic behaviours:* the Stop it Now! helpline is notable for its contribution in helping people who are concerned about their behaviour or the behaviour of others to come forward, and the relatively large number of calls from potential abusers suggests that such a service is needed. The helpline also shows that it is possible to combine advice and support with a clear commitment to reporting child protection concerns to authorities should the need arise.

- *The provision of specialist advice and support for potential abusers:* the helpline serves as more than just an information service – it enables callers to explore their attitudes and behaviours and actively seeks to challenge these. This is an intervention service that is committed to making the move from awareness raising to taking action and is mirrored in supervision work with offenders that seeks to 'change' behaviours.

CONCLUSION

There are difficulties with attributing success to the PHA in work with offenders and the public because there is little available research and the knowledge base in this area is growing. Furthermore, the community protection model still occupies a dominant position in policy and legislation, with increasing use of new technologies and approaches that seek to contain risk rather than work to change public and offender attitudes and behaviours (Kemshall and Wood 2007). The public have a larger role to play with the introduction of the public disclosure schemes, although these are still at 'arm's length' in the day-to-day operational management of sex offender risks (Wood and Kemshall 2008). Finally, the problem of selective media reporting persists with little obvious signs that sensible debate about the realities of child sex offending are likely to take prominence any time soon.

Despite the difficulties, there are a number of benefits that have been identified within this chapter that can be applied to work with sex offenders. The PHA offers the potential to strengthen prevention and early intervention strategies particularly at the primary level. Through work with the public, there is the possibility that myths and misconceptions about the types and incidence of sexual offending can be challenged and, in turn, the public may gain confidence in being able to act earlier to safeguard children. These early interventions are key given the longer-term psychological and physical health impacts that victims experience. The inclusion of the public also counters the dominant view that they are irrational vigilantes. The PHA therefore offers a constant commitment to public awareness, education and building public responsibility for the treatment of sexual offenders and the prevention of child sexual abuse.

Engaging the public is one strand: challenging the ways in which we work with offenders is equally important. Research suggests that, where approaches emphasise positive goal setting and pro-social modelling, offenders are likely to engage more effectively with criminal justice agencies. At the opposite end, where low-trust relationships persist, we are likely to see less positive impacts and weaker 'internal' controls – the elements offenders need strengthening in order to effectively manage their own risks.

The over-riding message of the PHA is that preventing child sexual abuse is an adult's responsibility. The approaches within this chapter have argued that such responsibility can be equally vested in members of the public, practitioners and offenders alike.

ACKNOWLEDGEMENTS

The author wishes to acknowledge the support of Hazel Kemshall and the colleagues involved in the studies referred to in this chapter. The responsibility for the chapter remains with the author.

REFERENCES

Brown, K., Spencer, J. and Deakin, J. (2007) 'The reintegration of sex offenders: barriers and opportunities for employment.' *Howard Journal of Criminal Justice 46*, 1, 32–42.

Brown, S. (1999) 'Public attitudes toward the treatment of sex offenders.' *Legal and Criminological Psychology 4*, 2, 239–252.

Brown, S. (2009) 'Attitudes towards Sexual Offenders and their Rehabilitation: A Special Case?' In J. Wood and T. Gannon (eds) *Public Opinion and Criminal Justice*. Cullompton: Willan.

Cawson, P., Wattam, S. and Kelly, G. (2000) *Child Maltreatment in the United Kingdom: A Study of the Prevalence of Child Abuse and Neglect*. London: NSPCC.

Collins, S. (2009) *Keeping the Public in Public Protection*. Birmingham: Lucy Faithfull Foundation.

Connelly, C. and Williamson, S. (2000) *Review of the Research Literature on Serious Violent and Sexual Offenders*. Edinburgh: Scottish Executive.

Craven, S., Brown, S. and Gilchrist, E. (2006) 'Sexual grooming of children: review of literature and theoretical considerations.' *Journal of Sexual Aggression 12*, 3, 287–299.

Craven, S., Brown, S. and Gilchrist, E. (2007) 'Current responses to sexual grooming: implications for prevention.' *The Howard Journal 46*, 1, 60–71.

Critcher, C. (2003) *Moral Panics and the Media*. Buckingham: Open University Press.

Eldridge, H., Fuller, S., Findlater, D. and Palmer, T. (2006) *Stop it Now! Helpline Report 2002–2005*. Available at www.stopitnow.org, accessed 30 September 2007.

Finkelhor, D. (1991) 'Child Sexual Abuse.' In M.L. Rosenberg and M.A. Fenley (eds) *Violence in America: A Public Health Approach*. Oxford: Oxford University Press.

Fitch, K. (2006) *Megan's Law: Does it Protect Children? (2), An Updated Review of Evidence on the Impact of Community Notification as Legislated for by Megan's Law in the United States.* London: NSPCC.

Glaser, B. (2009) 'Treaters or punishers? The ethical role of mental health clinicians in sex offender programs.' *Aggression and Violent Behaviour 14*, 248–255.

Home Office (1990) *Crime, Justice and Protecting the Public: The Government's Proposals for Legislation*. London: HMSO.

Home Office (2007) *Review of the Protection of Children from Sex Offenders*. London: Home Office.

Hughes, E., Kitzinger, J. and Murdock, G. (2006) 'The Media and Risk.' In P. Taylor-Gooby and J. Zinn (eds) *Risk in Social Science*. Oxford: Oxford University Press.

Kemshall, H. (2008) *Understanding the Management of High Risk Offenders*. Maidenhead: Open University Press.

Kemshall, H. and Wood, J. (2007) 'Beyond public protection: an examination of community protection and public health approaches to high-risk offenders.' *Criminology and Criminal Justice 7*, 3, 203–222.

Kemshall, H. and Wood, J. (2008) 'Risk and public protection: responding to involuntary and "taboo" risk.' *Social Policy and Administration 42*, 6, 611–629.

Kemshall, H. and Wood, J. with Westwood, S., Stout, B., Wilkinson, B., Kelly, G. and Mackenzie, G. (2010) *Child Sex Offender Review (CSOR) Public Disclosure Pilots: A Process Evaluation*. London: Home Office.

Kemshall, H., Mackenzie, G. and Wood, J. (2004) *Stop it Now! An Evaluation*. Birmingham: Stop it Now! UK and Ireland.

Kemshall, H., Mackenzie, G., Wood, J., Bailey, R. and Yates, J. (2005) *Strengthening the Multi-Agency Public Protection Arrangements*. London: Home Office.

Kitzinger, J. (2004) *Framing Abuse: Media Influence and Public Understanding of Sexual Violence Against Children*. London: Pluto Press.

Laws, R.D. (1996) 'Relapse prevention or harm reduction?' *Sexual Abuse: A Journal of Research and Treatment 8*, 3, 243–248.

Laws, R.D. (2000) 'Sexual offending as a public health problem: a North American perspective.' *Journal of Sexual Aggression 5*, 1, 30–44.

McCulloch, T. and Kelly, L. (2007) 'Working with sex offenders in context: which way forward?' *Probation Journal 54*, 1, 7–21.

Naidoo, J. and Wills, J. (2000) *Health Promotion: Foundations for Practice*. London: Bailliere Tindall.

Nash, M. (2006) *Public Protection and the Criminal Justice Process*. Oxford: Oxford University Press.

News of the World (2000a) 'Named, shamed.' 23 July, p.1.

News of the World (2000b) 'Sign here for Sarah.' 30 July, p.1.

News of the World (2001) 'Named, shamed.' 16 December, p.1.

Rosenberg, M.L. and Mercy, J.A. (1991) 'Introduction.' In M.L. Rosenberg and M.A. Fenley (eds) *Violence in America: A Public Health Approach*. Oxford: Oxford University Press.

Rutherford, A., Zwi, A.B., Grove, N.J. and Butchart, A. (2007) 'Violence: a priority for public health? (Part 2).' *Journal of Epidemiology and Community Health 61*, 764–770.

Sanderson, C. (2005) *The Seduction of Children: Empowering Parents and Teachers to Protect Children from Child Sexual Abuse.* London: Jessica Kingsley Publishers.

Wood, J. and Kemshall, H. (2007) *The Operation and Experience of Multi-Agency Public Protection Arrangements (MAPPA).* London: Home Office. Available at www.homeoffice. gov.uk/rds/pdfs07/r285.pdf, accessed on 20 July 2010.

Wood, J. and Kemshall, H. (2008) 'Risk Management, Accountability and Partnerships in Criminal Justice.' In B. Stout, J. Yates and B. Williams (eds) *Applied Criminology.* London: Sage Publications.

CHAPTER 11

ORGANISATIONALLY DANGEROUS PRACTICE: POLITICAL DRIVERS, PRACTICE IMPLICATIONS AND PATHWAYS TO RESOLUTION

MARTIN C. CALDER

INTRODUCTION

Recently Eileen Munro (2009) pointed out the difference a decade can make in the field of child protection: literally from elitism to escapism. In the 1990s, there was competition for front-line jobs and they were filled by experienced social workers or managers who stayed for several years, forming robust and supportive teams. Within a decade, the picture has changed dramatically with acute recruitment and retention problems. Indeed, the social work taskforce report (Children's Workforce Development Council Research Team 2009) pointed out that 'widespread staff shortages are seriously compromising its ability to deliver quality in the front-line', and that 'social work is struggling to hold its own as a durable, attractive public sector profession'(p.4). Unfortunately the taskforce report doesn't address why this shift has taken place, and thus all its recommendations are likely to fail. Context and causation are the key to understanding this alarming demise.

The convenience of deflecting responsibility from the top down has always been attractive to central government, and this is the key to understanding the current problems in child protection and indeed across all child care. This chapter will examine how the government has cultivated a dangerous and toxic environment within which organisations are expected to discharge their ever-increasing, ever-diversifying and under-resourced duties, which in turn provides the fertile breeding ground for professionally dangerous practice in which front-line professionals are held accountable for their actions or inactions.

Professional dangerousness can be summarised as relating to the risk of being caught in a system where the professional is psychologically and emotionally battered by clients, by colleagues, by the system, and defensively may make inappropriate and sometimes destructive responses, as well as 'the process by which individual workers or multi-disciplinary networks can, most unwittingly, act in such a way as to collude with, maintain or increase the dangerous dynamics of the family in which the abuse takes place' (Reder, Duncan and Gray 1993). Professional dangerousness can arise from embarking upon forms of intervention that fail to consider the assumptions and emotional responses of the people involved, which might include blunted emotional responsiveness, reduced sensitivity, inadequate reflection, high levels of stress, dangerous decision making, defensiveness, depersonalisation, detachment and denial. The danger then is that the professionals mirror the dynamics of the families identified as abusive.

Organisationally dangerous practice is where the organisation creates a working environment that doesn't address professional dangerousness or, as in recent times, can undermine front-line attempts to redress the organisational errors that have been created.

Some aspects of this problem are not new: social workers have always been pilloried for their perceived flawed decision making and the professional has come to realise that they are 'damned if they do, and damned if they don't'. What should be different, however, is the location of responsibility post-Laming (Laming 2003), which should lie in the higher management structures and which should have offered a welcome and overdue 'shock absorber' and support mechanism for workers, freeing them up to pursue creative practice in the pursuit of enhanced outcomes for children. Unfortunately, the political straightjacket of ill-conceived and incoherent policies and strategies has had the reverse effect: forcing many organisations to refocus professional time away from the work to unhelpful micromanagement and target issues. Munro (2009) pointed out that:

> The taskforce makes a strong case for the high level of intelligence and emotional wisdom needed to do the job well... However, social workers are not autonomous individuals. They are employed in complex organisations that shape their practice, for good or ill... We need radical reform of the inspection and management systems, eradicating the fantasy that social work can be reduced to a set of bureaucratic tasks and acknowledging that it requires skills in engaging with people and making fallible professional judgements about how best to help them... Only then can we expect skilled workers to stay and build up the profession's expertise. (p.4)

ORGANISATIONAL ISSUES (DEVELOPED FROM CALDER 2008a)

A systems perspective on organisational failure (errors and accidents) has been developed by Reason (1990a, 1990b, 1995, 1997) who introduced the related concepts of active failure and latent failure to express the multi-level nature of incident causation. He maintained that active failure is usually associated with the errors and rule violations of front-line operators (in child welfare, this translates to child protection investigators or direct service staff) and has an immediate impact upon the system. Reason argues that the effects of active failures or errors (i.e. errors of judgement and lapses in performance) are felt almost immediately and are associated with the actions of front-line workers.

Table 11.1 offers an overview of some of the key recent, current and potential issues raised about organisational practice that have featured in numerous child deaths.

The impact of these findings can be organised under three headings: policy, management culture, and actions and practice. The impact on policy has been the production of multiple examples of information-sharing guidance as evidenced by *Working Together* (Department for Children, Schools and Families 2006) contrasting with the Common Assessment Framework (CAF) and the Integrated Children's System (ICS) (see Calder 2007, pp.524–526 for more details); a lack of supporting duties to finance the required management accountability and the safeguarding children systems; and the emergence of an escalating prescriptive and punitive performance management regulation framework. As a measure of good practice following the death of Victoria Climbié, Area Child Protection Committees (ACPCs) were asked to undertake an audit using a set template. The aim was to gain an honest appraisal of where there were practice deficits, and most ACPCs responded with this aim in mind. However, they soon realised they were to be scored using the social work inspection matrix of performance; this resulted in several authorities being deemed to be failing, and so they fell within the failure framework with its associated restrictions on spending and lack of autonomy in decision making.

The subsequent impact on management culture and actions includes a fear of not being able to keep up with the initiatives and thus practitioners cannot operate in an informed or coherent way; a fear of informing elected members that the situation is deteriorating for fear of being scapegoated; a concern that their focus is shifting from casework to accounting; and a deepening isolation from colleagues within and across agencies. My experience of delivering training and consulting across England would suggest that, in practice, a lack of clarity persists about what safeguarding involves, and about the threshold for acting

Table 11.1: Issues from inquiries

Raised by inquiries	Raised elsewhere e.g. academic papers, research reports
The whole system of exchanging information.	The new initiative merry-go-round and expansion without evaluation or coordination.
The way information is collated and gathered on a variety of sophisticated yet inadequate information systems.	Unnecessary structural changes that have made communication more difficult and actually compounded the problem.
Unclear lines of accountability and responsibility.	Communication pathways have been disrupted and expert knowledge dissipated.
The absence of clear and strong leadership.	IT as a solution to all the presenting problems when Munro (2005) has noted that no consideration has been given to the reality that they carry many risks so that, overall, it may do more harm than good. In deciding what tools to develop or apply in a particular context, designers have tended to select those that are technically easy to operate. It seems to have been taken for granted that tools or formalisation of a work procedure are intrinsically good, and so the more the better. The trouble with this approach has been twofold. First, the tools have *not* been selected because they address the aspects of the task where the operators most urgently need help. Second, the introduction of tools alters the nature of the tasks that are left for the operators to carry out. The advent of IT systems do not deal with the more intractable problems such as helping professionals to know what information they need to collect and to have the skills required to collect it.
A failure of elected members and senior managers to appreciate the nature of the work that goes on in 'the front office'.	
A lack of clarity about information sharing, confidentiality and consent.	
The Laming report found evidence of profound organisational malaise and an absence of leadership as exemplified by senior managers' apparent indifference to children's services, which were under-funded and neglected.	
Local child protection procedures were very out of date and this was compounded by major staffing problems and low morale among staff who were invariably over-worked and 'burning out'.	
Front-line workers got little support or quality supervision and were uncertain about their role in child protection.	
Extremely poor administrative systems existed for tracking referrals and case information.	

Raised by inquiries	Raised elsewhere e.g. academic papers research reports
Poor or non-existent interagency communication.	There is a distinct lack of consistency in the messages emerging from government in relation to child protection services – not least the vocabulary related to risk and a strengths-loaded therapeutically driven assessment framework (Calder 2008b).
A consistent failure to engage with the child in any meaningful way as a service user or to assess the child's needs.	
A focus throughout on Victoria's carer, as the client in the case (reflecting the perpetrator-friendly assessment frameworks introduced by government) (Laming 2003).	The emphasis placed upon 'evidence-based' practice, effective communication and wide consultation at local authority level is not reflected at the national level. There is also no acknowledgement that different professionals operating in the arena of social care have a different definitional formula for evidence-based practice (Calder 2008c).
The social workers did not just have to deal with menacing and manipulative clients, but similar kinds of colleagues, including managers, and acted out distorted and abusive patterns with one another.	
Similar distorted relationships and communications extended to relationships between agencies: social workers were afraid to challenge doctors' opinions.	The major policy and structural changes imposed on welfare organisations by government are not 'evidence based' but politically driven. The demise of child protection was attributed to the failure of the child protection system to protect Victoria Climbié when in reality it was actually the failure of the system to identify her as a child in need of protection.
The 'bombardment factor' of the relentless work and the perceived 'conveyor-belt' processing.	
In total, there was a complete lack of attention to process and feelings, no space for reflection, for slowing things down, because the social work office itself was not a safe or nurturing space. The organisation reflects the perpetrator.	The advent of performance management (output measurement) at the expense of outcomes for children (Calder 2007).
	The prioritisation of performance in decision-making processes and some concern that the reorganisation of Ofsted has led to inspectors operating within and making judgements about areas of work in which they have little operational experience. Their security then becomes the non-negotiable enactment of the written word and has resulted in their creating a climate of fear within which they present as low on warmth and high on criticism.

Table 11.1: Issues from inquiries *cont.*

The impact of individual agency performance targets that militate against any real collaborative cross-agency work where practice becomes blinkered rather than landscape.

Naming and shaming as a means of scapegoating professionals – deflecting blame downwards and creating resentment in the process.

The mismanagement of information leading to faulty decision making by government that allowed many convicted sex offenders to resume their work in schools – with no sackings being reported either to the minister or civil servants – reflecting again that there is one rule for politicians and another for operational staff.

Organisational complexity – the workers need a compass and map with a satellite navigation system to actually keep track of the changing structures and job titles.

A shift from government to governance.

A lack of trust and the growth of vulnerability.

Child protection staff must often operate with excessive workloads, inadequate training and resources, poor supervision and a lack of organisational support. These conditions have been responsible for high rates of burn-out, job stress and staff turnover.

Note : The principal inquiry reports drawn upon here are those relating to Victoria Climbié (Laming 2003) and Baby P (Laming 2009).

where actual or likely significant harm is being debated; becoming business orientated with reduced time spent with children and families; and a real lack of opportunity to be creative and focus on enhancing outcomes for vulnerable children.

PERVERSE GOVERNMENTAL PRIORITIES
One of the pervasive features of the last decade has been the advent of performance management and audit mechanisms (Munro 2004a, 2004b). Originally seen as a way of driving up standards, maximising managerial efficiency and accounting for the allocated resources, the whole market economy approach has created numerous barriers to good practice, fuelling a focus on system outputs and de-skilling and de-motivating managers and front-line staff, many of whom have pursued premature exit strategies as a means of personal survival (Calder, forthcoming) Again the impact of these findings can be organised under three headings: policy, management culture, and actions and practice. In the policy area, a formula has emerged whereby each new initiative such as *Every Child Matters* (*ECM*) Department for Children Schools and Families 2003) has been accompanied by a stringent set of criteria against which success and/or compliance can be judged. This is linked to star ratings, resource allocation and freedom of spending. Ironically, creative reflection is only encouraged when you are deemed in need of 'special measures'. A culture of audit has flourished without a parallel realisation that 'quality doesn't protect'.

The recent example that the previous Labour government had again failed to grasp the points being made was when they heard staff believed the timeframes were counter-productive and so they suggested increasing the timeframe for initial assessment from 7 to 10 days. However, the point is that children's needs are so varied that it is a nonsense to have a rule, a 'one size fits all' (Munro 2009).

Procedural-driven practice predominates at the cost of outcomes and objectives, and this allows the politicians and sometimes senior managers to sit in their elevated protected bubble saying 'I told you what to do and you failed to comply' if anything goes wrong. They have also generated systems and exemplars to collect hard data leaving staff to develop their own evidence-based assessment tools, and again this requires time and reflection to knit the best of theory with research and practice wisdom. Professor Sue White of Lancaster University has done extensive research that backs this up (White, Hall and Peckover 2009). ICS not only poses a risk by taking social workers away from their time with families but also hampers good reasoning. Good practice, for example, requires assessment to be seen as an ongoing process with workers continually reviewing and revising their picture of a family.

ICS treats revising a completed assessment form as a rare event and makes it technically difficult, thereby giving the implicit and dangerous message that workers should get it right first time round. Policy has recreated the climate that allows a top-down blame culture to once again prevail.

The impact on management culture and actions is acute: managers are now focused on meeting the expectations of government departments as opposed to focusing on the accurate analysis of their organisation's capacity to manage 'risk' and take steps to minimise adverse outcomes; managers have to persuade and support staff to comply; managers and workers have to achieve the required performance for fear of consequence if they fall short, especially with the emergence of the 'name and shame' game; and, alarmingly, both managers and front-line workers are evaporating goodwill as their energy dips and they question the purpose of remaining in post – what matters has been lost and many are disillusioned and deflated. In practice, the realisation that the primary role is collecting and inputting hard data rather than spending time working with children has caused a great deal of resentment, as has the discredited tick-box assessment mentality; and all front-line staff are concerned about the day-to-day demands of the job, large and increasing caseloads and staff shortages, and the lack of focus on the child. Many staff find themselves swimming against a tidal wave of initiatives that is slowly drowning them and the energy expended in treading water is sapping creative potential. All staff should have their feelings recognised and attended to if we are not to add more fuel to the professional dangerousness fire.

GOVERNMENT: THE ORIGINS AND PERPETUATING DRIVERS OF ORGANISATIONAL DANGEROUSNESS

There are real policy issues present because they are the source drivers of much dangerous practice organisationally and professionally. The lack of any real professional consensus on what safeguarding constitutes is potentially a cleverly crafted move by government. No-one can argue against *ECM* (Department for Children, Schools and Families 2003) but if this is to be a reality rather than a vision it needs to be accompanied by:

- a duty to fund the activities it involves

- a commitment to evaluating initiatives, bedding them in and allowing time to gel them together rather than simply throwing initiative after initiative into the system and expecting organisations to have the capacity to coordinate and trouble-shoot them

- a resurrection of risk and associated language, and a freedom to talk about dangerousness and harm as opposed to needs, strengths, assets and early intervention

- a shift to encouraging truly integrated inter-agency work by freeing them all of individually focused performance indicators that preclude collaborative ventures.

There are also several key issues having an impact upon management culture and actions. The combination of market forces and government restructuring and funding affects the role of the manager directly. Managers have to steer their staff through changes in structure and philosophy and motivate them to work with change, and they also have to work indirectly, through an expanding public relations role, with other agencies concerned about the elevated threshold for the provision of a social work service, as well as being distracted from their ever-expanding front-line roles. The current first-line manager has a multifaceted role and functions include:

- ensuring safety first for children

- implementing organisational policy

- implementing strategies, establishing and maintaining forums for the participation of people using services in all aspects of the work

- managing partnerships with related services, both internal and external

- managing performance: including achieving targets, budgetary requirements

- managing the team: case management and decision making

- setting standards

- understanding the background of staff (in cultural terms as well as relating to varied qualification routes); ensuring or providing training and development opportunities, both formal and on the job

- establishing the role of computers in practice.

A review of the research and development work on first-line managers (Learner and Statham 2005) found that the role of team manager had grown incrementally and its complexity was often not recognised by the organisation. A consequence is that many first-line managers are under severe pressure, and the support systems they need are not in place.

Equally significant is that there is no qualification for them, although first-line managers are clear that moving from front-line worker to first-line manager is a very significant professional and personal step. For many, the entry qualification is that of practice teaching. This at least enables the first-line manager to think through supporting adults' learning to practice, and to be accountable for performance to standards of practice and service. However, it does not assist directly in being accountable to the organisation for the quality of practice of workers with a range of qualifications and experience, or in managing staff some of whom have more experience than themselves.

SUPERVISION IN CHANGING TIMES

Supervision is also changing considerably and the key changes and demands relate to:

- increased central government control

- performance targets

- performance management

- external audit, inspection and league tables

- multiple initiatives from government

- widening spans of control for managers

- uncertainty about funding

- rising public expectations especially about the management of risk

- increased use of litigation by service users

- continual restructuring of services

- turnover of staff and recruitment problems

- rising service thresholds resulting in more chronic presenting problems

- reduced demarcation between public and private sectors

- movement towards integrated services.

Organisational culture exercises a powerful influence in determining the dominant styles of problem solving, reward systems, role models and how change is managed (Morrison 1995). Social care organisations, in turn, are highly sensitive to the wider political context in terms of change, accountability and control. These institutional influences have the potential to distort and overwhelm the learning style preferences of individuals. For instance, the dominant learning style for organisations under pressure (in an environment where rules and expectations are changing rapidly and there is a strong emphasis on compliance) is a pragmatist style. This may ensure that targets are met, but at the expense of longer-term considerations or undesirable side effects, which might have been foreseen by the theorists. It may ensure that the required changes are made by the activists, but at a high cost to staff morale and motivation, which might have been anticipated by the reflectors.

In the current context, there ceases to be any role for leadership as the primary organisational objective becomes that of target attainment. This rather limited but politically significant feature of service delivery means that the overwhelming orientation within the public sector will be towards managerialism, where the management of targets becomes the central purpose of the organisation. Experience has informed me that, over a decade or more of their application, the use of targets has served to erode the value of individual skills and 'professional judgement' within the workforce. Instead the target culture has encouraged the revival of a management approach. Here managers and technical specialists act essentially as organisers and controllers of industrial operatives where the division of tasks is seen as a central factor in improving efficiency.

Three essential domains for leaders that are important despite the constraints are set out in Table 11.2.

Table 11.2: Essential domains for leaders		
Leading and developing others	**Personal qualities**	**Reading the organisation**
Has a genuine concern for others' well-being and development. Empowers, delegates and develops potential. Accessible, approachable, in touch. Encourages questioning and critical strategic thinking.	Transparency, honesty and consistency. Integrity and openness to ideas and advice. Decisive and risk taking. Charismatic, in touch. Analytical and creative thinker.	Inspirational communicator, networker and achiever. Clarifies individual and team direction, priorities and purpose. Unites through a joint vision. Creates a supportive learning and self-development environment. Manages changes sensitively and skilfully.

Empowering leadership and competent management are the cornerstones of the kind of workplaces that attract, retain and develop staff. Management and leadership is about developing knowledge, skills and behaviours, and having the ability to connect with people at both head and heart levels. While some may have a head start because of their personal attributes, all managers and leaders need to be developed. The bottom line is avoiding blame cultures.

Finally, there are several key impact areas on practice. The overwhelming response by welfare states to child deaths and other system failures has been to seek bureaucratic solutions by introducing more and more laws, procedures and guidelines. The more risk and uncertainty has been exposed, the greater the attempts to close up the gaps through administrative changes. While these are valid concerns, the problem surrounds the one-dimensionality of the approach and the relentless focus on new forms of organising child welfare work as the key to solving problems. Here, practice is regarded as little more than rule following and leads to:

- an erosion of the value of individual skills and 'professional judgement' within the workforce

- a stifling of creativity and discouragement of risk-taking

- a skewing of assessment tasks (e.g. the ICS as a business process).

Causes of poor performance may include:

- lack of clarity about the range of responsibilities

- lack of or poor induction

- irregular or poor quality supervision

- poor relationship between manager and worker

- mismatch between the culture of the organisation and the worker

- lack of resources to do the job

- lack of skills to do the job

- personal problems impeding performance

- poor motivation.

If social workers are to have any chance of working effectively to enhance outcomes for the children they work with, they need as a minimum to have:

- good observation and analytical skills

- an ability to:
  - o understand signs of non-compliance
  - o work alongside families
  - o reach safe and evidence-based judgements
  - o develop emotional resilience
  - o record information clearly
  - o present key case information
  - o reflect upon and analyse their observations
- good communication skills
- a thorough understanding of the legal framework surrounding safeguarding and child protection.

Social workers frequently look to their supervisors to assist them in these areas, but this is becoming significantly more difficult because the managers are becoming shock absorbers between organisational and political performance requirements on the one hand and promoting effective practice on the other: 'There is always the feeling that the agency will not go to bat for you…you have to walk the plank alone' (Scottish Executive 2005).

Disempowered workers are at best unlikely to be able to empower clients and at worst likely to dis-empower them further. Empowered workers, who believe in their ability to make a difference in their own lives as well as in others, are more likely to pass this skill on to those with whom they work.

The effects of poor or absent supervision are set out in Table 11.3.

Table 11.3: The impact of poor or absent supervision			
Services to patients/ clients/carers	*You, the worker and supervisee*	*Staff management relations and the organisation as a whole*	*Multidiscipli-nary working and interagency relations*
Loss of professional direction	Reduction in confidence	Increased sickness, disaffection, distrust	Role confusion
Reduced sensitivity/ empathy	Build-up of feelings of anxiety	Poor internal communication	Poor communication
Inappropriate use of authority	Training needs not identified	Organisational goals, values and policies unclear	Inappropriate services
Poor planning	Practice not reviewed		

KEY INGREDIENTS TO CULTIVATE SAFE ORGANISATIONAL PRACTICE

People matter

People make organisations work and they determine the quality of the output. The effectiveness of services provided is largely dependent on how the organisation supports and leads those people. (Department of Health (2000)

Organisations are the product of the way people think and interact. If we want to change organisations for the better we have to change the way people think and interact. (Senge 1991)

Key components of a learning organisation[1]

A 6-factor model

Shared vision: the extent to which there is a vision already in place that includes the organisation's capacity to identify, respond to and benefit from future possibilities. Part of this vision recognises the importance of learning at individual, group and system level to enable the organisation to transform itself continuously in order not only to survive but also to thrive in an increasingly unpredictable world.

Enabling structure: the extent to which the organisation has been designed and operates to facilitate learning between different levels, functions and subsystems. Also the recognition of the need for rapid adaptation and change.

Supportive culture: the extent to which expressed values and displayed behaviour by the organisation's leaders encourage challenges to the status quo, the questioning of assumptions and established ways of doing things, also the provision of opportunities for testing, experimenting and continuous development. Exploration and debate are valued and mistakes are treated positively.

Empowering management: the extent to which managers genuinely believe that devolved decision making and autonomous team working result in improved performance by those much closer to the work actually done and/or the customer. Managers see their role as facilitating and coaching rather than controlling and monitoring.

---

1   Kandola and Fullerton (2004), reproduced in Scottish Executive 2005.

Motivated workforce: the extent to which the workforce as a whole is motivated to learn continuously, is confident to take on new learning and seize opportunities for learning from experience, and is fully committed to self-development.

Enhanced learning: the extent to which the organisation has processes and policies to enhance, encourage and sustain learning amongst all employees.

An enabled and empowered workforce requires:

- 'good beginnings and endings: recruitment practices; induction; supervision; continuing professional development and exit interviews
- rewards: everything a person gains by working
- workloads and backroom systems: behind every good front-line worker there are processes, people and equipment behind the scenes making it happen!
- leadership, management and organisational culture: "how we do things here"
- performance management: how we know we are doing the right things well
- work–life balance: a critical factor for staff support, performance and morale.' (Scottish Executive 2005)

Learning organisations ideally have an organisational culture that:

- promotes openness, creativity and experimentation among members
- encourages members to acquire, share and process information
- provides the freedom to try new things, risk failure and learn from mistakes
- celebrates and shares good practice
- systematically gathers views from service users and carers and uses them to influence service planning
- creates opportunities for members to think and reflect and to learn from new evidence and research.

Many workers express their concerns that an organisational culture of blame prevails: one that fosters a fear of talking about incidents that could have, or actually did, go wrong.

CONCLUDING CORRECTIVES
From blame to quality

The result of so many inquiries into fatal child abuse is to foster a blame culture in child protection work. This is often the approach of politicians and the media. It is difficult to see how the benefits from inquiries positively inform policy, practice and learning. What is clear is that policy changes as a result of recommendations made by child death inquiries alone do not ensure improved practice and better outcomes for children. In environments where blame is individualised and society seeks scapegoats when errors and wrong decisions are made, practitioners are likely to develop defensive attitudes, which do not lead to ongoing improvement in the service provided. Johnson and Petrie (2005) highlight how organisational issues need to be given a higher profile to ensure avoidable tragedies do not occur as a result of organisational failure. Indeed, there are three relevant considerations.

- Physical risks are always created and effected in social systems – for example, by organisations and institutions that are supposed to manage and control the risky activity.

- The magnitude of the physical risks is therefore a direct function of the quality of social relations and processes.

- The primary risk, even for the most technically intensive activities (indeed, perhaps most especially for them), is therefore that of social dependency upon institutions and actors who may well be – and arguably are increasingly – alien, obscure and inaccessible to most people affected by the risks in question (Beck 1992).

Organisational culture is shaped by management style, the level of autonomy and expectations of the employees, and institutional function. Given the stressful nature of social work, particularly work in child protection, human service organisations may exhibit a culture of stress (Thompson, Stradling, and O'Neill 1996). Individuals respond to stress by avoiding anxiety through behaviour that is risk averse; agencies respond to stress by attempting to reduce uncertainty through the application of rules and procedures that regulate behaviour. The results of attempting to limit individual worker style, creativity, and decision-making autonomy have also been described as a culture of compliance (as compared to a culture of commitment).

Even within the confines of a large and sometimes disjointed system such as public child welfare, individual workers who are guided towards a sense of empowerment in their work will be able to help their clients believe the same. 'Empowerment', in this context, is defined as workers' belief that they have the capability to shape events in their jobs and their lives; that their actions are effective and that they have some control over their choices and action. Cearley (2004) examined several factors that might influence workers' sense of empowerment within a statutory child welfare agency. These included supervisory help-giving behaviours, the effects of organisational support, length of time as a child welfare employee and type of degree on worker empowerment.

Empowerment-oriented workers, supervisors and agencies understand that they best serve by recognising the strengths of help-receivers and how they have successfully used those strengths in past and current situations. The strengths then become part of the roles and tasks within the relationship and tools for change. The following table helps identify clearly what is needed to develop and sustain an enabled and empowered workforce.

Table 11.4: Enabled and empowered workforce	
To *enable* is to provide the means for a member of staff to do the job. This means:	To *empower* is to give staff the freedom and authority to use their skills, knowledge and experience to find the best way to achieve a particular task. This includes:
Defining the task or jobs to be done. Defining the role of the worker. Defining the structures, policies and procedures. Getting the 'back room' supports running smoothly. Ensuring the worker has the necessary knowledge and skills. Ensuring the worker has the right tools and equipment. Ensuring the worker has access to appropriate resources. Ensuring the worker has supervision and feedback on performance. Ensuring fair employment and reward strategies. Ensuring reasonable workloads.	Trusting workers to exercise professional judgement and to take responsibility for decision making and problem solving. Trusting workers to be responsible for balancing work requirements and lifestyle commitments. Trusting teams to solve problems, allocate work and maximise flexibility. Supporting staff and helping them to learn from mistakes and misjudgements. Welcoming challenges to the status quo and rewarding innovation and creativity. Building belonging and ownership – involving workers in service planning and review, organisational design and development, and decision making.
Enabled workers can *do what they have been told to do* but empowered workers *do what needs to be done and reflect on how it could be done better next time.*	

Source: Scottish Executive 2005, p.22.

Current organisational cultures and structures, and the governmental drivers shaping and reshaping them, are operating to constrain rather than enhance professional work with children and families in order to secure good outcomes. Leaders, managers and front-line staff working within this environment need to remain critically analytical about the process of change and the drivers that frame it. It is important that we do not lose sight of how to build effective work cultures and an environment that properly progresses core responsibilities for keeping children safe.

We are all operating in a climate of significant resource constraint. While we all have to do more with less, it becomes increasingly important that we create the structures, cultures and practices that ensure we do more of the right things with limited resources. This chapter has outlined the context and organisational culture in which we are becoming 'organisationally dangerous' and the governmental drivers that press us in that direction. However, the chapter also outlines the key themes that need attention in order to redress the balance, improve organisational safety and ultimately secure better outcomes for children, young people and their families. It is unlikely that solutions to this will come from without; therefore the challenge is to redress the balance from within. Local leaders, managers and staff within and across services need to grasp the risks inherent in the current context, and embrace the principal themes that point to a more positive and secure service environment when working with child protection. This will mean drawing upon already stretched resources, reviewing and redirecting service activity, and building more supportive and analytical cultures of practice when working with child protection.

REFERENCES

Beck, U. (1992) *Risk Society: Towards a New Modernity*. London: Sage Publications.

Calder, M.C. (2007) 'Child Protection in Changing Times: A Manager's Perspective.' In K. Wilson and A. James (eds) *The Child Protection Handbook* (3rd edition). London: Bailliere Tindall. 516–531.

Calder, M.C. (2008a) 'Organisational Dangerousness: Causes, Consequences and Correctives.' In M.C. Calder (ed.) *Contemporary Risk Assessment in Safeguarding Children*. Lyme Regis: Russell House Publishing. 119–165.

Calder M.C. (2008b) Risk and Child Protection.' In M.C. Calder (ed.) *Contemporary Risk Assessment in Safeguarding Children*. Lyme Regis: Russell House Publishing. 206–223.

Calder, M.C. (2008c) 'Professional Dangerousness: Causes, Correctives and Contemporary Features.' In M.C. Calder (ed.) *Contemporary Risk Assessment in Safeguarding Children*. Lyme Regis: Russell House Publishing. 61–86.

Calder, M.C. (forthcoming) 'Politically Dangerous Practice.' In M.C. Calder and S. Hackett (eds) *Assessments in Child Care* (2nd edition). Lyme Regis: Russell House Publishing.

Cearley, S. (2004) 'The power of supervision in child welfare cases.' *Child and Youth Care Forum 33*, 5, 312–327.

Children's Workforce Development Council Research Team (2009) *Newly Qualified Social Workers: A Report on Consultations with Newly Qualified Social Workers, Employers and Those in Higher Education*. Leeds: Children's Workforce Development Council.

Department of Health (2000) *A Quality Strategy for Social Care*. London: The Stationary Office.

Department for Children, Schools and Families (2003) *Every Child Matters*. Cm 5860. London: The Stationary Office.

Department for Children, Schools and Families (2006) *Working Together to Safeguard Children*. London: The Stationary Office.

Johnson, S. and Petrie, S. (2005) 'Child protection and risk management: the death of Victoria Climbié.' *Journal of Social Policy 33*, 2, 179–202.

Learner, E. and Statham, D. (2005) 'The role of the first line manager: new challenges.' *Management Issues in Social Care 10*, 1, winter, 36–45.

Laming, Lord (2003) *The Victoria Climbié Inquiry: Report of an Inquiry by Lord Laming*, Cmnd 5730. London: The Stationery Office.

Laming, Lord (2009) *The Protection of Children in England: A Progress Report*. London: The Stationery Office.

Morrison, T. (1995) 'Professional Dangerousness.' In P. Dale and T. Morrison (eds) *Dangerous Families*. Rochdale: NSPCC.

Munro, E. (2004a) 'The Impact of Child Abuse Inquiries since 1990.' In J. Manthorpe and N. Stanley (eds) *The Age of Inquiry: Learning and Blaming in Health and Social Care*. London: Routledge. 75–91.

Munro, E. (2004b) 'The impact of audit on social work practice.' *British Journal of Social Work 34*, 8, 1073–1074.

Munro, E. (2005) 'What tools do we need to improve identification of child abuse?' *Child Abuse Review 14*, 6, 374–388.

Munro, E. (2009) 'A job half done.' Parliamentary Brief, December, p.4.

Reason, J. (1990a) *Human Error*. Cambridge: Cambridge University Press.

Reason, J. (1990b) 'The Contribution of Latent Human Failures to the Breakdown of Complex Systems.' In D.E. Broadbent, A. Baddeley and J.T. Reason (eds) *Human Factors in Hazardous Situations*. London: Oxford University Press. 27–36.

Reason, J. (1995) 'A systems approach to organizational error.' *Ergonomics 38*, 8, 1708–1721.

Reason, J. (1997) *Managing the Risks of Organizational Accidents*. Burlington, VT: Ashgate.

Reder, P., Duncan, S. and Gray, M. (1993) *Beyond Blame: Child Abuse Tragedies Revisited*. London: Routledge.

Scottish Executive (2005) *Improving Front Line Services: A Framework for Supporting Front Line Staff*. Available at www.scotland.gov.uk, accessed on 25 March 2010.

Senge, P. (1991) *The Fifth Discipline: The Art and Practice of the Learning Organization*. New York: Currency Doubleday.

Thompson, N., Stradling, M.M. and O'Neill, P. (1996) 'Stress and organizational culture.' *British Journal of Social Work 26*, 647–665.

White, S., Hall, C. and Peckover, S. (2009) 'The descriptive tyranny of the Common Assessment Framework: technologies of categorization and professional practice in child welfare.' *British Journal of Social Work 39*, 7, 1197–1217.

Kerry Baker is based at the Centre for Criminology, University of Oxford, and has also worked with the Youth Justice Board for England and Wales. She has been closely involved in the development and implementation of the *Asset* assessment framework, now widely used across youth justice services in the UK, and writes regularly on the subjects of assessment, risk and public protection.

Georgia D. Barnett, BSc, MSc, C. Psychol., is a chartered forensic psychologist working in the National Offender Management Service (NOMS) sex offender treatment programmes team. She is particularly involved in research relating to the risk assessment and treatment of sexual offenders. Before taking on this post, Georgia worked in the risk assessment and delivery of treatment to medium to very high risk offenders in custody.

Thilo Boeck is a senior research fellow based at the Centre for Social Action at De Montfort University, Leicester. He worked in Youth and Community Development in Peru, where he initiated and managed development projects supporting people to set up community-led projects. In the UK, he worked in several participative research projects exploring social capital, diversity and community cohesion with young people and communities. He has worked with several local authorities in England advising them on their community cohesion policies, and he is currently an advisor and contributor to the Audit Commission's 'Diverse, Empowered and Active Communities Knowledge Network'. His work is influenced by his strong commitment to social justice and participative research, training and practice.

Dr Karen Broadhurst is a senior lecturer in social work and social science in the Department of Applied Social Science, Lancaster University. Karen's background is in social work with children and families, and her research interests also centre on this field of practice. Karen is co-editor of the book *Critical Perspectives on Safeguarding Children* (Wiley-Blackwell, 2009) and her work, spanning topics related to child protection and family support, has been published in a number of leading national and international journals.

Martin C. Calder established Calder Training and Consultancy in 2005 after 20 years in frontline child protection practice. His aim has been to generate and collate the available and necessary assessment tools for frontline staff and managers, especially in times of massive change. He also critiques central government guidance and attempts to provide remedial materials to help fill the gap left between aspiration and reality. He is currently an Honorary Research Fellow at the University of Durham.

Tina Cooper is the main family carer for her son James (age 27) who has profound and multiple learning disabilities, severe physical disabilities and complex health needs. When he was 25, James moved out of the family home and took up residence in a specially adapted bungalow under a shared ownership scheme, employing his own full-time carers. Tina then took part-time employment through the British Institute of Learning Disabilities (BILD) and now works as a family care link worker in a pilot personalisation project called 'Doing it your way' funded by the Worcestershire County Council Learning Disabilities Development Fund.

Jennie Fleming is Director of the Centre for Social Action and Principal Lecturer (Research). Before coming to De Montfort University, she had many years' professional work experience as a youth and community worker and social worker, and is professionally qualified in both disciplines. Jennie is committed to working in a participative and empowering way; while being at the Centre, she has been active in the development of participative research methodologies working with young people, community members and service users ensuring their input and contribution to research projects that affect them.

Jon Glasby is Professor of Health and Social Care and Director of the Health Services Management Centre at the University of Birmingham. A qualified social worker by background, he is involved in regular research, teaching, consultancy and policy advice around personalisation, inter-agency working and community care. He is a former board member of the Social Care Institute for Excellence (SCIE) and is currently a governor of the Birmingham Children's Hospital.

Dr Chris Hall is Social Care Researcher in the School of Medicine and Health at the University of Durham. Previously a social worker and team manager in local authority social services, he has held research posts at the National Foundation for Educational Research (NFER), Dartington Social Research Unit and the University of Huddersfield. In his present post, Dr Hall works in a team that provides advice on research design to academics, clinicians and other professionals. His own research interests include child welfare policy and practice, professional communication, and narrative and discourse methods. His most recent projects have been two ESRC-funded studies of information sharing, assessment and the use of information and communication technologies in child welfare.

Gill Kelly has been an independent trainer and consultant in youth justice for over a decade, supporting research and providing training and consultancy. She has developed in that time a significant body of work focusing on face to face work with both Adult and Young Offenders. She is an Honorary Fellow at De Montfort University in Leicester and an Honorary Lecturer at Birmingham University.

Hazel Kemshall is currently Professor of Community and Criminal Justice at De Montfort University. She has research interests in risk assessment and management of offenders, effective work in multi-agency public protection, and implementing effective practice with high risk offenders. She has completed research for the Economic and Social Research Council, the Home Office, Ministry of Justice, the Scottish Government, and the Risk Management Authority.

She both teaches and consultants extensively on public protection and high risk offenders, including training for MAPPA chairs and panel members in England and Scotland.

She has numerous publications on risk, including *Understanding Risk in Criminal Justice* (2003, Open University Press). She has completed three evaluations of multi-agency public protection panels for the Home Office (2001, 2005, 2007), and is currently researching polygraph use with sex offenders, and evaluating the public disclosure pilots. She is the lead author of the CD rom 'Risk of Harm Guidance and Training Resource' for NOMS PPU, and for the 'Assessment and Management of Risk' CD rom in Scotland for the RMA. Her most recent book: *Understanding the Community Management of High Risk Offenders* was published by the Open University in 2008.

Rosemary Littlechild is a senior lecturer in social work in the Institute of Applied Social Studies at the University of Birmingham. She is a qualified social worker and her research and publication interests are in work with older people, community care, partnership working between social care and health services, and service user and carer involvement.

Tony Maden is a forensic psychiatrist with a particular interest in violence risk assessment and the treatment of personality disorder. He trained at the Maudsley Hospital and the Institute of Psychiatry where he worked on national surveys of mental disorder in prisoners. He was an honorary consultant at the Bethlem Hospital and clinical director of forensic services at the Maudsley. He was appointed in 1999 to Professor of Forensic Psychiatry at Imperial College London and he is also Clinical Director of the Specialist Personality Disorder Directorate at Broadmoor Hospital.

Ruth E. Mann, BA, MSc, PhD C., Psychol., AFBPsS, is a chartered forensic psychologist who has worked first for the prison service and now for NOMS, for 22 years. For nearly all this time, Ruth has specialised in the assessment and treatment of sexual offenders. Her PhD, received from the University of Leicester in 2005, examined the role of cognition in sexual offending. She is currently responsible for the assessment and treatment of sexual offenders for NOMS and is also head of interventions research. Ruth has authored and co-authored numerous research papers and book chapters on sexual offender assessment and treatment.

Louise Niblett is a research, development and training consultant in the field of inclusion, education and transition. Louise has been in receipt of direct payments and Independent Living Fund payments since 1997. She was one of the 'pioneers' of mixed funding recipients of care packages in Birmingham. She was instrumental in the establishment of the Birmingham Direct Payments Service User Forum and was its first elected chair.

Dr Sue Peckover is a senior research fellow at the Centre for Applied Childhood Studies at the University of Huddersfield. Sue has recently been involved in two ESRC-funded research studies examining aspects of information sharing, assessment and the use of information and communication technologies in child welfare. Sue has a professional background in health visiting and has previously worked at the University of Sheffield. Her research interests include public health work with children and families, child welfare and domestic abuse.

Andrew Pithouse is Director of Research in the School of Social Sciences and a member of the Childhood Research Group at Cardiff University. He has been principal investigator in several child-safeguarding and parent/family-support projects that have helped promote conceptual development, practice innovation and system building across voluntary and statutory sectors in child and family services. Other interests in methodology and theory include voluntary services and community development, child and youth advocacy, child and adolescent mental health services, sociology of welfare organisations and action research.

Dr Amanda L. Robinson received her PhD in Interdisciplinary Social Science from Michigan State University, with concentrations in criminology, sociology, and industrial/organisational psychology and is now a Senior Lecturer in Criminology at Cardiff University. She has conducted empirical research into American and British criminal justice systems on topics such as police investigation, community policing, violence against women, and specialist courts. She recently concluded a national evaluation of Independent Domestic Violence Advisors (IDVAs) and Independent Sexual Violence Advisors (ISVAs) for the Home Office and is currently involved in a Daphne III project funded by the European Commission on protecting high-risk victims of violence. She has published in *Policing and Society, Criminal Justice & Behavior, Violence Against Women, Security Journal, International Journal of Applied and Comparative Criminal Justice,* and *the Howard Journal of Criminal Justice.*

Mike Titterton is director of the charity HALE (Health and Life for Everyone), which assists children and adults at risk of harm in the UK and overseas. He has worked on health, social care and educational projects in eastern Europe and central Asia, as well as working for government, social work, the NHS and third-sector agencies in Scotland. He has also taught and undertaken research at three universities in the UK. His PhD. was on the topic of risk and resilience in socially excluded groups. He has two grown-up children and plays in a blues band in Edinburgh.

David Wastell is Professor of Information Systems at Nottingham University Business School. He began his academic career as a psycho-physiologist, carrying out research on stress and technological innovation in collaboration with British Telecom. His current interests are in public sector reform, innovation and design, and cognitive ergonomics. He has held several research council grants and has extensive public sector consultancy experience. He has co-authored four edited books on technology and innovation, co-organised several international conferences and workshops, and published widely in a range of journals on information systems and psychology.

Sue White is Professor of Social Work at Lancaster University (from August 2010, University of Birmingham). She is a registered social worker and qualified at the University of Leeds in 1983. She was employed as a practitioner and manager in statutory children's services for 13 years and then took up an academic post at the University of Manchester. She has recently completed two influential ESRC-funded studies: the first focusing on electronic information sharing in multidisciplinary child welfare practice, and the second on the impact of performance management on social work. During 2009, Sue served on the Social Work Task Force, charged with undertaking a comprehensive review of front-line social work practice in England.

Jason Wood is Head of Research in the Youth and Community Division, De Montfort University. He has research interests in the community management of sex offenders including strategies that engage the public in risk assessment and risk management. He has conducted numerous national evaluations of the Multi-Agency Public Protection Arrangements (MAPPA) and other public protection schemes for the Home Office and the Ministry of Justice (with Hazel Kemshall).

SUBJECT INDEX

Note: The letter 'f' after a page number refers to a figure; the letter 't' refers to a table.